The Enterprise Engineering Series

Enterprise Engineering is an emerging discipline for coping with the challenges (agility, adaptability, etc.) and the opportunities (new markets, new technologies, etc.) faced by contemporary enterprises, including commercial, nonprofit and governmental institutions. It is based on the paradigm that such enterprises are purposefully designed systems, and thus they can be redesigned in a systematic and controlled way. Such enterprise engineering projects typically involve architecture, design, and implementation aspects.

The Enterprise Engineering series thus explores a design-oriented approach that combines the information systems sciences and organization sciences into a new field characterized by rigorous theories and effective practices. Books in this series should critically engage the enterprise engineering paradigm, by providing sound evidence that either underpins it or that challenges its current version. To this end, two branches are distinguished: Foundations, containing theoretical elaborations and their practical applications, and Explorations, covering various approaches and experiences in the field of enterprise engineering. With this unique combination of theory and practice, the books in this series are aimed at both academic students and advanced professionals.

Václav Řepa • Oleg Svatoš

Fundamentals of Business Architecture Modeling

 Springer

Václav Řepa
Prague University of Economics
and Business
Praha 3, Czech Republic

Oleg Svatoš
Prague University of Economics
and Business
Praha 3, Czech Republic

ISSN 1867-8920 ISSN 1867-8939 (electronic)
The Enterprise Engineering Series
ISBN 978-3-031-59034-4 ISBN 978-3-031-59035-1 (eBook)
https://doi.org/10.1007/978-3-031-59035-1

This Springer imprint is published by the registered company Springer Nature Switzerland AG
The registered company address is: Gewerbestrasse 11, 6330 Cham, Switzerland

If disposing of this product, please recycle the paper.

Preface

Standards and frameworks for modeling business architecture provide a vast offer of procedures, diagrams, and rules to follow. Novice analysts are so often overwhelmed by this range of possibilities and complexity translated into an endless number of pages of descriptions that many times analysts slip into using an intuitive approach, or a "how colleagues have done it before" approach, rather than delving into the rules of a systematic method. But systematic analysis based on general principles is always preferable to intuitively following some patchwork approach—it contributes to reusability, sustainability, readability, clarity, and consistency of the business architecture and the models that make it up.

In this book, we promote systematic analysis by presenting rules for a minimal business architecture based on Methodology for Modeling and Analysis of Business Processes (MMABP). We try to highlight what is essential for business architecture in the vast array of models and diagrams and related elements that the current standards and frameworks offer. We provide basic and fundamental principles and practices for capturing the core of business architecture so that it is complete and consistent while being minimal in the number of models and elements within them. In this way, we want to make business architecture modeling (whose principles we consider to be the basic way for business system modeling) more accessible to those who are at first discouraged by the complexity and extensiveness of standard frameworks.

From the point of view of business system (architecture) modeling, this book is about defining practical approaches for solving particular problems (smaller and larger, with respect to business architecture and what such a model entails), so that modeling is not seen as something that delays but something that is actually already the first version of a prototype, just on "paper."

The aim is not to provide some all-encompassing overview of all possible procedures and their variants but to provide a methodological basis on which it is possible to build further, to extend the methods according to needs, but with respect for the basic principles on which the methodology is based.

Additional digital resources, including the source code for the example implemented in CAMUNDA in Chapter 6, are available at http://www.e-bpm.org.

Václav Řepa
Oleg Svatoš

About This Book

This book is:

- A textbook focused on the basic principles necessary for business architecture modeling
- A reference book organized into parts, chapters, and sections so you can quickly find what you need, when you need it
- A comprehensive text that includes both common process analysis tools and ontology analysis tools and brings them together
- A practical, example-rich presentation of the MMABP methodology
- Step-by-step instructions for mapping the minimal business architecture
- A guide to how the various diagrams relate to each other and how the fundamentals presented in this book can be further developed

How This Book Is Organized

We have divided this book into six main chapters. Since the book presents a complex method of business analysis step by step, it is recommended to read the chapters one after another, so that one can gradually build up a comprehensive picture of the model of the real world that the method leads one to understand and capture.

Chapter 1: Introduction to the Field of Business Architecture Modeling

Chapter 1 introduces business architecture and the approaches and tools to model it. The sections on MMABP present the basic principles of the methodology and place the methodology, on which this book is based, in the context of other approaches to business architecture modeling. They also introduce the concept of the business system model, which is the foundation of the minimal business architecture described in this book.

Chapter 2: Intentions and Business Processes

Chapter 2 deals with modeling of the business system in terms of its objectives and what activities lead to their fulfillment in the form of business processes. The basic principles of process modeling, the distinction between global and detailed views of processes, and an approach to managing the detail of the process model in the form of four levels of process abstraction are introduced. The second half of this chapter outlines how to capture the process model and the step-by-step process of creating it using a practical example.

Chapter 3: Causality and Business Objects

Chapter 3 deals with the modeling of the business system in terms of the concepts it consists of and the description of the business rules that apply within the modeled business system. The basic principles of object modeling, the distinction between global and detailed views of objects, and the approach to capturing the object life cycles are introduced. The second half of this chapter outlines the approach of capturing an object model and the step-by-step process of creating it using a practical example.

Chapter 4: Integrating the Objects-Oriented and Processes-Oriented Models

Chapter 4 deals with the consistency of the created models of the business system. It presents a simplified metamodel that describes how all models of the business system are related and consistency rules that guide the analysts to avoid possible inconsistencies. Consistency checking is illustrated with a practical example.

Chapter 5: Implementation of Business System Model in an Organization

Chapter 5 focuses on the implementation of the business system in an organization. Based on the basic principles of the process-driven organization, we describe the role and specifics of its information system, explain the comprehensive procedure for building the process-driven organization from the first outline of the process system up to the implementation of organizational and technological infrastructures, and reflect on the organizational maturity and its role in the further development of the process-driven organization.

Chapter 6: MMABP Use Case

Chapter 6 contains the complex example of the application of MMABP in the field of transportation, including the functioning prototype of the process system. It starts with the global models: a process map and the corresponding excerpt from the concept model, complemented by the life cycle of a key object, illustrating how a detailed analysis of the object's life cycle affects the global model of concepts and improves its accuracy. The next part contains the complete set of the conceptual-level process flow models. The last part shows how to transform the conceptual-level models into technology-level processes in the CAMUNDA® workflow engine, which is necessary to create a working prototype in this environment. The prototype is then used to illustrate an essential difference between the conceptual and technology levels of models and the importance of distinguishing between them. We also include the source codes of the processes as a supplement to the book to allow the reader to run the prototype, which illustrates an essential importance of keeping the designed processes in harmony with the business ontology and the importance of respecting the natural parallelism of processes.

Where to Go from Here

Newcomers are advised to read the chapters one by one. The chapters gradually introduce the MMABP methodology and the individual models of minimal business architecture, how the models are related, how they form one business system model, and how this can be used in practice. Chapters 2–4 form a coherent block describing step by step the process of creating a business system model (minimal architecture), which is linked by an example that runs through all chapters.

However, there is no need to put the book in a drawer after reading it. On the contrary, the book is structured in such a way that it can be used as a reference book, since business analysis is a rather complex discipline that is learned mainly through practice, and this book is here to help you with that.

Experienced analysts who are already familiar in some form with the analytical methods presented in this book are encouraged to delve into Chap. 4 to get an idea of what models make up the presented minimal business architecture, how the models relate to each other, and how this can be used in practice.

If some parts inspire them, the book is structured in such a way that it can serve as a reference guide, and the reader can quickly find the part of the analysis that interests him/her.

Contents

Chapter 1
Introduction to the Field of Business Architecture Modeling

Abstract Business architecture modeling is a discipline that helps one align the overall structure and processes of an enterprise with the enterprise's business objectives and available technologies. It also helps visualize the business, enabling stakeholders to gain a holistic view of the enterprise's business and its interdependencies, bridge the gap between business strategy and its execution, and find a common unambiguous language for communication among various stakeholders, including executives, business managers, IT professionals, and other key decision-makers.

Business architecture modeling is a strategic discipline that plays a key role in aligning the overall structure and processes of an enterprise with the business objectives of the enterprise and the available technologies. It tries to provide a comprehensive framework for understanding and visualizing the interactions between the various components of the enterprise, enabling organizations to make informed decisions, optimize operations, and drive innovation.

The essence of business architecture modeling is to create a model of the enterprise in the form of a business system model that captures the essential elements of the enterprise, including its goals, processes, and capabilities. This model serves as a source for visual representation that allows stakeholders to gain a consistent holistic view of the business of the enterprise and its interdependencies. Business architecture model provides a common language for communication among various stakeholders, including executives, business managers, IT professionals, and other key decision-makers. It serves as a foundation for strategic planning, organizational transformation, and the development of targeted initiatives to address business challenges and opportunities.

The main purpose of business architecture modeling is to bridge the gap between business strategy and its implementation. The created blueprint of the business architecture model, when elaborated by appropriate modeling methods and tools, allows to materialize the vision into the design of specific procedures (processes) with respect to the business and environment in which the enterprise operates. This visual concretization of the plan "on paper" then allows for a deep discussion with

© The Author(s), under exclusive license to Springer Nature
Switzerland AG 2024
V. Řepa, O. Svatoš, *Fundamentals of Business Architecture Modeling*, The
Enterprise Engineering Series, https://doi.org/10.1007/978-3-031-59035-1_1

other stakeholders, its fine-tuning so that it does not contradict the objective reality and its further elaboration in such detail that it is then possible to proceed on its basis to its implementation in the enterprise.

The field of business architecture modeling is a relatively dynamic and evolving area that seeks to provide tools for analyzing the problems that inevitably arise with the development and growth of a business and the implementation and development of information systems to support the business in achieving its objectives.

Specific to this type of analysis is the need to respect that it models a dynamic system that is performed (or will be performed) daily by the specific people of a particular business, interacting both with each other and with the business environment. Analysis and modeling should therefore be approached as system modeling, which requires a complex multidimensional approach so that the resulting analysis captures the business system being modeled in all its complexity. The term business architecture modeling has been adopted for this system approach, which is based on a multidimensional approach, i.e., different diagrams (views) from different relevant perspectives of a modeled system. Although the model consists of different views, the desired output is then one consistent model of the reality of the business (consisting of different views) that respects its context—it is interconnected with the environment of the modeled business system and fits fully into it.

The modeling process, we call business architecture modeling, is not in the context of modeling primarily about the size, as the term architecture and the literature directly related to the field of business architecture might evoke, but about the style and method of modeling used.

1.1   Approaches to Business Architecture Modeling

The field of business architecture and its modeling is not uniform. There are different approaches that agree on the goals of the business architecture, but they differ in what aspects of these goals they primarily focus on and therefore in how exactly to achieve these goals and what tools to use to do so.

1.1.1   Business Architecture Guild

The Business Architecture Guild approaches to business architecture from strategic perspective, and according to it:

> Business architecture represents holistic, multidimensional business views of: capabilities, end-to-end value delivery, information, and organizational structure; and the relationships among these business views and strategies, products, policies, initiatives, and stakeholders. The value of business architecture is to provide an abstract representation of an enterprise and the business ecosystem in which it operates. By doing so, business architecture delivers value as an effective communication and analytical framework for translating strategy into actionable initiatives. [1]

The primary resource for this approach is the Guide to the Business Architecture Body of Knowledge—BIZBOK Guide [1]— and its main focus is on business architecture as a management discipline. In terms of modeling, it focuses exclusively on business architecture and how to map its different aspects. These are captured using so-called blueprints, which are proprietary tailored schemas or diagrams. The focus is on best representation of each aspect (blueprint) from the management point of view rather than on creating one formal consistent business model. This is consistent with the focus of this approach. The blueprints are tools for structuring reality, mapping it at a strategic level of detail and communicating with stakeholders. For this purpose, it provides the readers with so-called Industry Reference Models and case studies. BIZBOK does not forget about business architecture management either. It specifies business architecture governance as well as the interconnection with the higher level of detail, in form of guidance for business process modeling and management and case management, necessary for implementation of the strategic business architecture. It also specifies the Business Architecture Maturity Model for evaluating the business architecture. The primary focus on strategic level of business architecture does not mean that then BIZBOK neglects the context. Quite on the contrary, it provides guidance for business architecture and IT architecture alignment, and it connects the topic of business architecture with other management disciplines such as Lean Six Sigma and Business Performance Management.

1.1.2   The Open Group

The Open Group maintains, among many others, two core standards for business architecture: the Open Group Architecture Framework (TOGAF) and ArchiMate.

TOGAF sees the business architecture as "a representation of holistic, multidimensional business views of: capabilities, end-to-end value delivery, information, and organizational structure; and the relationships among these business views and strategies, products, policies, initiatives, and stakeholders" [2].

TOGAF works with the business architecture as a part of something bigger—the enterprise architecture. TOGAF is a comprehensive framework for enterprise architecture, providing a structured approach to developing and managing architectures, and so the business architecture is, for TOGAF, one of the four core architectures it works with [2]. The other core architectures are Data Architecture, Application Architecture, and Technology Architecture. TOGAF is very focused on models and provides its users with core diagrams, extension diagrams, catalogs and matrices specific for each architecture, and a metamodel that connects all these together in one architecture repository. TOGAF also provides an Architecture Development Method (ADM) that guides one in enterprise architecture development from its vision to its implementation and continuous development. In this method, we can also find how the TOGAF sees the purpose of the business architecture. The goal of the ADM is to "develop target business architecture that describes how the enterprise needs to operate to achieve the business goals and respond to the strategic drivers" [2].

The idea of multidimensional business views TOGAF materializes in modeling in the form of specification of core diagrams and extension diagrams. It specifies what the models should capture, their purpose, and what elements to use, but there is no method/technique on how exactly to do it. We can see this part of TOGAF as more of a recommendation, because when we look at ArchiMate [3], which elaborates the models and modeling for TOGAF into detail, these diagrams are not mentioned at all, and the multidimensional business views are represented by general, so-called architecture viewpoints. This is consistent with the promoted core idea of an architecture model as an instance of a common metamodel in one architecture repository that can be viewed from different perspectives—the architecture viewpoints.

TOGAF and ArchiMate stay at a strategic level of detail, and this is reflected in the models. For example, the atomic element of business architecture is a process, and if there is a need to model this in detail, it is outside the TOGAF/ArchiMate metamodel in other standards such as BPMN.

TOGAF is a very complex approach to enterprise architecture that has been shaped over many years by practicing professionals in a variety of industries. We can see it as a best practice-based standard that is constantly evolving. There are many extensions to the TOGAF core that try to link it to all the relevant methods that are relevant to enterprise architecture, such as architecture governance, risk management, security architecture, capability maturity models, agile methods, project management, and so on.

1.1.3   Enterprise Engineering

Enterprise engineering (EE) is a theory-based discipline that responds to the lack of coherence and consistency among the various components of an enterprise [4]. This approach to architectures is based on ontologies and relevant research and their methodologies and methods. These methods, domains of knowledge, constructs, and concepts, are used to analyze and design enterprises [5].

It is really a very theory-based approach that approaches an architecture and its development in a very different way than traditional best-practices approaches. In best-practice approaches such as TOGAF, methods evolve incrementally based on the experience of practitioners. EE works differently. EE is an ontological approach that builds on foundational science (theories) to ensure the coherence and consistency of the architecture model. It also evolves, but the core logic of this approach to architecture modeling was created as a synthesis of relevant scientific theories and remains stable, unlike best practices approaches, which are based on a synthesis of the practical architectural experience of practitioners in different domains.

EE defines an architecture as a coherent, consistent, and hierarchically ordered set of generic functional and constructional normative principles that guide the (re-)

development of the enterprise for a particular class of systems. The collective architectures of an enterprise are called its enterprise architecture [4].

The rules for the architectures are then common to all architectures. There is no classification of architectures as business, application, or technological, as in TOGAF, for example. Instead, there is the ontological model. This is a complete, implementation-independent model of how the system is built and operates. In addition, an ontological model must have a modular structure, and its elements are (ontologically) atomic. For enterprises, the meta-model of such models is called an enterprise ontology. For information systems, the meta-model is called information system ontology [4].

EE works with the models in full complexity. In General Conceptual Modeling Framework (GCMF), it shows that there are three levels in conceptual modeling and how they are related to each other. The levels are instance, schema, and meta schema [6]. For these models, it provides the General Ontology Specification Language (GOSL). This is a first-order logic language for specifying the state space and the transition space of a world. It is a language for specifying schemas and meta schemas, and syntax of GOSL comprises both graphical and textual symbols and constructs [6]. EE is not only about theory but also about practice, and for this, it offers Design and Engineering Methodology for Organizations (DEMO).

From the above, it is obvious that the EE has quite different and complex approach to business architecture modeling, and it requires an open mind to approach it successfully. Probably the most obvious example that illustrates this difference is the approach to business process modeling. Unlike the other standards, such as TOGAF or BPMN, the EE understands a business process as a tree of transaction processes, so it captures it as a structure, instead of a flow of activities or business processes as in BPMN or in TOGAF/ArchiMate.

The ontological approach to architecture modeling also provides a view that shows that business architecture does not have to end at the process level but that the detail of business processes can also be part of the (business) architecture.

1.1.4 Business Process Management

The field of business process management is probably not the first thing that comes to mind when thinking about business architecture modeling. While business processes are part of business architecture in standard methodologies or frameworks, the emphasis on process management and related methods are not so much a part of it. Yet when we look at TOGAF and the aforementioned business architecture goal, i.e., "to create a target enterprise architecture that describes how the enterprise must operate to achieve business goals," one cannot but conclude that this is the primary goal of process management too.

The reason for this distance from process management may be that process management is usually associated with process detail, for which many procedures and standards have been developed, but for a strategic (abstracting from process detail) view, standard tools of business process management are no longer sufficient. This can be well illustrated by a process map. It cannot be said that there is a standard, universally accepted procedure within process management methods to model the relationships between processes (without analyzing the process details). Process maps, process landscapes, value streams, and others have been written about, but none of these are standard. Standards like BPMN [7] and UML [8] have nothing like a process map, while ARIS [9] offers its value stream map, [10] its process map, and [11] its process landscape.

It may seem as if the two worlds, i.e., strategic and business process management, are separate. The opposite is true, as both of these approaches are still working with the same process model, and so not only does the process detail need to be consistent with the features listed in the process map, but conversely, what is listed in the process map (in the architecture) needs to be consistent with what is in the process detail. It is approaches such as Enterprise Engineering, based on ontologies, that show that from a modeling point of view there is no reason why business process detail (within a reasonable level of detail) should not also be part of the business architecture.

Process management offers procedures how to identify and model processes in detail and, in process map, how to measure their performance, and this is often not possible without knowing their details. It also offers best practices, for example, in the form of the APQC Process Classification Framework [12], linkages to the balanced scorecard [10], maturity models [10], etc. In short, it integrates everything even seemingly related to process management.

What process management leaves to others is the analysis of the structure of the real world, i.e., the objects with which processes work. Of course, we can find mention of business objects, but the details of the analysis are left to others.

1.1.5   MMABP

We describe Methodology for Modeling and Analysis of Business Processes (MMABP) in detail in a separate Sect. 1.3, but here at this point, we would like to put MMABP in the context of other approaches to business architecture modeling.

The abovementioned approaches to business architecture can, with their complexity, create the impression that it is always a big project, and for relatively simple problems, the use of architectural approaches is too robust. The opposite is true. A well-structured analysis, provided the right methodology and tools are used, is reusable and expandable after increments, so the goal does not have to be a global model of the entire company, but on the contrary, the right methodology will allow you to focus only on what is important and relevant to the problem being solved.

In this book, we try to achieve this goal by presenting rules for a minimal business architecture based on MMABP, so that the modeled business system model (architecture) can be developed step by step and allows to focus only on the specific problems to be solved and their solutions, not on a pile of documentation that may not be needed in the end. Thus, MMABP does not try to compete with the standards in use but tries to highlight what is essential for business architecture in the flood of a huge number of diagrams and related elements that the current standards and frameworks offer.

The MMABP goes across the above approaches, but it should be understood as a stand-alone methodology that stands on its own clear principles, not as an extract of what is essential from other methods and methodologies. The aim is to provide fundamental principles and practices for capturing the core of business architecture so that it is complete and consistent while being minimal in the number of models and elements within them. Nevertheless, everything is aligned in such a way that no one is prevented from using other diagrams and symbols that relevant standards offer.

MMABP is integrated with the standards used for the given modeling domain. MMABP respects TOGAF as the main enterprise architecture framework and uses the Event Diagram as the tool to capture a process map with the definition of core elements (business processes and functions) aligned. MMABP shares with Business Process Management and EE the idea that the detailed models of business processes are part of the business architecture and uses BPMN as the standard for their modeling.

MMABP sees the object model of the real world, the modelled business processes exist in, as undividable part of the business architecture. In this respect, ontological modeling promoted by EE is a powerful tool that is not driven by the "pure data analysis" that many analysts tend to slip into when modeling business and business architecture. Unfortunately, ontological approach is very complex for ordinary analysts, and they rather avoid it. MMABP takes core concepts from OntoUML and tries to extend the "regular" class diagram modeling approach with concepts that allow the analyst to capture the reality in the object model in a way that would not be possible using only the "data analysis" approach and yet does not require an ontologist to do so. Special focus is given to object life cycles, although, primarily captured in flow manner in state transition diagrams (state machine diagram from UML).

MMABP shares consistency concerns with EE. To avoid a lack of coherence and consistency among the different models, MMABP specifies a metamodel that describes how all its models of the business system are related and consistency rules that guide the analysts to avoid the possible inconsistencies.

MMABP does not exist in a vacuum. It specifies its relation to process management, maturity models, implementation of business processes through workflow, etc.

1.2   Standards and Frameworks for Business Architecture Modeling

There are many standards and frameworks for business architecture modeling. They are usually designed as a stand-alone standard/framework but often refer to a methodological framework for capturing the business architecture on which they are based. For example, ArchiMate is a stand-alone standard for enterprise architecture modeling (including business architecture), but it references TOGAF on which it is philosophically based. Conversely, TOGAF lists ArchiMate as one of the appropriate standards for modeling enterprise architecture, but not the only one.

In the overview of standards/frameworks for business architecture modeling that we present in this section, we have focused on those standards/frameworks that are relevant to the abovementioned approaches to business architecture modeling.

1.2.1   ARIS

Architecture of Integrated Information Systems (ARIS) is a long-time developed framework for architecture modeling [13]. Initially, as the name suggests, the focus was on the architecture of information systems, but as it evolved, the focus was broadened to include the entire enterprise architecture. The architectural approach to modeling in ARIS is reflected in its multidimensional approach to modeling the real world in the form of the so-called ARIS House.

The *ARIS House* concept is based on five viewpoints at the architecture. These five viewpoints, namely, organization, data, product/service, function, and control views, break down the complexity of the architecture into individual models and provide a comprehensive understanding of the architecture from different perspectives [9] (Fig. 1.1).

- *Function View*. The function view describes the activities, their relationships, and hierarchical structure within the business process. It often utilizes a function tree to depict the organization of functions. Goals associated with the functions are also assigned in this view, as functions support and are controlled by these goals.
- *Organization View*. The organization view offers an overview of the company's organizational structure, including human resources, machines, hardware, and their relationships. It helps visualize the roles, responsibilities, and interactions of various entities within the organization. This view can be represented through an organizational chart.

Fig. 1.1 ARIS House [9]

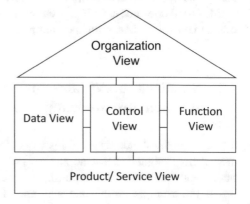

- *Data View*. The data view encompasses all relevant information objects within the company, such as correspondence, documents, and other data-related aspects. It focuses on capturing and organizing company-relevant data and can be represented using techniques like an Entity Relationship Model.
- *Product/Service View*. The product/service view provides a comprehensive overview of the organization's entire product or service portfolio. It encompasses offerings, including services, products, and financial aspects, helping to understand the scope and nature of the organization's offerings.
- *Control View*. This view captures business process which serve as a connecting link between all the other views. Techniques such as event-driven process chains or BPMN (Business Process Model and Notation) can be used to represent the flow and sequencing of activities within the process.

Even though the ARIS House was specifically developed for architecture of integrated information systems, its views also cover the important dimensions for the business architecture. Due to its universality and clarity for ordinary businesspeople, it became popular tool for modeling especially the *Value Chain diagrams* for global view at business processes and *eEPC diagrams* for their detailed view.

1.2.2 ArchiMate

The ArchiMate modeling framework [3], which builds on the TOGAF standard, is a popular and recognized framework for enterprise architecture modeling. ArchiMate is not just a visual notation for TOGAF, but from a modeling perspective, it is an extension of it and elaborates it into the detail needed for modeling. TOGAF provides only a basic metamodel, while the ArchiMate provides analysts with a modeling notation and elaboration of the basic TOGAF concepts into specific well-defined terms, which then as a whole form together complex modeling language. A clear example is the term "business process," which is present in the TOGAF specification only in the generic form "process," but the specific definition of what a business, application, or technology process is must be sought in the ArchiMate specification. This is the case for most TOGAF model elements, which are specific for each architecture (layer).

The ArchiMate Core Framework [3] consists of three core layers (Fig. 1.2) based on the three TOGAF architectures (business, application, and technology). The business layer captures the business services offered to customers, which are realized in the organization by business processes performed by business entities, the application layer captures the application services that support the business and the applications that implement them, and the technology layer captures both information and operational technologies.

ArchiMate distinguishes three different aspects on each layer (Fig. 1.2): an aspect of an *active structure* that represents structural elements such as business entities, application components, and devices that exhibit actual behavior, i.e., "subjects" of

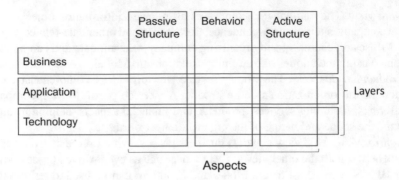

Fig. 1.2 ArchiMate Core Framework [3]

activity; the *behavioral* aspect, which represents the behavior (processes, functions, events, and other elements) performed by the *active structure* elements; and the *passive structure* aspect, which represents the objects on which the behavior is performed.

ArchiMate provides a generic metamodel for the ArchiMate Core Framework that defines for each layer a corresponding set of concepts with their interrelationships both within the layer and between the layers (and aspects) that can be used for modeling each layer.

Methodologically, ArchiMate relies on TOGAF and its Architecture Development Method (ADM) that guides the user through the steps of how the complete enterprise architecture should be developed, what the required inputs are, available models, and required outputs. A specific procedure on how to model each layer using the defined concepts is not specified in TOGAF or the ArchiMate specification.

1.2.3   Object Management Group Standards

Object Management Group (OMG) does not provide a single framework or methodology for how to model enterprise architecture; instead, it provides different standards with diagrams that have proven useful throughout the history.

The best known is the Unified Modeling Language (UML) standard [8], which provides many diagrams (views) that have proven useful throughout the history of systems modeling and a metamodel that links them together. It is then up to the user to choose which diagrams to use, and through the metamodel, the diagrams can be kept consistent with each other.

UML was created by merging three leading object-oriented methods (Booch, OMT, and OOSE), and from the point of view of object modeling, it represents the basic tool of object-oriented analysis. According to [8], the objective of UML is "to provide system architects, software engineers, and software developers with tools for analysis, design, and implementation of software-based systems as well as for modeling business and similar processes." It is clear from the objective that this is a tool for analyzing information systems, but many diagrams are not tied to implementation, but their object-oriented basis allows them to be used for other, more abstract, purposes. For example, let's mention the popular class diagram, which is used not only for describing implementation in an object-oriented programming language but also as a tool for conceptual analysis for the purpose of mapping business architecture or capturing abstract metamodels.

Another popular standard of OMG is the Business Process Model and Notation (BPMN) [7]. The BPMN standard, as the name suggests, is a widely accepted tool for modeling of detailed process flow models, especially in the field of business process management. The specification itself [7] states:

> The primary goal of BPMN is to provide a notation that is readily understandable by all business users, from the business analysts that create the initial drafts of the processes, to the technical developers responsible for implementing the technology that will perform those processes, and finally, to the business people who will manage and monitor those processes. Thus, BPMN creates a standardized bridge for the gap between the business process design and process implementation...Another goal, but no less important, is to ensure that XML languages designed for the execution of business processes, such as WSBPEL (Web Services Business Process Execution Language), can be visualized with a business-oriented notation.

BPMN is therefore a wide-ranging modeling language that, in the words of enterprise architecture, should be universally applicable across all layers of architecture in terms of capturing the process flow model. This broad scope leads to the fact that the notation is quite detailed and contains a lot of elements and their variants that are not comprehensible to ordinary business users, so when using BPMN, it is always necessary to consider the purpose of the model and what type of users will work with it and choose the element palette to be used in the diagram accordingly. BPMN also takes this into account. For example, BPMN contains a very comprehensive list of event types but also offers a palette of basic events without distinguishing types that are understandable to the ordinary business user.

OMG is the custodian of many other standards, many of which are relevant to architecture modeling, such as Business Motivation Model (DMM) [14], Semantics of Business Vocabulary and Business Rules (SBVR) [15], and Value Delivery Modeling Language (VDML) [16].

1.2.4 DEMO

Design and Engineering Methodology for Organizations (DEMO) is methodology based on EE with the objective to produce the essential model of an enterprise. DEMO is the result of scientific research from 1990 to 1994 at the University of Maastricht and from 1995 to 2009 at Delft University of Technology [6].

The essential model of an organization according to DEMO [6] consists of four integrated ontological models, each taking a specific view at the organization: the Cooperation Model, the Action Model, the Process Model, and the Fact Model.

All four submodels are modelled using the DEMO Specification Language (DEMOSL), which comprises diagrams, tables, and formal textual descriptions. Expressions in DEMOSL are basically formal textual descriptions, which look like structured English sentences, but they often also have a graphical equivalent. DEMOSL diagrams are intentionally kept simple. Any information that cannot be conveyed through a diagram must be expressed through additional formal text.

To create essential models, the DEMO offers the OER method (Organizational Essence Revealing). The concept of revelation is crucial in this case. The method is based on the assumption that the essential model is not devised or created in any other way but that the operational essence is already present in a running organization and only needs to be revealed. DEMO provides also techniques for validation of the essential model. Validation in the OER method means that one takes all the representations of the created integrated essential model (diagrams and tables) and checks the claims made in the model with the people who play the roles of actors in the essential model.

1.2.5   OntoUml and UFO

OntoUML is an ontologically well-founded language for ontology-driven conceptual Modeling developed by Giancarlo Guizzardi and first published in his PhD thesis "Ontological Foundations for Structural Conceptual Models" [17]. OntoUML extends the UML based on the Unified Foundational Ontology (UFO). The importance of UFO lies in the linking conceptual modeling and domain ontology engineering by enhancing the UML 2.0 metamodel. The basis of UFO (so-called UFO-A) allows to model and analyze the structural conceptual modeling constructs such as object types and taxonomic relations, associations and their mutual relations, roles, properties, data types and weak entities, and parthood relations among objects. During the later development, the foundational ontology has been enriched with ontology of events (UFO-B) and ontology of social and intentional aspects (UFO-C). OntoUML has been adopted by the academic community as well as by organizations worldwide for the development of conceptual models in a variety of domains.

1.3   Introduction to MMABP Essential Principles

Methodology for modeling and Analysis of Business Processes (MMABP) is a methodology for modeling business systems. Despite its traditional name, it is not focused only on the business processes but on the complete model of an organization (i.e., a business system).

In the following section, we introduce the reader to the Philosophical Framework for Business System Modeling, which serves as a base for essential principles of the methodology. The Framework determines the basic dimensions of the information model of an organization, their mutual relationships, and related underlying disciplines like logic, theory of algorithms, and others.

In the remaining subchapters of this chapter, we introduce the reader to the MMABP Minimal Business Architecture, its basic models, and their essential relationships.

1.3.1 Foundational Principles

MMABP is based on three fundamental general principles, as shown in Fig. 1.3: the *principle of modeling*, the *principle of abstraction*, and the *principle of three architectures*.

The *principle of modeling* posits that the basis for implementing a business system in an organization must be derived from tangible realities that exist outside of and independent of the organization. In essence, every organization, as an embodiment of a business system or idea, serves as a model of the Real World.

The *principle of abstraction* emphasizes the need to create abstract concepts when modeling the Real World, with hierarchical abstractions being particularly important.

The *principle of three architectures* describes the approach to create abstractions with primary consideration of the principle of modeling. According to this

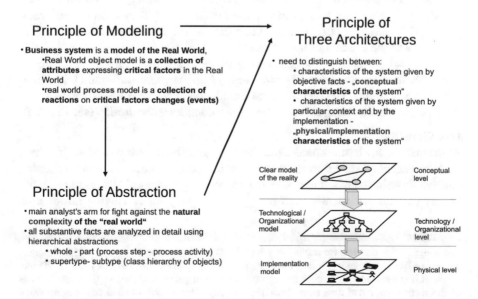

Fig. 1.3 Foundational principles of MMABP

principle, the highest level of abstraction should focus on a clear model of the Real World, unaffected by any general (technological or organizational) or individual (implementation) specific aspects. Subsequent levels of abstraction should take into account generic aspects of business system implementation, such as the technology and organization used, before dealing with individual specific aspects, such as individual skills, corporate culture, etc. This hierarchical structure, as shown in Fig. 1.3, implies that as one descends to lower levels of abstraction, the model becomes more complex, incorporating elements from previous levels along with the specific aspects relevant to that level. In essence, the Principle of three Architectures is a logical outcome of both the Principle of Modeling and the Principle of Abstraction, as illustrated in Fig. 1.3. The models in this book are mostly at the conceptual level of Three Architectures. For practical example of how models need to be modified when moving to lower architectural levels, see the example in Chap. 6.

1.3.2   Philosophical Framework for Business System Modeling[1]

The MMABP methodology is centered around the comprehensive description of a business system. In our understanding, a business system refers to any system that is created and continuously developed by individuals to achieve specific business goals. In this concept, the business system comprises a set of mutually collaborating business processes that collectively work toward attaining particular business objectives. The achievement of these goals is generally influenced by the overarching rules and regulations of the environment within which these processes operate. We refer to this collection of rules as business rules. Additionally, the MMABP methodology places significant emphasis on the information system as an integral component of the business system, recognizing that the information system itself serves as a model of the overall business system.

Figure 1.4 presents our understanding of the fundamental nature of business, which revolves around *achieving goals in a given environment*. Within this definition, two key phenomena that form the foundation of the MMABP framework for business system modeling are identified: *intentionality* and *causality* (see Fig. 1.4).

Intentionality
At the core of any business endeavor, there are specific intentions and goals. These goals are accomplished through actions organized into processes, often requiring collaboration in today's interconnected society. Effective collaboration relies on quality communication, which in turn paves the way for leveraging information

---

[1] Warning: In this chapter, we use a fairly high level of abstraction as we aim to fully explain the roots of the methodology. It may therefore be difficult to understand on first reading. We recommend that the reader first skims through the chapter to get an overview of the main features of the methodology and then come back periodically after getting more detailed information on specific topics in order to maintain a global overview at the same time.

Fig. 1.4 Business system
as an equilibrium of
intentions and causality

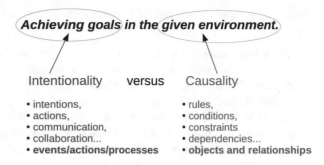

Within the context of the business system's intentionality, we work with business processes comprised of actions driven by events.

Causality

Beyond processes, the business system encompasses individuals, entities, relationships, values, meanings, and other tangible or abstract elements known as (business) objects. These objects are interconnected through rules, conditions, constraints, dependencies, and various types of relationships. These relationships establish the system-like nature of the collection of business objects, imbuing it with logical coherence. When considering business processes as an essential phenomenon, causality emerges as a vital aspect of the business system's logic. It involves the general determination of the consequences resulting from events, actions, and changes within the business objects.

These two phenomena are closely intertwined, as they jointly shape the business system and require harmonization. A well-calibrated business system can be characterized as an *equilibrium between intentionality and causality*. In the following text, we delve into how MMABP methodology supports and maintains this equilibrium.

Philosophical Framework for Business System Modeling determines the basic dimensions of the information model of an organization, their basic mutual relationships, and related underlying disciplines. The creation of the Framework is primarily driven by the imperative to gain a comprehensive understanding of the essential aspects of the real world that should be incorporated into an information system. This need arises from the recognition that an information system, serving as the information infrastructure for a business system (representing the real world), is intended to provide accurate, truthful, and timely information about the system's state, history, and potential future events. To achieve this holistic understanding of the Real World, it is essential to develop a general grasp of its fundamental dimensions. This understanding should be as universally applicable as possible, drawing insights from various research fields focused on the Real World, including philosophical disciplines, particularly logic. Considering its broad applicability, we refer to our framework for business system modeling as "philosophical."

The framework is founded on the premise that the depiction of a given business domain (the Real World) is influenced by two fundamental phenomena, *being and behavior*, as well as two critical perspectives, *system view and particular (temporal) view*.

- *Being* represents the Real World in its existing state and its potential states. It encompasses fundamental facts about the presence of real-world objects, their capacity for change, and their relationships. *Modal logic* provides a formal means of describing being.
- *Behavior* captures the events that occur in the real world as a result of actions performed by real-world actors. These actions encompass goal attainment, plan execution, and intentional behavior. *Process-oriented* descriptions serve as a formal representation of such behavior.
- The *system view* perceives the Real World as a collection of individual elements forming a cohesive system. Given the objective of describing system attributes, this model must encompass the entire system. Adopting a system-level perspective involves abstracting individual attributes of system components, especially excluding temporal aspects that are inherently partial. Consequently, the system model can be characterized as a static view.
- The *particular (temporal) view* focuses on real-world events and their consequential changes. To achieve sufficient precision, this model does not cover the entire system but instead focuses on its specific segments. Temporal aspects of the Real World can be formally modeled using algorithmic descriptions, which do not account for parallelism. Therefore, each particular model must be developed from the perspective of a single system element, as the temporal view restricts the description just to the characteristics of that specific element.

By combining these two phenomena with the two perspectives, we can establish four fundamental models (refer to Fig. 1.5):

1. *The Model of Real-World Modality*. This model presents the static view of existence, delineating the system of real-world objects and their potential relationships.

Fig. 1.5 Philosophical framework for business system modeling

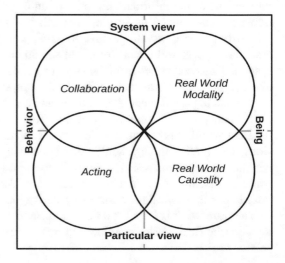

2. *The Model of Real-World Causality*. This model embodies the temporal view of existence, delineating the possible states in the life cycle of a specific real-world object and the transitions between them.
3. *The Model of Collaboration*. This model captures the static view of behavior, portraying the system of business processes and their interrelationships. Given the intentional nature of the behavior, the relationships among processes consistently signify their collaboration in attaining predefined goals.
4. *The Model of Acting*. This model represents the temporal view of behavior, illustrating the sequences of actions within a specific business process aimed at accomplishing the designated process goal under all possible circumstances.

Figure 1.5 depicts the four fundamental types of models and their interconnected nature, underscoring that these models partially mutually overlap. While some facts about the Real World are uniquely expressed in a specific model type, others are articulated from different perspectives, resulting in overlapping content. This overlap arises due to the inherent interconnectedness of the basic phenomena and viewpoints within the framework. The notion of being without behavior holds no meaning, as every change in the Real World is a consequence of purposeful actions within the business system. Similarly, particulars lack significance in isolation from the larger system to which they belong. Each element in a particular model is intricately linked to the corresponding system model, which provides the necessary contextual framework. Recognizing the fundamental relationships among different informatics models, stemming from their collective depiction of the complex Real World, lays the foundation for consistency rules (see the following subchapter).

Figure 1.6 illustrates the basic analytical models, aligning them with the specific model types defined in the Framework. In the context of information modeling, *Real World Modality* pertains to the static rules of the Real World, which are expressed through basic modal logic. In the field of informatics, this perspective finds representation in the traditional data-oriented conceptual model, exemplified by [18]. Such a model encompasses the relationships between Real World objects and their corresponding circumstances. Currently, the commonly used diagram for this type of model is UML Class Diagram [8, 17]. Traditional conceptual models are data-oriented, where objects are represented only by their attributes. MMABP understands the Real World objects in an object-oriented way as a unity of attributes and their life cycle operations. To avoid misunderstanding, MMABP calls this model the *model of concepts*.

Real-World Causality focuses on the temporal rules of the Real World, which are captured through causal logic. Unlike modal logic, focusing on relationships in general, causal logic focuses on temporal dependencies. Thus, one should speak rather about interactions instead of relationships. Informatically, this perspective can be captured by the *object life cycle* model, which describes the causal evolution of Real World objects through defined states and their sequentiality under specific circumstances. This type of model is standardly represented by UML State Machine Diagram [8].

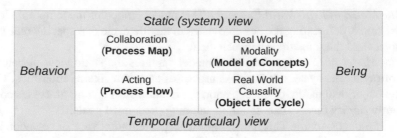

Fig. 1.6 Kinds of business system models in MMABP

The *model of collaboration* shows the interrelationships among business processes and their shared context. Given the intentional nature of behavior within the business system, the relationships between processes are viewed as collaborative efforts toward achieving goals. In the informatics field, this perspective can be represented by the *process map*, commonly associated with the methodology developed by Erikson and Penker [19]. Currently, this model can also be made using the TOGAF Event Diagram [2, 20].

The *model of acting* refers to the algorithmic description of specific business processes, encompassing various behavioral variants aimed at accomplishing the process goal. This perspective on behavior in the Real World can be captured using the *process flow* model. Notations such as the standard Business Process Model and Notation (BPMN) [7], as well as others like ARIS [21] and IDEF [22], are widely accepted as diagrams for process flow models.

1.3.3 MMABP Minimal Business Architecture

As noted above, the MMABP builds its theoretical background on principles expressed in Philosophical Framework for Business System Modeling. MMABP as a methodological framework is intended to use these principles to achieve its goal, i.e., to provide principles and methods suitable for the design of a Minimal Business Architecture that builds on the ability to capture the architecture of a business system using as few diagrams and symbols as possible while taking into account that even so, the resulting model and views (diagrams) must be complete, mutually consistent, understandable to the average user, and relatively resistant to common changes in business and thus represent a stable foundation for business architecture.

The Minimal Business Architecture described in this book as model of a business system focuses on the analysis at the conceptual level. We intend to provide readers with a general approach to business system modeling that can be adapted to meet the specific needs of individual businesses. MMABP does not delve into implementation details as those are specific to each enterprise's current business, application, and technological architecture. Additionally, numerous methodologies have already been introduced for this purpose, including both traditional [3, 23, 24] and agile [25] approaches.

The MMABP is built upon the widely recognized enterprise architecture standard, TOGAF [2], which we integrate with UML [8] and BPMN [7]. Additionally, we consider ArchiMate [3] due to its extension of TOGAF concepts and its ability to provide more tangible representations. While TOGAF and ArchiMate acknowledge UML and BPMN as valid extensions for detailed architecture elaboration, they lack specific details on their interrelationships. Likewise, BPMN and UML standards do not elaborate on their connections in depth. To address these gaps, we utilize MMABP, which maps the relevant relationships among these standards and suggests for each standard a minimum set of specific diagrams. This holistic approach enables a comprehensive view of the modeled business system, facilitating the evaluation of business architecture's completeness, correctness, and mutual consistency.

We also emphasize the practical perspective of business system modeling. Creating a minimal business architecture requires a capable computer-aided software engineering (CASE) tool. This tool should support the individual modeling standards and capture the relations between entities across different diagrams and standards. To fulfill this need, we have developed the Enterprise Assistant tool [26], which fully covers all the models specified in MMABP, including their interconnections and consistency rules. With Enterprise Assistant, users can seamlessly create, manage, and interlink these diagrams and models, ensuring their coherence and accessibility within a single tool.

1.3.4 Models of the Minimal Business Architecture

In contrast to the extensive range of diagram types specified by conventional modeling standards for specific scenarios, MMABP takes a different approach. It advocates for a minimal set of model types that need to be developed to create a concise and cohesive business architecture.

As derived from the earlier discussion on the Philosophical Framework for Business System Modeling (see Sect. 1.3.1), there are two fundamental types of models for the business (Real World) system (see Fig. 1.7).

The MMABP utilizes the UML modeling language [8] to represent the *Real-World ontology* through models that capture the essential characteristics of the business environment, namely, modality and causality. These models, also known as structural models in the field of informatics, focus on the structure of the business system, including its objects and their interactions.

For modeling the Real-World modality, the *UML Class Diagram* is employed. This diagram provides a static representation of the fundamental aspects of the Real World in terms of the model of concepts. The model of concepts, often referred to as the system model, describes the interconnectedness of the business objects within the system. However, this type of description primarily focuses on the common aspects of the entire system and does not explicitly capture the temporal aspects (i.e., causality) that are specific to individual elements of the system.

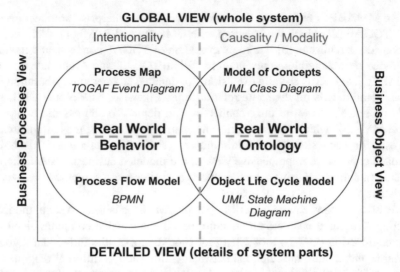

Fig. 1.7 MMABP models that the business system model consists of

To incorporate the temporal aspects of causality associated with Real-World objects, the *UML State Machine Diagram* is utilized. This diagram provides representation of object life cycle model and represents the causality in terms of an object's life cycle, providing a complementary perspective to the system model. Each object life cycle model is dedicated to a single object and describes the temporal causality relevant to that object throughout its life cycle.

UML defines some basic relationships between both diagrams, which are also a part of the MMABP rules for modeling the Real-World ontology.

To represent the *Real-World behavior*, the MMABP relies on the *BPMN* (Business Process Model and Notation) standard [7]. BPMN is used to model the temporal aspects of process flows, while the *process map* is employed to describe the system of business processes. Although the process map is not included in the BPMN standard, it is a necessary and commonly used diagram type that complements BPMN. MMABP utilizes the *TOGAF Event Diagram* [2, 20] to fulfill the role of the *process map*.

MMABP distinguishes between two fundamental types of models within both kinds of Real-World models (see Fig. 1.7):

- *Global (system) models.* These models focus on the overall characteristics of the system and therefore are referred to as system models. As their purpose is to provide an overview of the entire system, they abstract from the temporal aspects of the Real World. Consequently, these models represent a static view. MMABP utilizes the model of concepts (UML Class Diagram) for the global ontological model and the *process map* (TOGAF Event Diagram) for the global behavioral model (as mentioned earlier).
- *Detailed models.* These models concentrate on the specific details of the Real World, considering both ontological and behavioral temporal aspects. To capture the temporal dimension, each detailed model must focus on a specific, unam-

biguous part of the system, described as a single algorithm. Hence, these models are termed detailed. MMABP employs the object life cycle model (UML State Machine Diagram) for the detailed ontological model and process flow model (BPMN) for the detailed behavioral model (as discussed previously).

For a more comprehensive understanding of these types of models, detailed explanations are given in the following chapters. They not only provide detailed explanations, but they also include comprehensive guide on how to approach the modeling process.

1.3.5   Consistency of the Minimal Business Architecture

In practice, the time to create a very detailed enterprise architecture to enable simulation is limited. Such an effort would be time-consuming, costly, and resource-intensive. However, ensuring the completeness and correctness of the business architecture remains critical, as any significant partial change during system evolution could jeopardize the integrity of the entire business system.

The models presented here give us four different but complementary views of the same reality, the same trading system. For this to be true, the individual diagrams must be consistent with each other so that together they form one compact and consistent business architecture. Since in the analysis phase of many business/IT projects there is usually nothing tangible yet, only diagrams that together form one future business architecture, it is the consistency of the individual diagrams that is available as the main tool for business architecture verification. It is up to the analyst to check for consistency conflicts, clarify them, and refine the business architecture to match the expected reality from all modeled perspectives. Only when the proposed architecture is correct and complete can one properly evaluate whether, at least on paper, the proposed business architecture is feasible. Therefore, MMABP defines the necessary consistency of models using a set of metamodels. The MMABP business system meta-model [27] consists of three basic related models:

- The Business Substance meta-model, which defines the basic concepts and their underlying relationships used to model the business object domain in terms of ontology/conceptual modeling. This meta-model is based on the UML Core definition [8] extended with special concepts to define other aspects of modeling, especially life cycle modeling aspects.
- The business process meta-model that defines the basic concepts and their underlying relationships used for business process domain modeling.
- The Business models consistency model, which defines the basic relationships between concepts from the two metamodels above, defining in this way the required consistency between the ontology/conceptual model and the business process model describing the same business system.

Set of specific consistency rules is implied by these metamodels, and they are elaborated and described in detail in Chap. 4.

1.4   Further Reading

The standards for enterprise architecture and therefore also for business architecture today are the TOGAF [2] together with ArchiMate [3], so we recommend reading up on what these standards look like and how they relate to each other. You can find information about their use in [28].

Business processes are the core of the business architecture, and so it is good to know something about the basics of business process management, presented, for example, in [10].

The modeling of enterprise and therefore business architecture can also be approached from the position of ontological modeling. A comprehensive ontological approach to enterprise architecture modeling can be found, for example, in Enterprise Engineering. As an introduction to enterprise governance and Enterprise Engineering, one can start with [5]. For further detail on enterprise ontology, one can see [6] that includes also description of the DEMO methodology. Approaches and principles on how to approach enterprise (business) architecture modeling and its management in the context of EE can be found in [29] and [30]. For MMABP basic structure and metamodel, see [27].

1.5   Summary

This chapter presents the business architecture modeling filed as a discipline that includes different approaches to architecture modeling, represented by different standards and frameworks. One of the approaches is the MMABP, which this book focuses on.

Section 1.1 Approaches to Business Architecture Modeling introduces different approaches to business architecture modeling. It provides an overview of not only the industry standard approaches to enterprise architecture, which also include the business architecture, like the TOGAF or BIZBOK, but also of ontological approach, specifically the Enterprise Engineering, and business process management approach.

Section 1.2 Standards and Frameworks for Business Architecture Modeling presents the different standards and frameworks for business architecture modeling that are relevant for the previously discussed approaches to business architecture modeling, namely, ARIS, ArchiMate, BPMN, UML, DEMO, and OntoUML.

Section 1.3 Introduction to MMABP Essential Principles introduces MMABP and its core principles. MMABP understands the fundamental nature of business as *achieving goals in the given environment* and captures its architecture in a business system model that consists of four different interrelated models: process map, concept model, process flow models, and object life cycle models. The concept of minimal business architecture is presented, which has wide applicability for business system modeling (not only in the field of business architecture), and we elaborate on it in the following chapters of this book.

References

1. Business Architecture Guild: A Guide to the Business Architecture Body of Knowledge® 8.5 (BIZBOK® Guide) (2020).
2. The Open Group: The TOGAF® Standard, 10th edn. Van Haren (2022)
3. The Open Group: ArchiMate® 3.2 Specification. Van Haren (2023)
4. Dietz, J.L.: Enterprise engineering the manifesto. In: Advances in Enterprise Engineering V, pp. 1–3. Springer (2011)
5. Hoogervorst, J.A.: Practicing Enterprise Governance and Enterprise Engineering. Springer (2018)
6. Dietz, J.L., Mulder, H.B.: Enterprise Ontology: A Human-Centric Approach to Understanding the Essence of Organisation. Springer Nature (2020)
7. Object Management Group: Business Process Model and Notation (BPMN) Specification Version 2.0.2 (2014). http://www.omg.org/spec/BPMN/
8. Object Management Group: Unified modelling Language (UML) specification v2.5.1. https://www.omg.org/spec/UML/ (2017)
9. Scheer, A.-W.: ARIS – Business Process Frameworks. Springer Science & Business Media (1999)
10. Dumas, M., et al.: Fundamentals of business process management. Springer (2018)
11. Weske, M.: Business Process Management: Concepts, Languages, Architectures, (2019).
12. APQC: APQC Process Classification Framework (PCF). https://www.apqc.org/process-frameworks (2023)
13. Sheer, A.: Architecture of Integrated Information Systems, (1992).
14. Object Management Group: Business Motivation Model Version 1.3. http://www.omg.org/spec/BMM/1.3/ (2015).
15. Object Management Group: Semantics of Business Vocabulary and Business Rules (SBVR) Version 1.5. https://www.omg.org/spec/SBVR/1.5/ (2015).
16. Object Management Group: Value Delivery Modeling Language (VDML) Version 1.1. https://www.omg.org/spec/VDML/ (2018)
17. Guizzardi, G.: Ontological Foundations for Structural Conceptual Models. Telematics Instituut; University of Twente, Centre for Telematics and Information Technology, Enschede (2005)
18. Chen, P.P.-S.: The entity-relationship model—toward a unified view of data. ACM Trans. Database Syst. 1, 9–36 (1976). https://doi.org/10.1145/320434.320440
19. Eriksson, H.-E., Penker, M.: Business Modeling with UML: Business Patterns at Work. Wiley, New York (2000)
20. Desfray, P., Raymond, G.: Modeling enterprise architecture with TOGAF: a practical guide using UML and BPMN. Morgan Kaufmann, Amsterdam (2014)
21. Scheer, A.-W., Nüttgens, M.: ARIS architecture and reference models for business process management. In: van der Aalst, W., Desel, J., Oberweis, A. (eds.) Business Process Management, pp. 376–389. Springer, Berlin (2000). https://doi.org/10.1007/3-540-45594-9_24
22. IDEF3 Process Description Capture Method. https://www.idef.com/idef3-process-description-capture-method/
23. Ashworth, C.M.: Structured systems analysis and design method (SSADM). Inf. Softw. Technol. 30, 153–163 (1988). https://doi.org/10.1016/0950-5849(88)90062-6
24. Jacobson, I., Booch, G., Rumbaugh, J.: The Unified Software Development Process. The Addison-Wesley Object Technology Series. Addison-Wesley, Reading (1999)
25. Al-Zewairi, M., Biltawi, M., Etaiwi, W., Shaout, A.: Agile software development methodologies: survey of surveys. J. Comput. Commun. 05, 74–97 (2017). https://doi.org/10.4236/jcc.2017.55007
26. Neit Consulting: Enterprise Assistant. https://www.popisto.online/

27. Řepa, V.: Business system modeling specification. In: Chu, H.-w., Ferrer, J., Nguyen, T., Yu, Y. (eds.) Computer, Communication and Control Technologies (CCCT '03), pp. 222–227. IIIS, Orlando (2003) ISBN 980-6560-05-1
28. Jung, J., Fraunholz, B.: Masterclass Enterprise Architecture Management. Springer (2021)
29. Greefhorst, D. et al.: Architecture Principles: The Cornerstones of Enterprise Architecture. (2011).
30. Ziemann, J.: Fundamentals of Enterprise Architecture Management: Foundations for Steering the Enterprise-wide Digital System. Springer Nature (2022)

Chapter 2
Intentions and Business Processes

Abstract Business process analysis focuses on mapping business intentions and actions that lead to their fulfillment. For their capturing, we use two models. Process map, which allows one in a systematic way using the TOGAF event diagram to get an overview of the analyzed business, identify its business processes and their relationships, specify the scope and context of the process analysis, structure the analysis, and let one decide what should be subject to detailed process analysis.

Process flow model, which allows one in a systematic way using the BPMN diagram to capture the details of a business process at two consistent levels of detail (process steps and tasks), map process steps and tasks of business process, their possible sequences, and all possible outcomes, and analyze and capture the points at which business processes synchronize with their environment. For both models, we specify a step-by-step modeling process for their creation.

Over the past three decades, the incorporation of business process thinking into organizational management has become a common practice. However, Business Process Re-engineering (BPR) and Process-Based Management (PBM) signify much more than what is typically recognized in conventional managerial practices. At its core, it represents a profound paradigm shift in management theory. The intricacy of this paradigmatic change makes its practical implementation challenging, and grasping the fundamental idea of this approach is not straightforward. Consequently, the full realization of process-driven management concepts remains relatively uncommon.

Many narratives about the adoption of process-based thinking often emphasize peripheral aspects such as incremental improvements in documentation, time reduction, cost-cutting, and process automation. However, they often fall short of achieving the substantive and fundamental transformation of business performance—the true essence of the idea. Conversely, there is no business domain where the implementation of Process-Based Management cannot yield significant improvements.

In their seminal work, Michael Hammer and James Champy [1] contextualize the imperative of "Business Process Re-engineering" within historical evolution.

V. Řepa, O. Svatoš, *Fundamentals of Business Architecture Modeling*, The Enterprise Engineering Series, https://doi.org/10.1007/978-3-031-59035-1_2

They trace the traditional milestones from the division of labor through organized production and management to the "Growing economy" of the 1940s to 1980s. They characterize the present situation as the "end of economic growth," a consequence of market saturation altering the conventional roles of customers, collaborators, and competitors. This shift labels typical issues like an overgrown middle management, the separation of management from customers, goal definition challenges, heavy-handed management, and global-local goal coordination difficulties as no longer acceptable for future organizational development. These issues must be unequivocally and immediately addressed.

The authors describe the turbulent situation as the "3C" challenge: customers, competition, and change. They advocate for change across various dimensions, emphasizing the continuous nature of change in markets, competition, business nature, and organizational dynamics itself. Hammer and Champy highlight two essential characteristics encapsulating the essence of process-oriented management:

1. *Flexibility for Environmental Adaptation* The primary rationale for this approach is the necessity of making the organization flexible enough to adjust its internal behavior in response to changes in the external environment. This encompasses shifts in customer preferences, requirements, and technological developments.
2. *Shift to Collaborative Organizational Concept* The key consequence of the aforementioned rationale is the transformation of the business organization from a strictly hierarchical structure to a collaborative one.

Achieving this shift entails numerous partial changes across all aspects of organizational life, each of which is considered critical. Moreover, the interplay between these changes generates additional challenges that need to be addressed.

Business Process-Driven Management (BPM) offers a revolutionary departure from the conventional methods of enterprise management. It aims to position the enterprise organically to swiftly leverage the benefits of technological advancements. To achieve this, an enterprise must be flexible in adapting its behavior to the opportunities presented by new technologies, allowing for immediate adjustments to its business processes. Consequently, these processes cannot be rigidly dictated by the inherently static organizational structure.

BPM introduces a paradigm shift in management, where *business processes take center stage as vital assets driving the enterprise's performance*. Instead of adhering to a traditional organizational structure, BPM views processes as the essential foundation of enterprise functionality. In this perspective, other crucial elements of enterprise management, such as organizational structure and information systems, serve as the supporting infrastructure for these processes.

Despite being the core value of BPM, this approach has not yet gained universal acceptance in practical applications. Current methodologies in Enterprise Architecture (EA) and Information System Development (ISD) still predominantly rely on the organizational structure as the primary determinant of enterprise configuration. This not only influences the structure of information systems but also shapes the design of business processes. Consequently, the true potential of process-driven management remains underutilized. This prevailing approach also

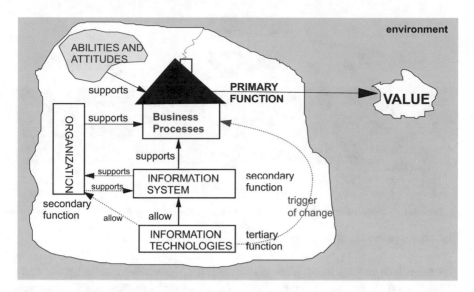

Fig. 2.1 Process-driven organization—essential factors

contributes to the traditional tendency to prioritize predefined structures over the genuine requirements of business processes, further underscoring the historical oversight of human-centered considerations in Information Systems.

Figure 2.1 describes the main components of process-based management of an organization. It shows the organization (the white area) as part of the socioeconomic system (the grey area).

The fundamental significance of an organization derives from its impact on other entities within the system. Its primary purpose should perpetually align with external goals rather than focusing internally. The *primary function* of an organization lies in *delivering values to other actors in the system*. Process-driven management adheres to the principle that these external values, emanating from the organization, are rooted in its business processes. Information and organizational systems serve as secondary functions, acting as infrastructures supporting these business processes. Information technologies, facilitating the operation of these infrastructural systems, take on a tertiary function. Simultaneously, IT plays a *pivotal role in evolutionary changes within business processes*. This *dual role of IT* encapsulates the essence and core objective of process-driven management, enabling a transformative approach where technology development allows us to "do things differently," implying a simplification of processes to their inherent essence.

In a customer-centered philosophy, all business processes in process-driven management should be clearly categorized into two main types: *key processes*, which directly meet customer needs, and *support processes*, which encompass all other essential infrastructure functions and activities. The distinction between key processes and support processes is fully consistent with Michael Porter's [2] concept of the *value chain*, whose work can be seen as a direct precursor to the idea of

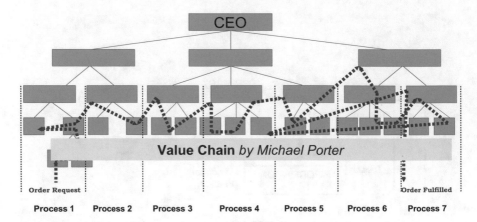

Fig. 2.2 Fragmentation of the key process by the hierarchical structure

process-driven management. This classification of processes encourages a more sophisticated use of specialization than in traditional organizational structures, where specialization is often limited to the organizational hierarchy.

In traditional hierarchies, key processes are fragmented into organizational functions, fixing each business process as a static sequence of tasks (see Fig. 2.2).

The figure shows that the naturally continuous key process is fragmented into the sequence of seven processes that belong to the different organizational units according to the required specializations. In this way, the global structure of the process is hardwired into the organization structure, and the only way to change the process structure is to change the organizational structure.

Organizational hierarchy, as the traditional way of exploiting the effect of specialization, has been the main source of the growth in efficiency that lies behind the industrial revolution. However, the fact that the only way to change such fragmented processes is to change the organizational structure excludes the possibility of adapting the process structure flexibly to the changed conditions. In this way, the effect of specialization can only be exploited at the cost of a *loss of flexibility*. The organizational structure-driven management approach, which severely restricts the organization's flexibility, is understandable given the level of technology in the nineteenth and twentieth centuries, which did not allow for the immediate sharing of information across the organization, nor did it directly support collaboration. With the current state of technology, there is no reason to stick with this type of management.

Process-driven management unlocks the potential of specialization without compromising the ability to adapt processes quickly when needed. In this innovative approach, specialization is not limited to organizational units; instead, *the processes themselves are specialized*, making *specialization independent of the organizational structure*. As a result, *organizational hierarchy loses its primary function*. Proponents of process-driven management herald this shift as a *revolutionary change* in management approaches [1, 3]. This transformational perspective triggers significant changes in various facets of an organization's life, as eloquently outlined in the relevant literature [1, 3]. The reorganization of competencies and responsibilities based on process requirements rather than organizational functions naturally leads to the decentralization of competencies traditionally concentrated in hierarchical managerial roles. This shift underlines the need for *increased empowerment and competence of all employees*. A paradigm shift toward a people-centered approach is unfolding, in line with the visionary ideas of figures such as William Deming [4] and Michael Porter [2], both advocates of a *people-centered approach to organizational management*.

Process-driven management offers an alternative, more sophisticated way of exploiting the effect of specialization as a primary tool for increasing the effectiveness and efficiency, based on process collaboration. To understand the "business essence" of process collaboration, it is important to distinguish between two basic functional types of processes:

- *Key processes* are those processes in the organization that are directly linked to the customer and cover the entire business cycle from the identification of the customer's need to one's full satisfaction with the product/service.
- *Support processes* are indirectly linked to the customer through key processes. While the key processes ensure the complete service to the customer, the support processes support other process(es) with specific products/services.

In this way, *each process is ultimately linked to customer value*, either directly (key process) or by serving the other processes. Key processes therefore represent a specific way in which an organization satisfies customer needs, while support processes represent more standard functionality, usually associated with a particular technology. As a result, key processes are very dynamic, often changing, and constantly evolving; each instance of the key process is different from the others because each business case is specific and each customer has his specific needs and other circumstances. On the other hand, support processes are mostly static and stable, providing standardized and reusable services (see Table 2.1). Therefore, the main effort in the process of designing the system of processes must be to create a *balance between the necessary dynamics of the key processes on the one hand and the necessary stability of the system with its maximally standardized support processes on the other*.

Table 2.1 Essential differences between key and support processes

	Key process	Support process
Customer's needs	Fulfilled directly	Fulfilled indirectly, through key processes
Responsibility	Management-oriented Responsible primarily for the context of the whole business case from the customer point of view	Production-oriented Responsible for the quality of its service, not for the context in which it is used
Dynamics	Very dynamic, often changing, permanently developing; every instance is an original	Rather static, stable, offering standardized and multiply usable services

Thinking in terms of key and supporting processes is essentially present in all of the process-related methodological principles and activities presented in this book, such as the procedure for building a process-driven organization, the Normalization of Processes technique, the organizational maturity concept, etc.

Figure 2.3 shows the example of the process map in TOGAF event diagram. It shows how the events represent the interaction of different elements of the business system. For example, the *Service demand* event represents the action of the *Client* business actor, the *Service Request* and *Complaint Processing Request* events represent the actions of the *Client Management* process to request support from the *Service Providing* and *Complaint Management* processes, and so on. All events in the model represent an action of either a business process or a business actor. The *Client Management* process is the key process of the *Clients Care* business function. It corresponds to the structure of the processes' collaboration, which can be characterized as a centric network. Supporting processes with services support the central key process. The example also shows that the *key process is an inherently relative concept*. If the *Clients Care* is only one of the company's business functions, and there may be other customer-oriented business functions (and thus other primary functions of the company), then there may consequently be other key processes, each relative to its business function. Moreover, even the apparently supporting business functions should have their local key processes since every business function has its customers, even the internal ones. For example, the local key process of the *Services Management* business function is the process that provides the service to the *Service Providing* supporting process of the *Clients Care* business function. This service is the "local primary function" of the *Services Management* business function, since the *Service Providing* process is actually its customer.[1] In the organization that has only one primary function, there is no need to have the business function to which its key process is local, and the key process then usually does not belong to any business function (a libero).

The essential difference between key and support processes discussed above must also be supported by the information system. The differences between key and support process types, summarized in Table 2.1, actually outline the necessary classification of types of information system components in the process-driven organization, as discussed in more detail in Chap. 6.

---

[1] The relativity of the primary function is essentially related to the *principle of outsourcing* as one of the basic principles of the process-driven organization. Any business function or support process can potentially be easily outsourced, since there is no essential difference between the internal and external services. The only difference is in the technical aspects of their implementation. This feature boosts the business development toward effectiveness and efficiency, breaking the main barrier of division of work among different market actors.

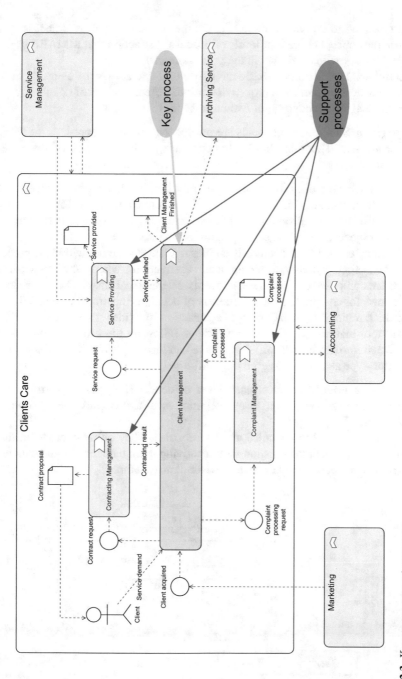

Fig. 2.3 Key versus support processes

2.1   Introduction to Four Levels of Process Abstraction

Before going on to describe how to capture the process model, it is necessary to introduce the concept of the four levels of process abstraction that MMABP uses to manage the work with detail within the process model.

Hierarchical abstraction is a basic modeling tool that allows the elements of the modeled business system to be broken down into different levels of detail.

Hierarchical abstractions are of two basic types [5]:

- *Aggregation* Subordinate elements are part of the parent concept.
- *Generalization* The subordinate elements are particular types of the parent concept.

The aggregation type of abstraction is typically used to decompose business processes, i.e., complex activities, into sub-activities (refined using the Top-Down procedure), while the generalization type of abstraction is typically used to decompose conceptual objects into sub-objects (specialization into object types).

In this chapter, we focus specifically on hierarchical abstraction within the process model, i.e., aggregation-type hierarchical abstraction, where the higher-level concepts are composed of lower-level concepts. Hierarchical abstraction in a process model allows for an infinite number of levels of detail, as illustrated in Fig. 2.4.

The hierarchical aggregation-type abstraction provides the analyst with a powerful tool that not only has its advantages (allowing the process model to be broken down into levels of detail), but its use can lead to pitfalls if the hierarchical aggregation-type abstraction is used only intuitively:

- Inconsistent level of detail of each level of detail. This typically arises when multiple analysts work on a model and each approaches the abstraction differently.
- Created models are too detailed and too abstract. They either overwhelm their users with too much information without giving them a chance to understand it or are so abstract that they explain the user almost nothing.

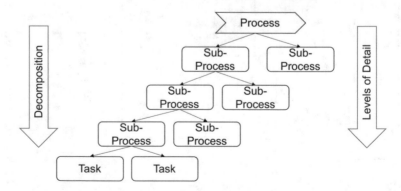

Fig. 2.4 Aggregation-type hierarchical abstraction in process model

- By just looking at the existing process models, it can be hard to learn what rules for abstraction the analyst, who created them, followed, and then it is hard for another analyst to be consistent with them.
- The freedom left to the degree and use of abstraction often gives the impression that the main factor of abstraction is the size of the paper used.

All of these potential pitfalls threaten the basic properties of the model that are necessary for it to be usable and maintainable. Therefore, to produce consistent process models, abstraction must be managed, and the different levels of abstraction (detail) must be given purpose and meaning.

MMABP [6] approaches this through four predefined levels of process abstraction (Fig. 2.5). Each level of detail (abstraction) has its own purpose, and the way the process model is created is adapted to this (see the following chapters).

Each of the four levels of process abstraction has its own specific meaning and thus allows the creation of both a complex hierarchical process model and a model that is formed by only one layer of abstraction. Thus, four different models are available.

The two global models are as follows:

- *Map of business functions*, which describes the functional structure of the enterprise. This way of structuring enterprise activities is close to the traditional view of management and allows the analyst to apply the principle of process-oriented enterprise structuring to the correct/optimal parts of the complex enterprise system—the so-called enterprise domains.
- A *map of business processes* that describes the system of processes characterizing the behavior of actors in one business area. The processes in the map of business processes are of two basic types: key and supporting processes. This means that in each enterprise domain (business function), there are local key and

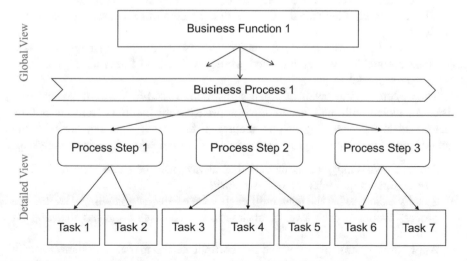

Fig. 2.5 Four levels of process abstraction according to MMABP

supporting processes, regardless of whether this domain plays a key or supporting role in the overall enterprise system. This relativism supports process-
oriented thinking, such as the principle of outsourcing.

The two global models can be captured using the process map. The process map
allows one to capture the business processes (see *Book Order Processing* business
process in Fig. 2.6) and business functions (see *Human Resources Management*
business function in Fig. 2.6) alone or interconnected as illustrated in Fig. 2.6 by
business functions *Purchasing*, *Logistic Management*, *Warehouse Management* and
Book Order Processing business process.

Two detailed models:

- *A process step model* that describes the algorithmic logic of a particular business
  process that is managed based on collaboration with other processes and actors.
  The level of process steps can be expressed by a simple rule: "The only reason to
  divide a process into multiple process steps is synchronization of the business
  process with its environment." In terms of a business process, an external influence means an event (set of events) for which the execution of the process waits.
  Such a place in the process represents the state of the process.
- *A task model* that describes the internal algorithmic structure of a process,
  specifying the detail of individual process steps. Tasks are the elementary elements
  of the process model. Unlike the process step model, which reflects the closest
  higher-level model (the business process map), the task-level model reflects not
  only the closest higher-level model (the process step model) but also the causality
  model of the business system, in particular the so-called object life cycle models
  (see Figure 2.7 and the association of object states with individual tasks).

Two detailed models can be captured using the detailed process flow model. The
process flow model allows one to capture process steps alone with hidden details
(see *Order Preparation* process step in Fig. 2.7) or openly with fully specified
details in the form of individual tasks (see *Placing Order in Processing* process step
in Fig. 2.7).

As mentioned above, these four models can be used both separately and as a
complex hierarchically interconnected whole, which then forms together a complete process model.

The system of four levels of process abstraction used in MMABP reduces the
risks associated with the loose intuitive approach, which suffers from the pitfalls
mentioned at the beginning of this chapter. It is explicit, and together with the
defined model development process (see Sects. 2.2.5 and 2.3.5), it leads an analyst to:

- Produce consistent process models that always use the same level of process
  abstraction within each level of abstraction
- Specify exactly what the content of each level of abstraction will be, so that the
  process model at each level of abstraction is consistent and has meaning on
  its own.
- Apply pure abstraction rules and not complicate the model with unnecessarily
  considerations of what all could be the reason for abstraction (e.g., the abovementioned size of the paper on which the model is being captured).

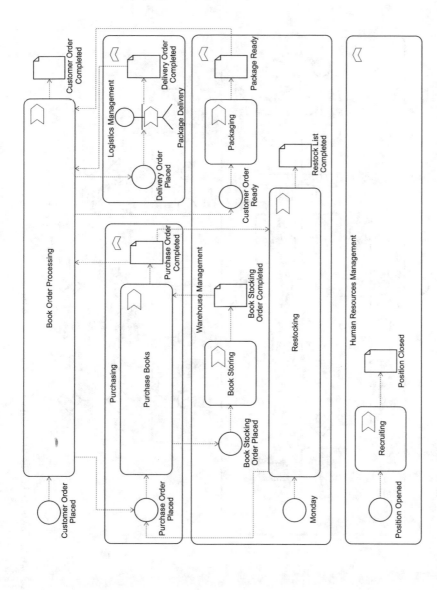

Fig. 2.6 Example process map of a bookshop

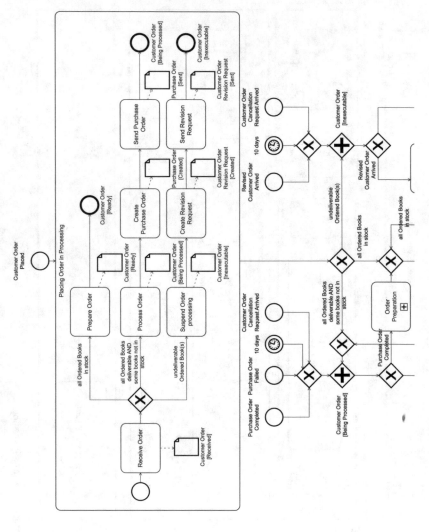

Fig. 2.7 Excerpt from flow model of the Book Order Processing business process

2.2   Process Map

Process map is a model that allows one in a systematic way to:

* Get an overview of the analyzed business
* Identify its business processes and their relationships
* Specify the scope and context of the analysis
* Structure the analysis and let one decide what should be subject to detail analysis

We recommend using the TOGAF Event Diagram [7] as an enterprise architecture compatible diagram (Fig. 2.8). The notation used is from [8].

In the minimal business architecture, use the following key elements listed in Table 2.2 to capture the process map in TOGAF Event Diagram.

2.2.1   Process Map Introduction

The global process map is one of the four basic models of MMABP (Fig. 2.9), and it is the one with which business analysis usually starts. The main objective of the process map is to identify the system of business process and, this way, to get an overview of the analyzed business and specify what the scope of the analysis is.

The process map maps the system of business process and describes:

* For each business process, what events trigger it, what its target state is, and which business function it belongs to
* How business processes collaborate, i.e., how they synchronize—what triggers which process and what feedback each business process awaits from other processes

One should always bear in mind that the purpose of the process map is not to capture what all the data the processes share with each other but mainly the moments of synchronization (relationships) between the modelled processes (the dependence of each process on the others). The process map is a global model and therefore operates at a relatively high level of abstraction and does not have a sufficiently detailed context for analyzing all the data that business processes share with each other. Such analysis belongs to detailed analysis where it can be treated systematically, not just intuitively.

Use the TOGAF Event Diagram (Fig. 2.8) as a tool to capture the process map formally. The process map (Table 2.2) uses only a few elements to capture the business processes and their synchronization with respect to targeted minimalism.

Although the process map imposes strict rules because it is a model, it is quite flexible. The basic concept of a process map is business processes, and a process map should focus on them, but it is always possible to work with the two available levels of process abstraction—business processes and functions.

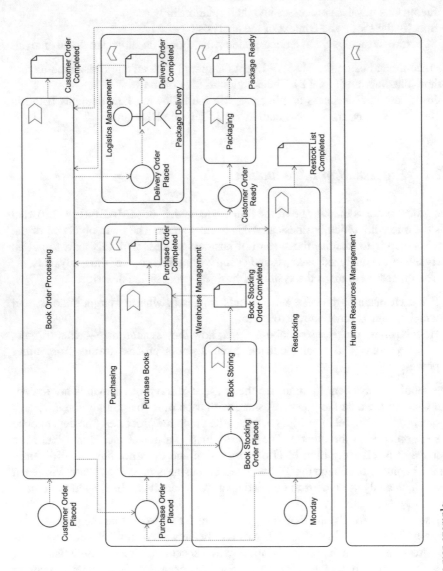

Fig. 2.8 Process map example

Table 2.2 Overview of the key elements needed to capture the process map in TOGAF Event Diagram

Element	Description
Business Function	*Business function* is a grouping of the business processes of an enterprise into a logical whole that delivers one of the capabilities that enable the enterprise to meet its objectives
Business Process / Outsourced Process	*Business process* is a series of activities by a business deliberately seeking to create a target output (product or service) that is essential to the satisfaction of the specific needs of the customer of the process. A business process covers the entire cycle leading to the satisfaction of a customer need from its expression to its satisfaction by a realized service or product. A business process can also be outsourced
Event	*A triggering event* represents occurrence of a significant change in the environment of a business process at a specific moment that triggers the business process. It can be of two kinds: an occurrence of an ad hoc change in an object or objects (change of object state or state of affairs[a]) or the passing of time (absolute or relative)
Target State	*The target state* of a process is represented by a business object in such a state of its life cycle that it signifies the satisfaction of the specific needs of the customer of the process
·······>	*Triggering relationship* represents the relationship of a business process to events or target process states that the business process either generates or resolves

[a]Occurrence of a particular attribute value or association instance

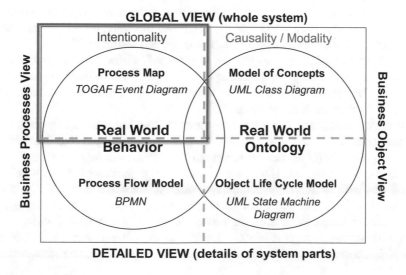

Fig. 2.9 Position of the process map within the business system model

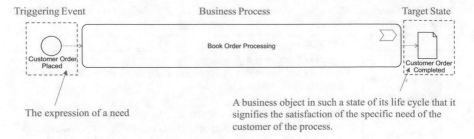

Fig. 2.10 Capturing a business process in a process map

As Fig. 2.8 illustrates, a business function does not have to have its detail (the business processes they consist of) specified if it is not needed for the particular analysis, and at the same time key processes of the enterprise do not necessarily have to be part of any business function as their nature is to run across the entire enterprise in order to coordinate individual support business processes from different business functions of the enterprise.

2.2.2   Capturing Business Processes in a Process Map

According to the MMABP, a business process is defined as a series of activities of a business deliberately seeking to produce a target output (product or service) that is essential to satisfy the specific needs of the customer of the process. A business process covers the entire cycle leading to the satisfaction of a customer need—from its expression to its satisfaction with a realized service or product. In current literature [9], is this process characteristic called "end-to-end" (E2E).

A business process represents the undertaking of a significant effort toward satisfying a customer need, the success of which is not a given. The expression of a need does not always have to be explicit (e.g., an incoming order) but can also be implicit (e.g., an incident whose resolution is defined within an SLA).

The definition of a business process is reflected in how business processes are captured in the process map (compare Fig. 2.10 with the business process definition). The triggering event(s) and the target state of the process must always be specified for each business process.

In reality, it happens that a business process does not reach its target state for various reasons. A systematic analysis of these reasons and possible final states of business processes (other than the target one) requires much more detail than a process map can provide. This is why this matter is left to the process flow models, and the process map focuses only on the target process states.

This does not mean that possible failures to achieve the goal are completely abstracted from when modeling the process map. For example, if a failure is the reason for starting a support process that has to solve the problem, this should be taken into account in the global analysis, and this process should be included in the process map.

2.2.3   Capturing Business Functions

Business function is a grouping of the business processes of an enterprise into a logical whole that delivers one of the capabilities that enable the enterprise to meet its objectives.

As Fig. 2.11 shows, the business functions in a process map represent supporting activities of the enterprise for the key enterprise process(es), and they can be described with (Fig. 2.8) or without (Fig. 2.11) the business process(es) they consist of. It only depends on the purpose of the analysis and required detail for such goal.

The process map in Fig. 2.11 is close to what could be called a capability map. But it is the key enterprise process that makes the difference. The key enterprise process has to always be the starting point of the process analysis, if one is serious about process management. The analysis of business functions should always be done after key enterprise process(es) identification, and the analysis of business functions has to be always done with the respect to key enterprise process(es).

2.2.4   Capturing Process Relationships

The fact that one process supports another is captured in the process map by the triggering relationships between the supported process and the triggering event and the target state of the supporting process, thus mapping what triggers the support process and what business process waits for its output (Fig. 2.12).

It can also be seen from Fig. 2.12 that the supporting processes must conform to the business process definition. In contrast to the commonly used "Sub-processes" according to MMABP and principles of business process management, supporting processes cannot be hidden somewhere in the details of the supported process; instead, they must be explicitly specified in the process map.

The process map allows to capture the synchronization between processes not only for cases like in Fig. 2.12, i.e., that a process triggers its support process and waits for it to reach its target state (schematically shown as (1) in Fig. 2.13), but also for more complex cases. Processes may synchronize not only when the support process starts and when it reaches its target state but also when the support process runs in parallel with the supported process (2 in Fig. 2.13). Synchronization at the beginning (start of the support process) or at the end (reaching the target state of the support process) is also not always the case, as illustrated in Fig. 2.13 as 3 and 4. A support process may be triggered, and the process that triggered it is no longer "interested" in its progress (3 in Fig. 2.13), or conversely, a support process may be triggered by a process other than the process it supports, and the supported process only waits for its target state to be reached (4 in Fig. 2.13).

In general, the process map focuses on processes and their targets and does not attempt to go into the detail of processes for which the process map model does not

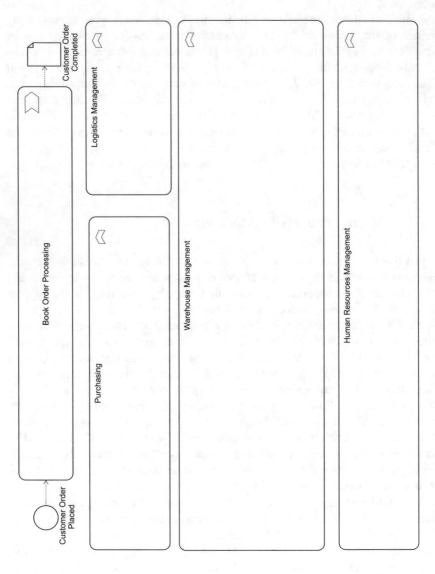

Fig. 2.11 Process map capturing the key process and relevant business functions

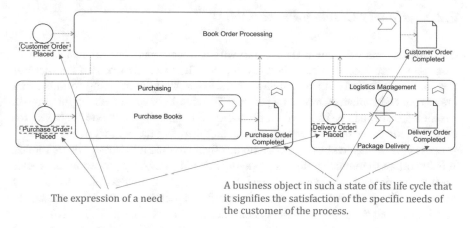

The expression of a need

A business object in such a state of its life cycle that it signifies the satisfaction of the specific needs of the customer of the process.

Fig. 2.12 Support processes must conform to the business process definition too

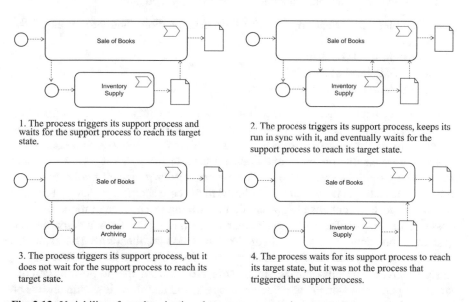

1. The process triggers its support process and waits for the support process to reach its target state.

2. The process triggers its support process, keeps its run in sync with it, and eventually waits for the support process to reach its target state.

3. The process triggers its support process, but it does not wait for the support process to reach its target state.

4. The process waits for its support process to reach its target state, but it was not the process that triggered the support process.

Fig. 2.13 Variability of synchronizations between processes in a process map

have the necessary detail. For example, in a process map, we do not address all possible ends of processes (except reaching the target state) because for their systematic identification, we would need a detailed process flow model of each process. In this case, it is implicitly assumed that when a business process waits for the target state of a support process to be reached, it also expects a response that indicates that the support process has failed to reach that state. Of course, the moment we also have detailed process models available, it is possible to explicitly include these synchronizations in the process map.

2.2.5   *How to Create a Process Map*

The business analysis should always start with a process map. Not all business functions and process need to be elaborated in detail. It always depends on the focus of the analysis. Similarly, it is not always necessary to start the mapping from the first step of the recommended modeling process. The step-by-step model creation process presented below can be used even if the focus is on mapping only one business process. It is therefore possible to start with a later step, but the context of the business process must be taken always into account. When creating a business system model, it is important to remember that its modeling it is not a one-way procedure but rather an iterative process where each change in just one of the models that the business system model consists of can mean a change in another related model that needs to be made so that the entire business system model remains consistent. The basic consistency rules presented in Chap. 4 are a good help in finding related changes.

By following the recommended modeling process, you get:

- A complete and clear map of the business functions and processes of the enterprise
- Consistent levels of abstraction
- Appropriate level of detail
- TOGAF/ArchiMate compatible model

The process map creation process is illustrated below with a specific example of a business that anyone can imagine—a small bookstore that processes incoming book orders from the retail customers. It has its own small warehouse and also offers customers books that the bookstore does not have in stock, but it can obtain them from its suppliers. The bookshop uses a delivery service to deliver books to its customers. The example is, of course, simplified to the core activities of such a business for the purpose of model's clarity and demonstrating the presented modeling process. This example of a bookstore is interwoven throughout the whole process of creating a business system model (minimal business architecture). The examples build on each other as the chapters on process and object model and their consistency progress. The illustrative examples are provided for the purpose of demonstrating a particular step in the modeling process, and therefore, it should always be kept in mind that these are simplified excerpts from an otherwise complex model.

The modeling process described in the following chapters focuses on how to capture the reality of the business system in the model. On the topic of designing the processes of a process-driven organization, see Chap. 5.

The process of creating a process map consists of the following steps:

- Identify all relevant customers of the enterprise
- Identify the key process(s) that satisfy customer needs
- Identify supporting business functions
- Identify support processes
- Identify the support processes of the identified support processes down to the level of elementary support processes

- Identify the business processes that realize the identified supporting business functions
- Identify the support processes of the identified support processes down to the level of elementary support processes

In the following text, we will go through the steps in detail.

Identify All Relevant Customers of the Enterprise

At the beginning, review the business partners that the enterprise has, and if such a partner is the source of a need that the enterprise is responding to and trying to satisfy, then classify such a partner as a customer. Remember that the expression of a need does not always have to be explicit (e.g., an incoming order) but can also be implicit (e.g., an occurrence of incident whose resolution is defined within an SLA). Business processes have their customers, and the value they deliver to their customers is what makes them important.

In our simplified bookstore case, we take into consideration only retail customers. But if we think about the definition of a customer in its full meaning, we can find other customers who are not obvious at first glance, for example, the tax office that expects tax returns to be filed every year. Its need is imposed by law, so it does not have to ask for anything, and it is up to the company to be aware of this need and to meet it on time.

Keep in mind that a business customer is a relative concept. If the analysis focuses only on the support part of the business (i.e., only on the "inside" of the business), it is possible to approach this step in this context and thus focus on the (internal) customers of the support business functions, which have their key processes too.

Identify the Key Process(es) That Satisfy Customer Needs

Identify the key business processes that handle the satisfaction of expressed customer needs completely from the expression of a customer need (triggering event) to its satisfaction with a service or product (target process state).

For each key process, identify:

- A triggering event(s), which either represents an explicit expression of a customer need to which the business must respond or an implicit expression of a need, which represents the point at which the key process is triggered so that the business can meet the agreed satisfaction of the need on time
- The key process triggered by the identified event(s)
- The target state of the key process, which signifies the moment of satisfaction of the need expressed by the customer of the process

In the case of our bookstore, the key process is *Book Order Processing* (Fig. 2.14). It is triggered by the placed *Customer Order* and the target state, which signifies the moment of satisfaction of the need expressed by the customer in the *Customer Order* is when the *Customer Order* is completed.

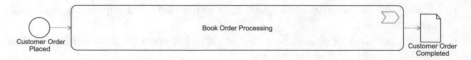

Fig. 2.14 Bookstore key enterprise process

Identify Supporting Business Functions

Key process(es) directly responsible for meeting customer needs typically needs resources and services to run. Identify capabilities that key process(es) requires for their proper execution. Based on these needed capabilities, identify the business functions that provide them. If the analysis focuses only on the support (internal) part of the business as mentioned above, identify the business functions to which each identified key process(es) belong(s) too.

The analysis of business functions is often performed by companies themselves as part of an analysis focused on the necessary business capabilities—the creation of so-called capability maps. Business functions are the elements that provide these business capabilities [7], and these capability maps, for example [10], can therefore provide inspiration for identifying business functions when one is not sure what such business function look like.

It is important to remember that the process of identifying business functions is in principle an iterative process. Later on, in the identification of support processes phase, we may also find out that we have unintentionally omitted some business functions, and they will need to be added.

In the case of our bookstore, we identified four additional business functions that the *Book Order Processing* process needs to run (Fig. 2.15). Thus, by completing this step, we obtain a process map at the business function level that captures the key process(es) and maps the individual capabilities/business functions needed to run the key processes to satisfy the needs of the business customer.

Identify Support Processes

The identification of support processes is based on the decomposition of the goal (target state) of the business process for which we are trying to identify supporting processes. Look for support processes that realize the fulfillment of the goal of the supported process, and their goals therefore represent significant milestones along the way of satisfying a specific customer need of the supported business process.

It is important to remember that the process of identification of support business processes is an iterative process. Later, during the analysis of the business process details, we may also find out that we have not identified some business processes in the global analysis (they remained hidden in the details of another process—see also Sect. 2.2.4), and it will be necessary not only to capture their details but also to add them to the process map.

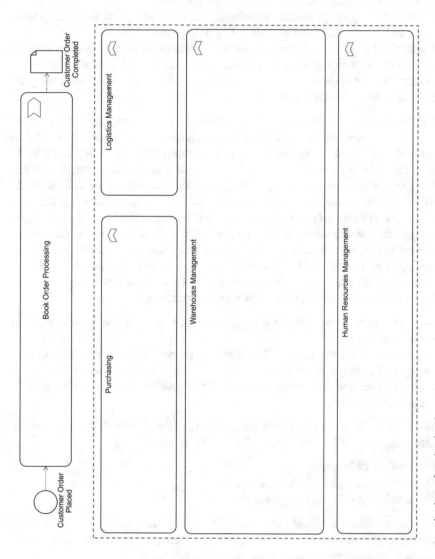

Fig. 2.15 Process map at business function level

When identifying support processes, proceed as follows:

1. Identify the critical milestones within each business process being analyzed that represent significant points along the path to satisfaction of a specific customer need for that business process. Based on the identified milestones, determine the target states corresponding to the identified milestone.
2. Identify the support processes that directly support the achievement of the identified milestones, and determine their triggering evets.
3. Capture the identified support processes in a process map. Add synchronization relationships in the process map whenever a support process is initiated by another business process or when a business process synchronizes with the completion of its support process.

The milestones are checkpoints within a business process represented by object states that are necessary to deliver a service or product to a business process customer. For the business process, these object states represent milestones to be achieved and also points of possible decisions on what to do next. It can be said that within the process map, when identifying support processes, we can look at the analyzed process as a project with a clear goal, which has its milestones in the form of target states of support processes, necessary activities in the form of support processes and their interdependencies in the form of relationships between processes.

We can try to identify milestones intuitively or systematically, as we would recommend, based on a functional view of the business process, i.e., as an activity that transforms inputs into outputs. According to this view of the business process, we can usually distinguish three types of supporting processes:

- Support processes that provide the supported process with the necessary inputs for its execution
- Support processes that provide the supported process with the transformation of its inputs into target outputs
- Support processes that provide the supported process with the delivery of its outputs to its customer

In our example of an online bookstore, we can therefore find in this way the following milestones of the *Book Order Processing* process:

- Ordered books in stock
- Ordered books ready for shipment
- Ordered books delivered to customer

Next, it is necessary to identify the support processes whose output is the one that fulfils the identified milestones. That is, we are looking for processes that have target process states corresponding to the identified milestone.

As illustrated in Fig. 2.16, some milestones can be achieved by multiple ways—by different processes. In the case of our bookstore, there are two ways to get books into the warehouse: through inventory management, where we try to manage stock levels based on our expectations, or ad hoc, when a customer orders a book that is out of stock.

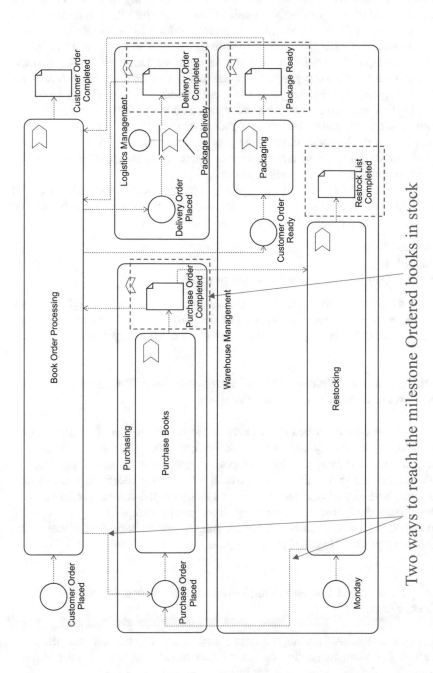

Fig. 2.16 Identified support processes based on milestones

For the identified support processes, we also need to specify triggering events, which are expressions of the need that the process is trying to fulfill. Often, the identification of the trigger events is intuitive (resulting from the nature of the process), but when in doubt, a good place to start is to look for where the processing unit of the process (the object associated with the process trigger event) changes.

In our example, the bookstore does this in the *Book Order Processing* process when it processes requests to purchase ordered books that are out of stock (*Purchase Order*) and orders the delivery of the books ordered (*Delivery Order*) since not everything that was in the customer's order has to be in the delivery package.

Finally, capture the identified support processes in a process map. Add synchronization (triggering) relationships in the process map whenever a supporting process is initiated by another business process or when a business process synchronizes with the completion of its supporting process.

In our bookstore example, four support processes were added to the model (Fig. 2.16). The three directly support *Book Order Processing* on demand and whose outputs are awaited by the *Book Order Processing* process:

- Purchase Books
- Packaging
- Package Delivery (outsourced business process)

And one supports the *Book Order Processing* process indirectly through inventory level management and uses the services of the *Purchase Books* process to do so, which is in effect a support process that supports two different processes.

Identify the Support Processes of the Identified Support Processes Down to the Level of Elementary Support Processes

Apply the procedure described in the previous step to all the identified support processes until you have identified all the underlying support processes.

Support processes can also have supporting processes, so again, you need to determine through milestone analysis whether the newly identified support processes also have any support processes (ones that meet the definition of a business process). If so, determine them according to the previous step.

In the case of our bookstore, we have identified one such support process—the *Book Storing* process (Fig. 2.17).

Identify the Business Processes That Realize the Identified Supporting Business Functions

Within each relevant supporting business function, identify the business processes that affect the quantity, quality, or other characteristics of any of the identified resources that the supporting business functions provide.

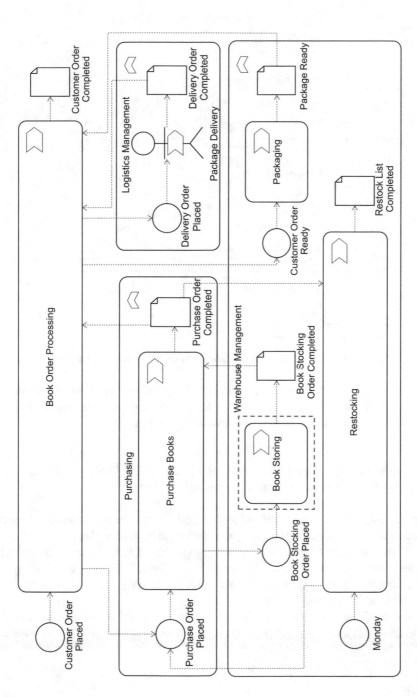

Fig. 2.17 Support process of the support process

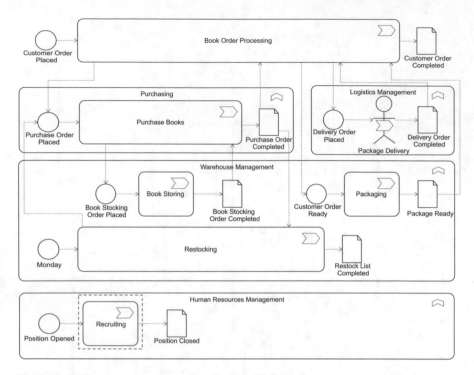

Fig. 2.18 Business processes that realizes the identified supporting business function

In the case of our small bookstore, just for the sake of clarity of the process map, we have identified only one such support process in *Human Resources Management* that provides for the acquisition of new employees (Fig. 2.18).

Identify the Support Processes of the Identified Support Processes Down to the Level of Elementary Support Processes

Apply the support process identification procedure above to the identified support processes until all underlying support processes have been identified.

As above, for newly identified supporting processes, it is necessary to determine whether they use the services of other support processes. If they do, the above procedure for identifying supporting processes should be used until all underlying support processes have been identified.

In our bookstore example, since it is simplified, this was not necessary, but one can imagine that the *Recruiting* process may have a support process such as assessment of the applicant, for instance.

2.2.6   Summary of the Basic Rules for Process Map Modeling

Summary of rules described in the process map modeling process above:

- Each business process has, according to its definition, at least one triggering event and just one target state.
- Business processes are named in terms of the activity leading to the target state of the process.
- Each business process is part of at most one business function.
- Business functions do not overlap or duplicate in content.
- Each business process meets the MMABP definition of a business process and covers the entire business cycle: from the expression of a customer's need to its satisfaction.
- Outsourced business processes are also included in the model (but not described in detail).
- Events are named as a description of the meaning of occurrence of a significant change in the environment of a business process at a specific moment, i.e., occurrence of change of object state or state of affairs or passing of time (absolute or relative).
- The target states are named as state of an object.

2.3   Process Flow Model

Process flow model is a model that allows one in a systematic way to:

- Capture process detail at two consistent levels of detail: process steps and task
- Capture process steps and tasks of business process and their possible sequences
- Capture all possible outcomes of the business process and the sequences that lead to them
- Analyze and capture the points at which business processes synchronize with their environment
- Capture the process detail so that it is consistent with the business rules specified in the object life cycle models and process description specified in the process map

We use the BPMN standard [11] to capture the details of the process that allows us to capture two levels of detail in one diagram. A BPMN process flow diagram allows us to view and capture the process flow model at the level of process steps (Fig. 2.19), for which it is also possible to specify their processing flow in the form of chains of tasks that can be executed without waiting for any outside feedback (Fig. 2.20).

In the minimal business architecture, we use the following key elements listed in Table 2.3 to capture the process flow model in the BPMN diagram.

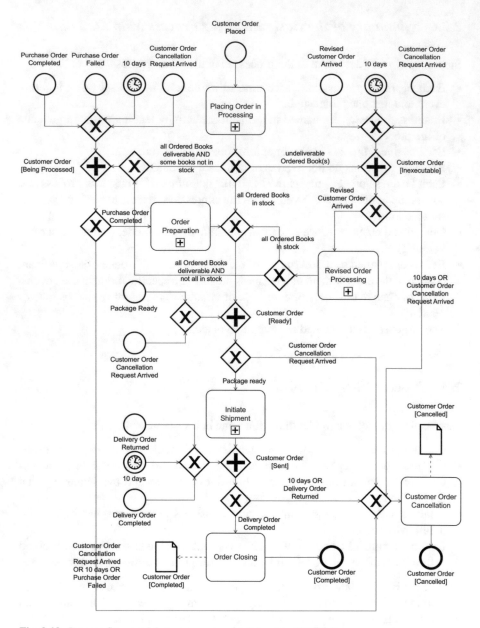

Fig. 2.19 Process flow model at process step detail level in BPMN diagram

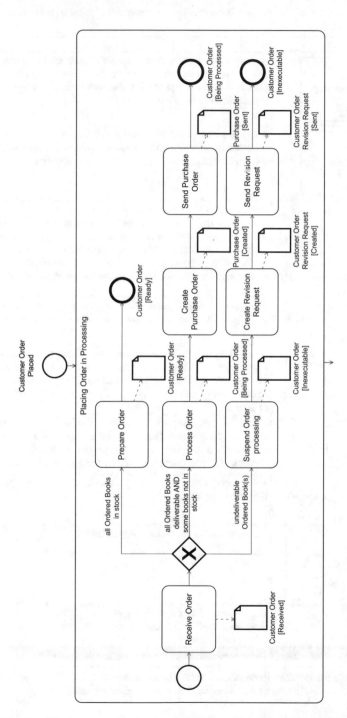

Fig. 2.20 Process step detail unfolded in BPMN diagram

Table 2.3 Overview of the key elements needed to capture the process flow model in the BPMN diagram

Element	Description
Process Step ⊞	A *process step* represents a sequence of tasks of a business process that can be executed without any interruption from outside the business process. It does not represent any support process in the context of MMABP
Task	A *task* is a clearly defined activity, the execution of which changes the essential state of one significant object to another essential state in accordance with the life cycle of that object
Process State	A *process state* is a place in a process where the process execution stops and waits for an event that will determine which direction the execution of the process will continue. This pattern is used to capture all synchronizations of the modeled process with its environment (support processes, customers, suppliers, etc.). For further explanation, see Sect. 2.2.2 and recommended readings
Process End	*The process end* is a pseudo process state that represents the point in the process at which the processing of the process ends
Time Event Ad-hoc Event	An *event* represents occurrence of a significant change in the environment of a business process at a specific moment. It can be of two kinds: an occurrence of an ad hoc change in an object or objects (change of object state or state of affairs[a]) or the passing of time (absolute or relative)[b]
Object[State]	*Data Object* represents either a class of objects (role, input or output of the associated task, etc.) or, if a specific object state is also specified in the element's description, an object state from an object's life cycle (state achieved by the associated task)
XOR OR AND	*Logic gates*, which are the only ones that allow one to split and merge processing flows
Process Step Process Step End	*Start and end* of the process step detail
⟶	*The sequence flow* connects the elements of the process flow diagram to each other and determines the order in which they follow each other
- - - - - - ->	*The association* links the task and the data object

[a]Occurrence of a particular attribute value or association instance
[b]Which usually signals the absence of an ad hoc event in the given period

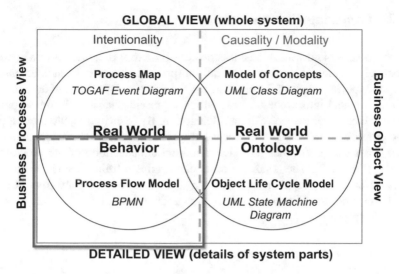

Fig. 2.21   Position of the process flow model within the business system model

2.3.1   Introduction to Process Flow Model

Process flow models represent a detailed view of the business processes specified in the process map (Fig. 2.21). They capture goal-oriented intentional behavior and consist of two levels of detail:

- The process step level, which focuses on the description of particular business process in terms of synchronizing its running with its environment. It describes what requests to its environment the business process generates and what reactions, feedback, it expects from the environment (Fig. 2.19 for our bookshop example).
- The individual process steps can then be elaborated in detail into individual tasks (Fig. 2.20 for our bookshop example). This level of detail focuses on describing the chain of specific tasks that need to be performed in order to achieve the target state of the business process or one of the other regular ends of the process.

In the analysis, we use only a subset of BPMN elements, which not only fits the MMABP metamodel but also in practice has proved to be the basic set used by regular business analysts [12], and therefore, it can be assumed that it is understandable to common business users. As noted in the introduction, we focus on the minimal required elements in order to capture the essence of the modeled business system, but it does not mean that we limit an analyst to this minimum.

2.3.2   Capturing Process Details

By definition, we know that a business process is a series of activities of a business, deliberately seeking to create a target output (product or service) that is essential to satisfy the specific needs of the customer of the process. This series of activities can be firstly divided into process steps, which represent chains of business process tasks that can be performed without interruption. By interruption, we mean a point in the process, i.e., a state of the process at which the process flow stops and waits for an event that determines in which direction the execution of the process will continue (Fig. 2.22). The pending events can originate from outside the company (from the customer, supplier, etc.) or from the modelled company (output of the supporting process). The process flow then ends at one of the possible specified ends of the process.

Process State

From the above, it is clear that the process state is a key concept for the process flow model.

A process state should be named appropriately so that it best describes the state in which the process flow stops and waits for an event. Usually, this is the state of a significant object whose setting is the output of the task that precedes the process state (Fig. 2.22).

Process states have to be captured according to a set pattern (Fig. 2.23) that guides the analyst to ask the right questions, in particular what can occur while waiting for external input.

Process flow models must capture in process states all relevant feedback from around the process that may occur in particular process state, and to avoid deadlock, the time event (the amount of time it takes to wait for the other events) must always be considered (Fig. 2.24). This avoids waiting for "something didn't happen" events, which is logical nonsense.

When creating a process flow model, consistency with the process map must not be forgotten, where synchronizations between processes are already captured. The events the process processing is waiting for in the particular process state must correspond with the occurrence of object states that are triggered by the support process whose output we are waiting for in that particular process state (Fig. 2.25).

The necessity of the process states in a process flow model directly follows from the essential principle of cybernetics, which has been firstly expressed in [13]. In this seminal article, the authors articulated a notion that profoundly shaped the evolution of cybernetics: "*all purposeful behavior may be considered to require* negative feedback." The essence of negative feedback is elucidated as follows: "...the behavior of an object is controlled by the margin of error at which the object stands at a given time with reference to a relatively specific goal. The feedback is then negative, that is, the signals from the goal are used to restrict outputs which would otherwise go beyond the goal."

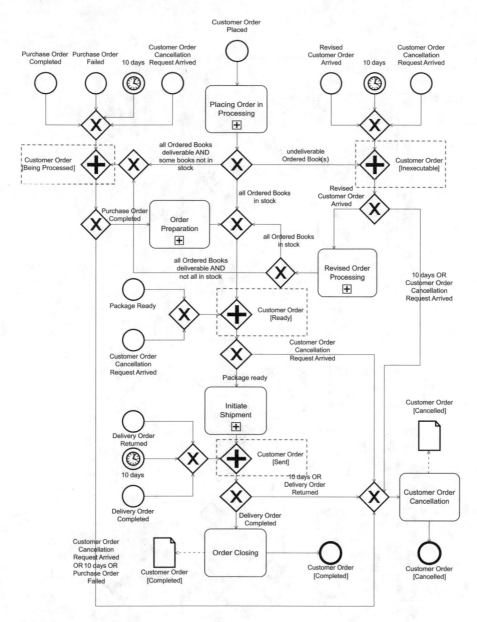

Fig. 2.22 Process states

According to foundational work in the area of process-driven management [1], a business process always pursues a goal. The goal stands as a fundamental attribute of a business process, a concept routinely used in mature methodologies such as [14]. This implies that a business process is inherently an intentional process. By "intentional process," we refer to purposeful behavior orchestrated by an interested entity that is striving toward a specific goal. Therefore, since a *business process* is

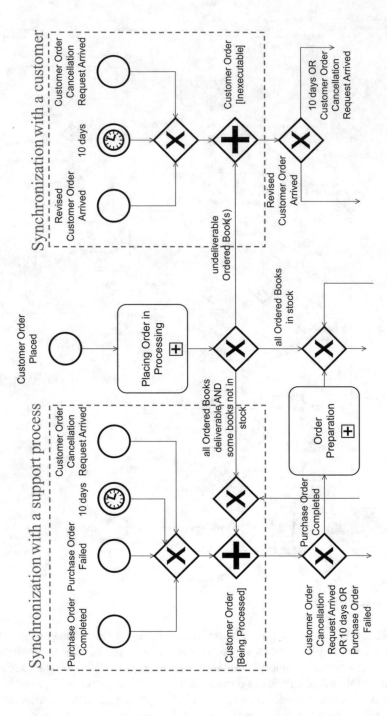

Fig. 2.23 Modeling pattern for process states

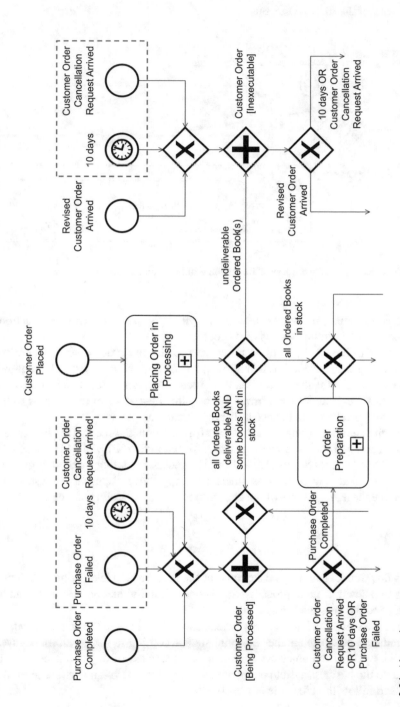

Fig. 2.24 Alternative events

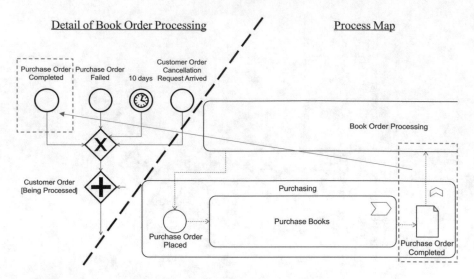

Fig. 2.25 Consistency of process synchronization within the process model

intentional in nature, it *must incorporate negative feedback* to regulate its actions and keep them within the bounds of its goal.

Feedback in business processes is represented by the process state, where the process waits for the event that will allow it to perform the next step. The required "negativity" of the feedback requires the process decision immediately following the process state. This decision limits the possible next steps of the process to the only one that is relevant to the event that has occurred.

Given the paramount importance of the aforementioned issue and the inadequate support in many process modeling standards including BPMN [11], it can be asserted that the primary imperative for any process modeling methodology is to facilitate the modeling of process states, ensuring the indispensable presence of negative feedback, regardless of the chosen notation or modeling standard.

Task

Process flow model can only be captured at the process step level without creating process step detail. If more process detail is needed, individual process steps can be elaborated to the task level (Fig. 2.20).

A task is a clearly defined activity whose execution changes the essential state of one significant object to another essential state according to the possibilities given by the life cycle of the object. A significant object (class of objects) is one that is essential to the business system being modeled and for which it makes sense for the business to follow the life cycle of the object.

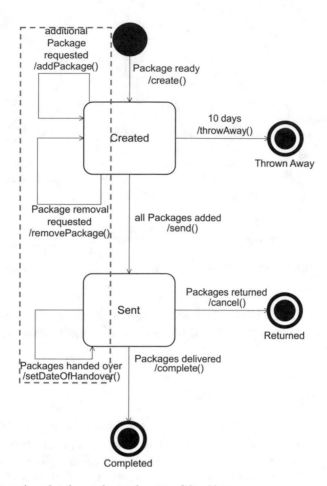

Fig. 2.26 Operations that do not change the state of the object

For the process model, the essential states of the objects determine the lowest level of detail. If an operation does not change the essential state of one object to some other essential state (as shown, for example, in Fig. 2.26 for the add and remove Package operations), and if a task would contain only that operation, it is not a task from the MMABP perspective, and the operation would be the content of another task that already contains an operation that changes the state of one object to another.

For tasks and their associated object states, the rule is that a task always has one goal, so it changes the state of only one object. The exception is alternative endings/ goals, where a task may end with the achievement of one of the possible states (but again, only one occurs), e.g., an Order Validation task, where the outcome may be that the received Order was evaluated either valid or invalid is captured as in Fig. 2.27.

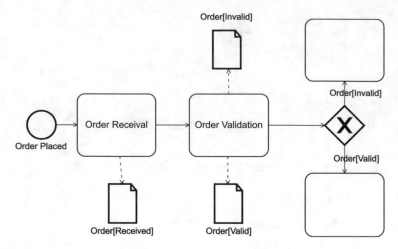

Fig. 2.27 Alternative results of one task

If a process step contains only one task, we can capture the task directly in the processing flow of the process flow model (Fig. 2.28) without having to wrap it in a process step.

Flow Splitting and Merging Gates

The splitting and joining of process processing flows using the gates has also its rules (Fig. 2.29). One should always keep in mind the logic that binds the gates, so as to avoid constructs that conflict with the underlying logic (e.g., combining a splitting XOR gate with a merging AND gate, etc.). Further on, when using the parallel paths in the model, one should get very suspicious whether this should not be resolved using support processes (see Sect. 2.2.4). This is relevant for AND gate but also for the inclusive OR gate, which due to its ambiguity at the time of modeling (only the evaluation of the conditions in particular instance of the model will determine what processing flows will be taken) should be rather avoided.

When describing decision-making, it is also important to remember that the business process, according to MMABP, exists in environment modeled as system of objects. The formulation of conditions should then correspond to this. There are four basic possibilities on the basis of which decision-making takes place (Fig. 2.30). Their combinations are also possible.

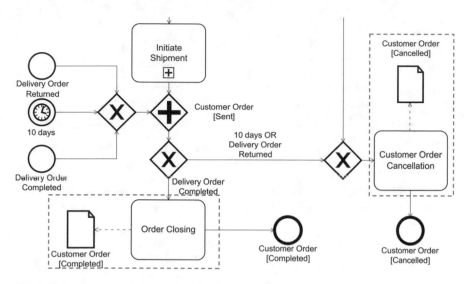

Fig. 2.28 Tasks without process steps

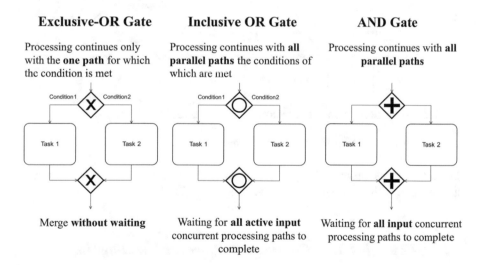

Exclusive-OR Gate	**Inclusive OR Gate**	**AND Gate**
Processing continues only with the **one path** for which the condition is met	Processing continues with **all parallel paths** the conditions of which are met	Processing continues with **all parallel paths**
Merge **without waiting**	Waiting for **all active input** concurrent processing paths to complete	Waiting for **all input** concurrent processing paths to complete

Fig. 2.29 Processing flow splitting and merging gates

Business Process Boundaries

Often in modeling, the question arises as to what is and what is not already part of the detail of a particular business process. As a general rule of thumb, everything that is performed by process actors that are directly managed by the process owner can be part of the business process. The activity performed is their primary activity in the company. On the other hand, sending a request to perform an activity outside

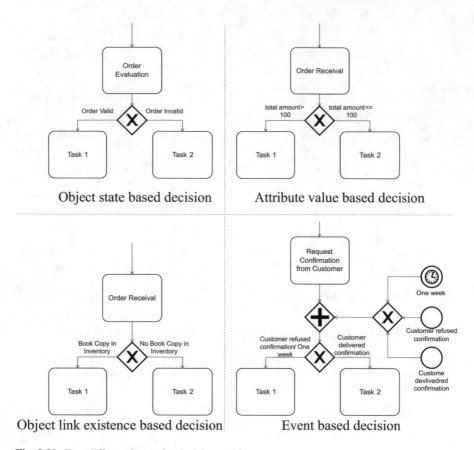

Fig. 2.30 Four different inputs for decision-making

the control of the process owner (e.g., approval by external authority) signals synchronization with the environment—waiting for feedback.

2.3.3   Capturing Task Context in a Process Flow Diagram

Tasks can have a context (actor, organizational unit, average duration, etc.) which, although it does not affect the process flow, is often part of the process models. Capturing this context is recommended to do through the attributes of tasks (in the CASE tool). Capturing it through additional symbols in the process flow diagram is possible, but this risks overwhelming the diagram with symbols, making it unreadable and unclear. The focus should always stay at sequences of process steps and tasks of the process.

Data inputs and outputs are a separate chapter. Again, these can be captured as task attributes or even as separate symbols in the diagram, but as discussed above, this risks overwhelming the diagram with symbols that have no direct impact on process flow. The possibility of capturing inputs and outputs in a process flow diagram also makes it tempting to do this analysis at the level of individual tasks, which is not a good idea because this level of detail is not sufficient for this. As discussed below, at the level of process flow model this is mainly an intuitive analysis.[2] For appropriate analysis, a different diagram must be used—see Sect. 3.1.3.

It can be said that the detail of a business process model has two basic dimensions:

- The level of abstraction of the process (granularity)
- The level of detail provided in the business process model (context)

The first dimension of detail (the level of abstraction of the process) is addressed by the MMABP methodology using predefined levels of process abstraction. For more detail, see Sect. 2.1.

The second dimension of business process detail (the relevant context of tasks) is not so easy to structure. The process context detail level domain is much more fuzzy and variable than the process abstraction domain. It is always driven by the different focus of business process modeling standards, related methodologies, and individual analyst needs. Current standards allow analysts to record large variety of contexts as individual symbols in the process flow diagram, and analysts using these contexts are able to populate the process flow diagrams so heavily that the process sequence flow, representing the processing flow in the process, can become almost invisible. In order for a process flow diagram to be usable, it is necessary that attention remains focused on the processing flow. Of course, other items that provide context for individual activities within a process can be valuable information, but not all of them need to be included in the diagram as a symbol, and not all details are relevant at particular level of process abstraction.

Popular standards such as ARIS, ArchiMate, BPMN, etc. are not very helpful in this case. You can add almost anything you want to a process flow diagram. There is no real method or guide—any context that a modeling tool or language has at its disposal can be added to a process flow diagram as an individual symbol. The level of detail of the process context is then governed by the analyst's intuition and the capabilities of the tools used, which, of course, are very flexible. This is very dangerous because the volume of available context items is quite large and can degrade the process flow diagram when applied arbitrarily.

The context of the business process tasks as such does not affect the process flow. It is supplementary information (usually to individual activities) and, in the context

---

[2] From a process flow point of view, only the input to the process that represents the point of synchronization with another process/actor is important (for explanation, see the principle of negative feedback in Sect. 2.2.2). Such inputs are represented by events in the process states. The need for other information is then related to the internal content of individual process activities, which is below the level of detail in the process flow model and should be reflected either in the object-oriented models or in the implementation of the process tasks. From a process model perspective, MMABP uses the term "process memory," which means that all necessary information is automatically available throughout the process, i.e., the problem of availability of information is irrelevant in the process flow model.

of minimal business architecture MMABP, leaves this context up to the analysts' discretion. The only required is the object states that represent the goals that the tasks achieve. Generally, the task context needs to be approached carefully and usually very restrictively if it is to be displayed as separate symbols in the diagram, if only because there are other diagrams in which it can be viewed.

The common context that one usually always encounters is:

- The roles/organizational units associated with each task
- The inputs and outputs of each task

But there are many others, e.g., in ARIS:

- Goal
- Machine
- HW
- SW Application
- Risk

If the context is captured using the CASE tool as a task attribute, its quantity and detail are entirely at the discretion of the analyst as to whether such detail is necessary and maintainable in the future. However, when it comes to capturing task context in the form of symbols in a process flow diagram, then the spirit of the minimal business architecture of MMABP applies to context too, and that means that less is more. We illustrate this with the example of two types of context commonly used in process flow diagrams.

Roles/Organizational Units Associated with Each Task

Roles or organizational units are a common context for tasks, and the analytics try to capture which role or organizational unit performs which task in the process flow diagram. There are several ways of capturing this, and they vary according to the modeling notation.

The simplest approach is the eEPC approach [15], where organizational units or roles have their own separate symbol and are associated with the activity (in eEPC function) by simple association (Fig. 2.31).

BPMN, for example, takes a different approach. This uses "swim lanes," where each swim lane corresponds to one role/organizational unit and the individual process activities need to be placed in the corresponding lanes (Fig. 2.32).

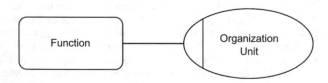

Fig. 2.31 Organization unit in eEPC

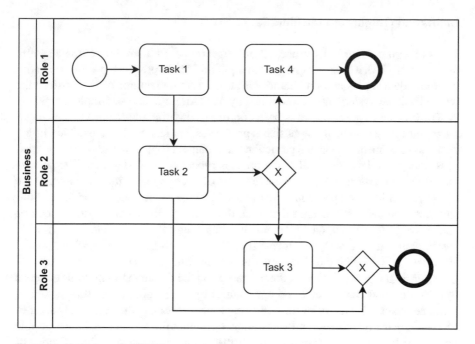

Fig. 2.32 Swim lanes in BPMN

In terms of the minimal business architecture and therefore focusing on the minimum required, the question here is whether the organizational units and roles need to be explicitly stated in the process flow diagram at all. If they stand out as a separate symbol, they unnecessarily fill the diagram with many symbols and many arrows representing their associations. In the case of swim lanes, it is even worse. The entire flow of the modelled process has to be subordinated to how the individual swim lanes are organized, and as a result, in more complicated models, the process flow becomes difficult to read as it jumps from one swim lane to another, often skipping multiple swim lanes at once. But swim lanes are a major hazard for analysis in terms of process management objectives. They provide an opportunity to view processes as components of the main, i.e., organizational structure and thus create the illusion that the process architecture is just an add-on to the organizational structure. However, this is in direct conflict with the objectives of business process management. The business processes are primary and organization structure secondary (Fig. 2.1).

In the end, however, it is still just additional information to the process task, and there is always the question of whether it is not enough to put the organizational unit or role into the properties of the individual task, either in the form of a task attribute in the CASE tool used or in a separate table.

Inputs and Outputs of Individual Tasks

Tasks in a process typically process inputs and transform them into outputs.[3] From this point of view, it looks simple, and there is nothing to prevent a person from adding individual inputs and outputs to the process flow diagram. If we consider the whole business system model as defined by MMABP, it is not so simple.

The business system model is based on the basic principles of process management and focuses on mapping business processes that lead to the satisfaction of the business customers' needs in a particular environment (object world bound by business rules). The level of detail of the process model is adapted to this. The process model has the task as the most detailed unit of change execution. In contrast, the object model has the operation as the unit of change execution. Since the relationship between task and operations is such that multiple different operations can be performed within a task (see metamodel addressing relations of elements used in the diagrams in Sect. 4.3), the process model is more abstract than the object model and does not work with individual operations but with groups of them in the form of tasks. From the point of view of the process model, i.e., the mapping of a sequence of activities, that change states of significant objects, leading to the satisfaction of customer needs, this is sufficient. Within each task, it is up to the actor—the actor of each task, using one's skills and knowledge, combines the execution of the available operations in a way that is appropriate for the situation and to meet the objective of the task.

The inputs and outputs of a task are the inputs and outputs of the various operations that are performed during the execution of that task. Thus, the process model does not allow a systematic approach to analyze the inputs and outputs of each task, as we lack information about which specific input is transformed into which specific output (by what operation). This can only be analyzed at the level of single operations that have their inputs and outputs, but not at the level of tasks in which multiple possible operations are executed.

The identified inputs and outputs at the level of single operations can then of course be associated in a process flow model with tasks, depending on which operations are performed within the task, but the systematic analysis must take place at the level of operations in the object model—see Sect. 3.1.3.

The actual association of inputs and outputs in a process flow diagram also has its pitfalls. Again, it must be emphasized that this is additional information to the process and has no effect on the process flow description itself. For the clarity of the process flow diagram, it remains the best solution if the inputs and outputs of activities are listed outside the process diagram (in a CASE tool, in a table, etc.). If the inputs and outputs have to be listed in the process flow diagram, it must be remembered not to overwhelm it. An example of such overwhelm is the eEPC diagram in Fig. 2.33, where the inputs and outputs of the activities create their own network of

---

[3] To avoid any confusion, it must be emphasized that task-associated object states, as required by MMABP, do not represent output in the classical sense but the target of a task, and so the discussion on inputs and outputs is not relevant to them.

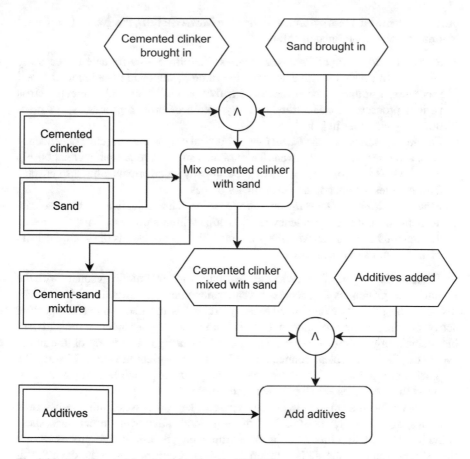

Fig. 2.33 Mix of material and activity flow in eEPC [15]

data/material flows that clutter the key sequence flows that the processing of the individual process activities follows.

This again nicely documents that the basic rule for diagrams is less is more.

2.3.4   Normalization of Processes

The concept of Processes Normalization draws inspiration from E. F. Codd's technique for the Normalization of Data Structures, initially introduced in [16], further elaborated by R. F. Boyce in [17] and comprehensively explained in [18]. While Codd's original intention was primarily technical, aimed at database system design, this technique evolved to reveal the fundamental Principle of Modeling in information systems development, as later defined by P. Chen in [19]. Given the universality of this principle across Real World models' dimensions, it becomes imperative to apply it to process descriptions. Aligned with the essential unity of objects and processes in the business system, as defined in MMABP [20], the goals of Processes Normalization are outlined as follows:

- *Reduce Redundancy of Process Activities* The aim is to eliminate unnecessary repetition of activities with essentially the same content and meaning in different processes. Redundant occurrences of activities with identical contents across various processes are identified as a "symptom of broken processes," as mentioned by Hammer in [1].
- *Ensure Dependency on the Initial Event* This goal emphasizes the clear dependency of all activities on the initial event. This not only supports a transparent relationship with the customer-oriented value of the company's performance but also ensures that activities are anchored in the primary process goal.
- *Eliminate Hidden Dependency Relationships* The objective is to eradicate unnecessary hidden dependency relationships within a process. This, along with the previous goal, aligns with the principle of key processes as the central drivers of all activities in organizations.

These goals, as part of the Processes Normalization technique, resonate with the fundamental principles of process-driven management, as articulated in [1]. For instance, the goal of reducing redundancy addresses the need to avoid repeating activities with similar meanings in different processes, a phenomenon indicative of hierarchical organizational issues. The goal of ensuring dependency on the initial event contributes to a clear connection with customer-oriented values. Meanwhile, the goal of eliminating hidden dependencies supports the principle of key processes, ensuring that activities are aligned with the primary process goal.

Processes Normalization effectively separates key processes from non-essential activities, signaling the existence of more general, supporting processes. These activities, previously embedded in the normalized process as sub-processes, are then recognized as stand-alone support processes,[4] contributing to the overall efficiency of the normalized process and revealing essential relationships between the original process and its support activities. This method ensures that the normalized process focuses on essential activities, removing non-essential elements to more general support processes.

The assumed conditions for the normalization procedure are:

- The logical process mirrors a segment of the Real World comprising inherent process sequences and their interconnections.
- Every activity within the process corresponds to an activity within a natural process sequence or a relationship among process sequences.
- Each event in the process signifies an activity involving an external actor or a connected (collaborating) process sequence.

---

[4]This means that they can no longer be seen as sub-processes but rather as co-processes that run independently of the original process and are only connected to it only by the service they provide.

- Every concealed natural process sequence in the logical process can be distinctly identified by an event or by the logical arrangement of events. This event (structure of events) is referred to as an "initial event."

The *procedure of process normalization* is defined as a sequence of steps by particular normal forms. The initial condition for each step is that the process is in the previous normal form (i.e., fulfills its required characteristics). Particular normal forms are defined as follows.

First Normal Form (iterative generalizable structures free)
The process is in the First Normal Form if the bodies of all its repeating non-elementary structural parts (iterations) have been removed to stand-alone processes and replaced with process states. Each removed part of the process has been identified with the corresponding business system object. Its starting event has been defined as a request from the original process. Its product has been defined as a service and corresponding event from the point of view of the original (i.e., receiving) process.

Second Normal Form (alternative generalizable structures free)
The process is in the Second Normal Form if it is in the First Normal Form and the bodies of all its mutually alternative non-elementary structural parts (selections) have been removed to stand-alone processes and replaced with process states. Each removed part of the process has been identified with the corresponding business system object. Its starting event has been defined as a request from the original process. Its product has been defined as a service and corresponding event from the point of view of the original (i.e., receiving) process.

Third Normal Form (parallel generalizable structures free)
The process is in the Third Normal Form if it is in the Second Normal Form and the bodies of all its mutually parallel non-elementary structural parts (simultaneities) have been removed to stand-alone processes and replaced with process states. Each removed part of the process has been identified with the corresponding business system object. Its starting event has been defined as a request from the original process. Its product has been defined as a service and corresponding event from the point of view of the original (i.e., receiving) process.

Fourth Normal Form (hidden generalizable sub-structures free)
The process is in the Fourth Normal Form if it is in the Third Normal Form and the bodies of all its non-elementary structural parts (sequences) that are not fully specific to the starting event of the process have been removed to stand-alone processes and replaced with process states. Each removed part of the process has been identified with the corresponding business system object. Its starting event has been defined as a request from the original process. Its product has been defined as a service and corresponding event from the point of view of the original (i.e., receiving) process.

From the perspective of the process system, Process Normalization can be seen as a method for revealing the inherent supporting processes concealed within a particular process. This unfolds in distinct steps:

1. *Uncovering Repeatedly Used Support Services* In the initial step, all support services that are repeatedly employed are brought to light within the process.
2. *Uncovering Conditionally Used Support Services* The subsequent step exposes support services that are conditionally utilized.
3. *Uncovering Substantially Different (Parallel) Services* The third step involves revealing substantially different (parallel) services that exist within the same process step.
4. *Uncovering Remaining Standalone Services* In the final step, all remaining portions of the process, which can be treated as standalone services, are uncovered.

The order of these steps is crucial, like the normalization of data structures. To accurately interpret alternative sub-structures (branches) in the process, it is essential to first eliminate all repeated structures of activities (First to Second Normal Form). This is because the decision about repetition (end of the loop) might otherwise be misconstrued as a fork, signaling mutually alternative sub-structures. The pursuit of parallel structures is irrelevant between different alternative structures; thus, the structure must be in the second normal form before progressing to the third normal form. Additionally, identified sub-structures must not extend beyond the boundary between alternative or parallel branches of the process. These guidelines are rooted in the theory of structured thinking, extensively elaborated in [21, 22].

Example of Process Normalization

Figure 2.34 illustrates the unnormalized *Customer Order Management* process in BPMN notation [11]. The process description adheres to the MMABP methodology [23], emphasizing communication with external collaborators. In its unnormalized state, the process collaborates solely with the customer. Note the process states (Parallel AND gates) at the beginning (order negotiation) and just before the conclusion (payment) of the process.

The notation employed in this example is a reduced version of BPMN, aligned with the MMABP methodology and its business process meta-model [20]. To ensure methodical consistency with MMABP principles, the BPMN notation is simplified to include only the fundamental set of language constructs. Events are consistently defined as external influences on the process, and the absence of the process state concept is compensated for by the AND join construction, which signifies the essential synchronization with external influences (events) in the process state. Further clarification regarding the necessity to enhance BPMN can be found in Sect. 2.2.2 and as a further reading [23].

Figure 2.35 depicts the alterations in the process resulting from its transformation into the first normal form. Repeating segments that correspond to the management

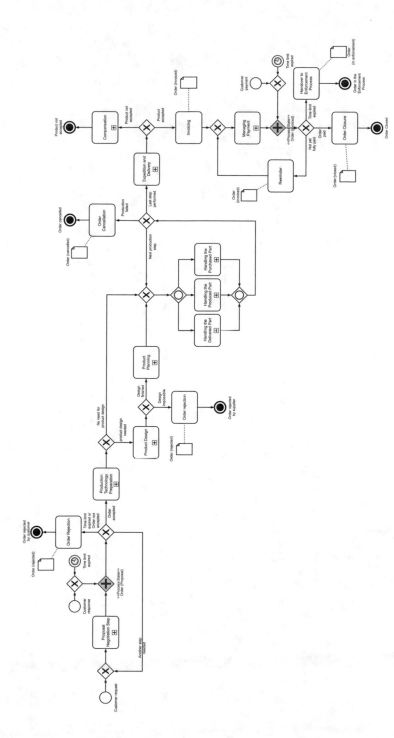

Fig. 2.34 Example: unnormalized process Customer Order Management

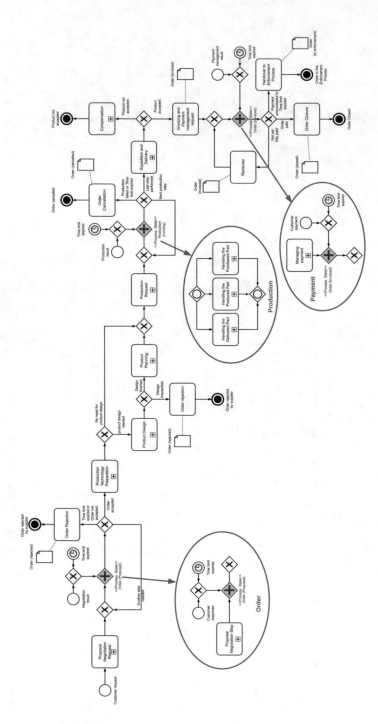

Fig. 2.35 Example: process in the First Normal Form

of *Order*, *Product*, and *Payment* entities have been recognized, extracted to independent support processes, and substituted with new process states, each signifying the anticipation of external services.

The process illustrated in Fig. 2.36 has attained the second normal form subsequent to eliminating two conditional sections, which can be viewed as independent standard support services. *Product Preparation* is executed solely if the customer requests a nonstandard product and the *Order Finalization* branch only if the customer accepts the delivered product. Since there are no remaining parallel parts in this process, it also conforms to the third normal form.[5]

In the fourth normal form (Fig. 2.37), the process has been streamlined by removing two sections that represent stand-alone standard services: *Production Technology* and *Expedition & Delivery*. Consequently, all remaining parts of the process are entirely specific to the starting event, which is the *Customer request*.

Figure 2.38 shows the resulting process map after complete normalization of the original primary process. In addition to the newly established support processes discussed in the preceding comments on the various normal forms of the process, several other processes have been created through the normalization of these new support processes. These include *Product Design* and *Product Planning*, extracted from the *Product Preparation* support process, and the former three parallel segments of the *Production Step Management* process.

The *Payment Management* process, which was initially derived from the key process during its transition to the first normal form, has been completely decoupled in the second normal form. The *Order Finalization* process is also decoupled and is no longer directly linked to the key process.

The process map illustrates the configuration of mutually collaborating processes united by a shared objective—the final product of the key process *Customer Order Management*. This structure impeccably embodies the fundamental traits of a process-driven organization:

- All processes adhere to a network structure, indicating their general independence. Their connections indicate collaboration, with each process providing mutual support through services. There is no overall hierarchy between processes.
- The collective significance of all processes in the map is determined by the key process, which acts as the ultimate consumer of supporting services. Consequently, the final product of the key process defines the purpose of each process's presence in the map.
- This structure of generally independent yet collaboratively aligned processes can be termed a purpose-centric collaboration network structure.

---

[5]The parallel services represented by the process steps "Handling (delivered, produced, and purchased) part," which would be the subject of the transition to the third normal form, have been removed as a block due to the fact that this block can be used repeatedly in the process (see Fig. 2.36). Thus, they will cause the transition to the third normal form as far as in the further analysis of the newly created support process *Production Step Management* (see the result at the process map in Fig. 2.39).

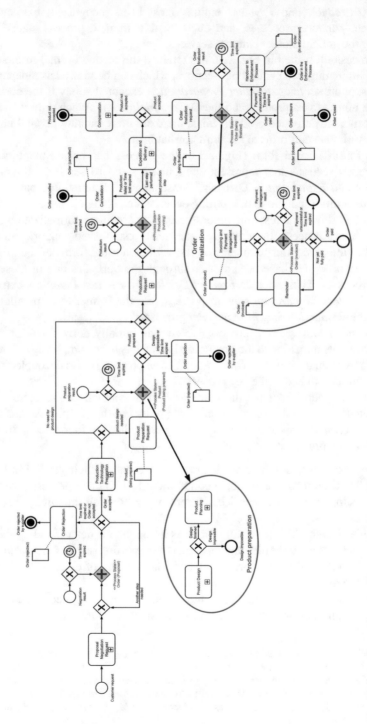

Fig. 2.36 Process in the Second and Third Normal Forms

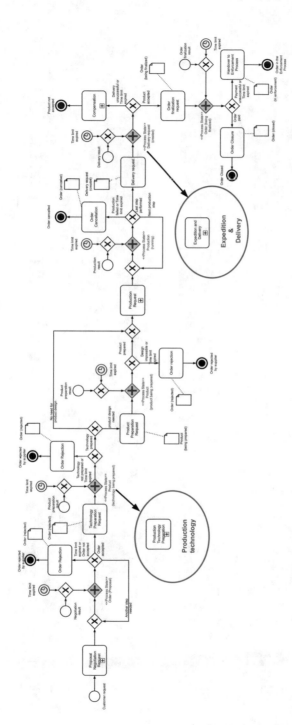

Fig. 2.37 Process in the Fourth Normal Form

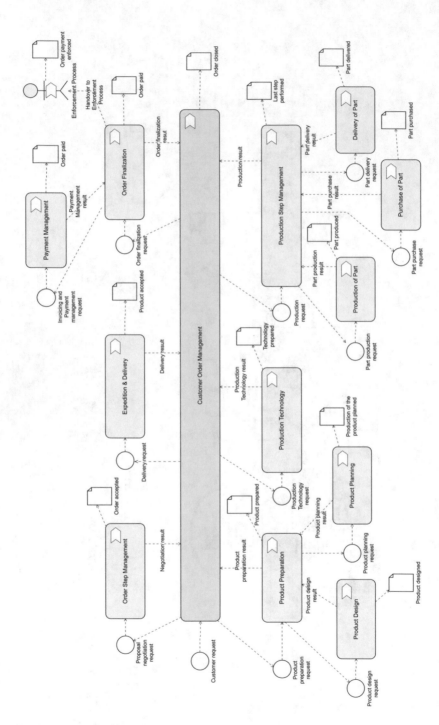

Fig. 2.38 Process map of the process normalization example

- The central position in the structure (key process) signifies direct interaction with the customer, serving as a representative of the shared purpose of the entire structure. Given that the core idea of process-driven management is to enhance organizational flexibility in response to customer needs, the central (key) process naturally emerges as the most dynamic and purpose-specific component in the structure.
- Consequently, other (support) processes become more universal, generally oriented, and naturally static as their distance from the center of the structure increases. For instance, the "first-order" support processes—*Product Preparation*, *Production Step Management*, and *Order Finalization*—are evidently closer to specific customer aspects than the more general "second-order" support processes like *Product Design*, *Purchase of Part*, or *Enforcement Process*.

Such distribution of work among the processes allows the maximum flexibility of the process system with respect to the future changes. For example, the *Payment Management* process can be thought of as a black box and is used completely independently of the payment technology used. Any future technology change that does not completely change the nature of this service will not affect other processes such as *Order Finalization* or the key process itself. Similarly, any change in the logic of the key process, which is assumed to be highly dynamic by default, that does not completely change the required nature of the supporting services will not affect the support processes. In this way, the process normalization fulfills the fundamental principle and value of the process-driven management.

2.3.5   How to Create a Process Flow Model

Looking at the basic MMABP scheme (Fig. 2.21), it is clear that the detailed analysis can be approached from two directions. We have the option to start with either process flow models or object life cycle models. When creating a detailed model, of course, there is inevitably a simultaneous development of both detailed views (process and object) and their interlinking, but one has to start somewhere.

The initial situation can be distinguished according to the state of the business whose business system model is being created. If the business being analyzed has well-established and well-articulated business rules, then it makes sense to start with object life cycle models, focusing primarily on the business rules of the existing business, and then add process flow models. On the contrary, if the business being analyzed is new, usually yet to be designed and implemented, the analysis will primarily focus on the design of a new business that does not exist yet, so it makes sense to start with process flow models and then add object life cycle models.

By following the recommended modeling process, you get:

- A complete and clear process flow models with consistent levels of abstraction

- Models with an appropriate level of detail that can be understood by regular business stakeholders
- BPMN compliant diagram

When modeling a business system model, it is important to remember that its creation process, even if described sequentially, is iterative. While modeling the individual models that MMABP business system model consists of, new information is often identified that affects not only the currently modelled model but often also other models related to this model. In this case, it is therefore necessary to make changes, resulting from this new information, in all relevant models so that they remain consistent. The basic consistency rules presented in Chap. 4 are a good help in finding related changes.

The step-by-step process flow model creation process is illustrated below with a specific example of a small bookstore described in Sect. 2.2.5. This example of a bookstore is interwoven throughout the whole process of creating a business system model (minimal business architecture). The examples build on each other as the chapters on process and object model and their consistency progress. The illustrative examples are provided for the purpose of demonstrating a particular step in the modeling process, and therefore it should always be kept in mind that these are simplified excerpts from an otherwise complex model.

As mentioned above, there are two starting points, depending on the state of the business whose business system model is being created. If the business to be analyzed has well-established and well-articulated business rules, follow the steps outlined below in the section Analysis Based on Business Rules of Existing Business. If the business to be analyzed is new, usually yet to be designed and implemented, go to page 93 and follow the steps outlined in the section Analysis Focused on the Design of a New Business.

Analysis Based on Business Rules of Existing Business

The process of capturing process flow models comes in the second phase, and the analyst therefore has the outputs of the analysis of the individual life cycles of important objects available right from the start of the detailed process flow analysis.

The process of creating process flow model, based on business rules of existing business, consists of the following steps:

- Determine the boundaries of the business process
- Identify all other possible ends of the process
- Identify all process states
- Complete the events associated with the process states
- Identify the activities performed
- Specify the beginning and end of each process step
- Specify the detail of each process step
- Identify the tasks of each process step
- Review the process flow model

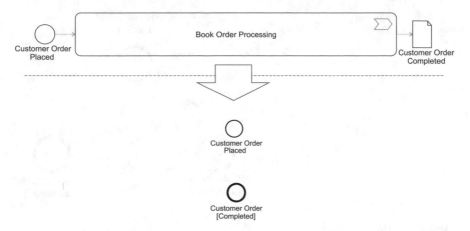

Fig. 2.39 Business process boundaries according to the process map

In the following text, we will go through the steps in detail.

The creation of a process flow model for each business process starts with the event that triggers the process, and from there, the process flow model is developed step by step in close relation to the relevant object life cycles.

Determine the Boundaries of the Business Process

First, based on the global process map, capture the triggering events and the target process state for the business process in the process flow model.

In the case of our bookstore, we start with the key process *Book Order Processing*. Based on the process map, we capture one triggering event and one process end (target state) in the process flow model of the *Book Order Processing* process (Fig. 2.39).

Identify All Other Possible Ends of the Process

Try to identify all possible ends of the process. Name each end of the process as the object state that best describes the state of the process at which the execution of the process ends.

It may not be possible to identify all possible ends of the processing right from the start. This is to be expected. The aim of this step is a basic awareness of where the modelled process begins and ends, but the detail of this knowledge will of course develop further as the process detail analysis progresses to map the entire flow of the analyzed process.

In the case of our bookstore, we identified only one other end of the process— *Customer Order [Cancelled]* (Fig. 2.40).

Fig. 2.40 Ends of the
process Book Order
Processing

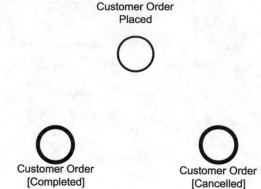

Identify All Process States

First, focus on what should be the result of the activities performed—the process states. The process states are points in the process flow where each activity that preceded that point in the process flow has been completed, and now the processing is stopped, waiting for the necessary input from the business process environment to continue.

Starting from the triggering event(s), identify each processing path step by step with all the process states on the way to the end process states. For each process state, select the object state from the already existing modeled object life cycles that best describes the state at which the process execution stopped, and identify the inputs from outside the process (in the form of events) that the process execution is waiting for in that particular process state.

Use gates to split and merge the process flow. For decision gates (XOR and OR), identify the conditions under which processing continues along a particular path. Do not list or analyze individual actions yet.

Identification of process states starts from the points we already know from the process map—the synchronizations of the modeled process with the support processes. These are places in the supported process where its processing is stopped, and it is waiting for feedback from the processing of the support process.

In the case of our bookstore, we start with the process states related to the three support processes of the process. First, we capture the process states and the expected outcome the *Book Order Processing* process is expecting from its support processes (Fig. 2.41).

Next, using the existing object life cycles, we name the process states as the object states that best describe the process state and in which we are waiting for an event analogous to an event in the corresponding object life cycle—usually, but not necessarily, life cycle of the key object for the process, in this case, the *Customer Order* (Fig. 2.42).

We continue to add process states to the model, where process processing waits for input from the environment of the business being modeled. These can be found in the life cycles of the objects that the modelled process is working with.

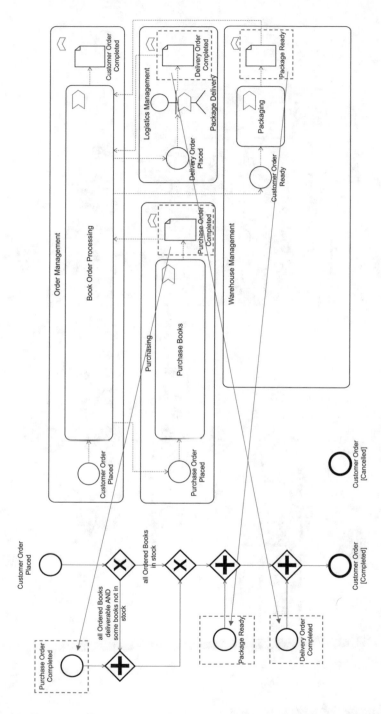

Fig. 2.41 Detail of Book Order Processing process and its links to the process map

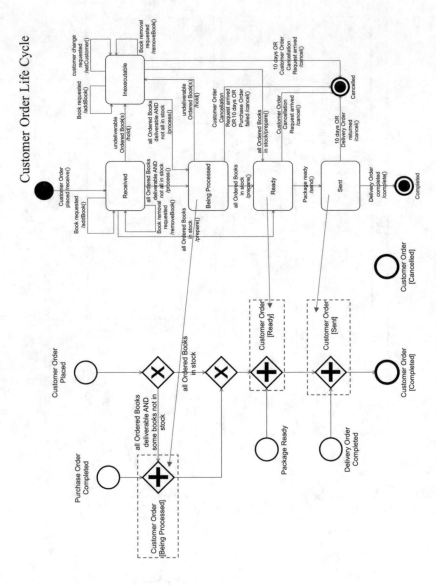

Fig. 2.42 Naming process states in detail process flow of Book Order Processing process

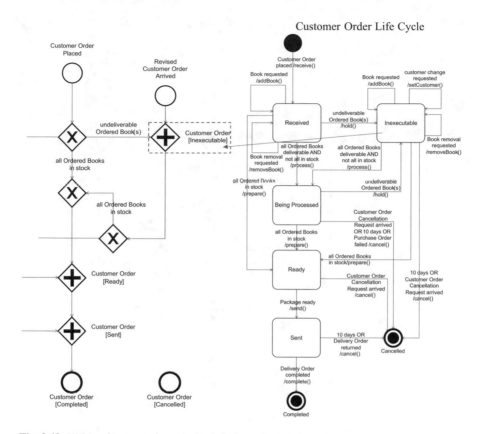

Fig. 2.43 Waiting for events from the business's environment

In the case of our bookstore, we can find a point in the *Customer Order* life cycle where the order is inexecutable, and we wait for the customer to modify it (Fig. 2.43).

We name the newly identified process state as the object state that best describes the process state and modify the processing flow of the process according to the alternatives that can occur if the revised *Customer Order* arrives. (Fig. 2.44).

It may be the case that none of the object states identified so far adequately describes a particular process state. Thus, if one identifies a new class of objects or a new object state that is more appropriate for a particular process state, it should be also captured in the class and life cycle models.

Complete the Events Associated with the Process States

Review each identified process state so that the events associated with it capture all relevant events that may occur while waiting for expected inputs. All alternatives need to be captured, e.g., what if the information being waited for never arrives,

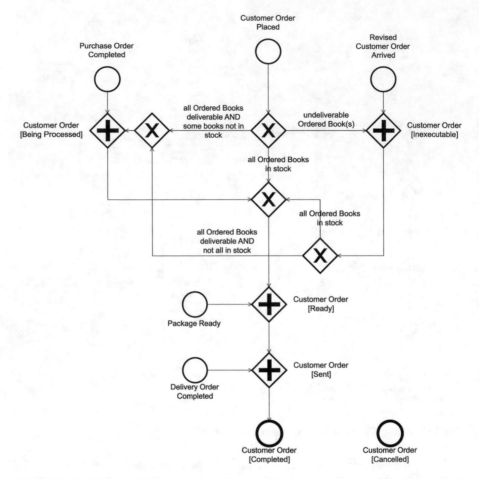

Fig. 2.44 Process flow model after adding all process states

what if the response is negative, etc. As alternatives are added, alternative process-ing flows also need to be added. In general, the process model must include all pos-sible external influences so that a process constructed in this way cannot be caught off guard by a situation to which it will not be able to respond. Timed events are used by default to avoid deadlocks. Again, the existing object life cycle models can be helpful—the relevant events for the particular process state we can find in the rules specified in the object life cycle for object state, according to which we named the process state.

In the case of our bookstore, we have identified multiple alternative events in each process state (with the help of *Customer Order* life cycle), and we have extended the alternative processing flows of the process to include this (Fig. 2.45).

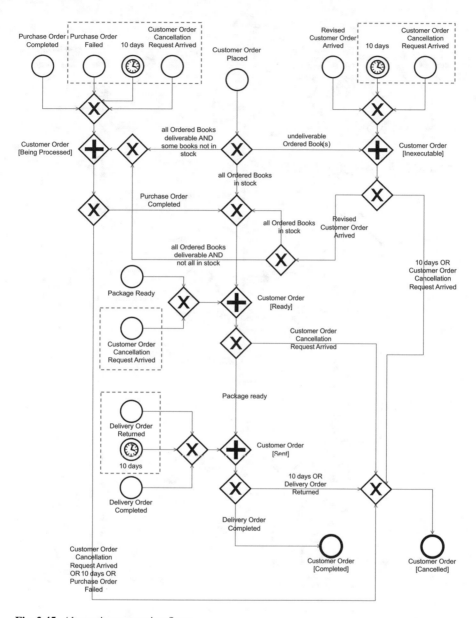

Fig. 2.45 Alternative processing flows

Identify the Activities Performed

Add the activities that lead to the identified process states and ends to the model. Activities that are immediately subsequent to each other should be captured in the aggregate form of process steps, individual activities as tasks. Name the process steps to best represent the collection of activities they aggregate.

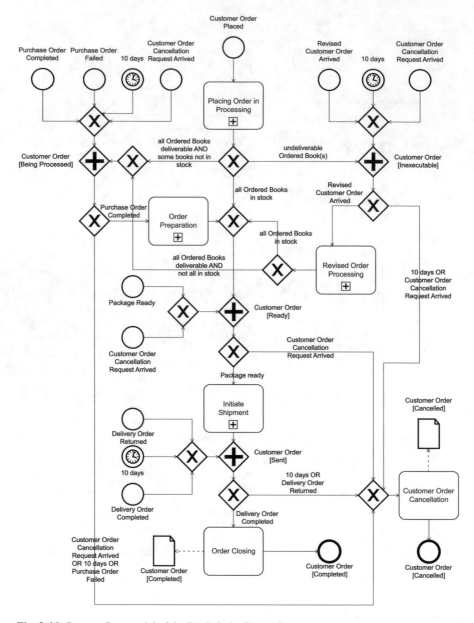

Fig. 2.46 Process flow model of the Book Order Processing process

An example of a completed *Book Order Processing* process from our bookstore is captured in Fig. 2.46. Activities leading to process states *Customer Order [Being Processed]*, *Customer Order [Inexecutable]*, *Customer Order [Ready]*, and *Customer Order [Sent]* are captured as process steps aggregating chains of particular activities (tasks) and activities leading to process ends *Customer Order*

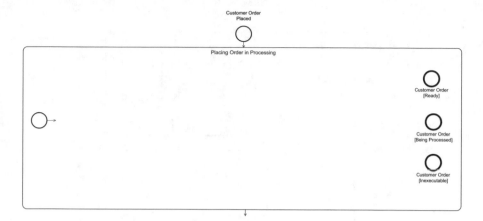

Fig. 2.47 Start and end of the Placing Order in Processing process step

[Cancelled] and *Customer Order [Completed]*, each representing particular activity and captured as single task at this level of detail.

Specify the Beginning and End of Each Process Step

Once the process flow model at the process step level is complete, one can proceed to modeling the details of each process step.

Always start the process step detail with one general starting point and specify the ends of the process step. From the identified object states, select the names of the process step ends that best describe the state at which the process step execution stops.

As an illustrative example from the *Book Order Processing* process, we select the *Placing Order in Processing* process step. We specify the start and end points of the process step in Fig. 2.47. The ends of the process step correspond to the process states of the *Book Order Processing* process in which processing the *Placing Order in Processing* process step precedes them.

Specify the Detail of Each Process Step

Again, first focus on what is to be the result of the tasks performed—the object states that represent the results of the execution of each task. Respect existing object life cycles when creating a process flow. The proposed process processing must not conflict with the business rules captured in the object life cycles.

Starting from the starting point, specify each processing path step by step with all the object states on the way to the final states of the process step. Use gates to branch and close the processing flow. For decision gates, determine the conditions under which processing continues along a particular path (Fig. 2.48).

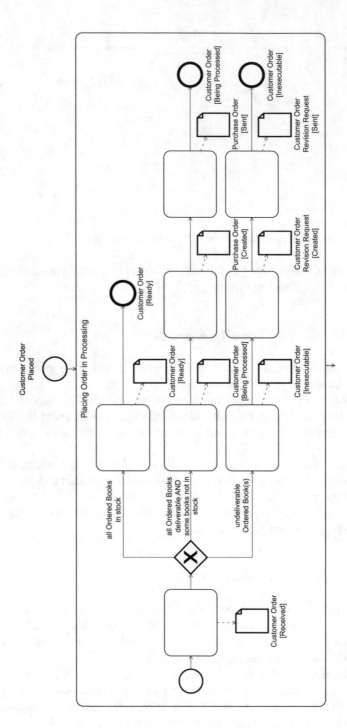

Fig. 2.48 Specification of object states in process step detail

If you identify a new class of objects or a new object state that is more appropriate to a particular sequence of object states, it should be also captured in the class and object life cycle models.

Identify the Tasks of Each Process Step

For each object state listed in the process step detail, capture the task whose execution leads to that object state. Name the tasks so that the name describes the activity leading to the associated object state and is not in conflict with the name of the life cycle operation whose execution leads to the object state associated with the task in the process model (Fig. 2.49).

Review the Process Flow Model

After completing the previous steps of the modeling process, the model needs to be revised in the context of the other models and the business process definition.

- Decide whether the modeled process is really a business process, i.e., that it corresponds to the above MMABP definition of a business process. It may happen that after modeling the flow model of a support process, that was identified within the process map, one finds out that it is not a business process but only a series of activities that belong to the flow model of the supported process. If it is the case, merge the flow model of the support process with the flow model of the supported process, and align the process map so that the process model remains consistent.
- Apply process normalization rules to the modeled process flow models (see the Process Normalization chapter). Using the normalization procedure, you can identify support processes that remained hidden to you at the level of the process map. If this happens, it is necessary to modify both the process map and the flow models of the processes affected by this modification.

Analysis Focused on the Design of a New Business

The process of capturing process flow models comes first, and the analyst therefore does not have the outputs of the analysis of the individual life cycles of important objects available to him right from the start of the detailed process analysis.

The process of creating process flow model, focused on the design of a new business, consists of the following steps:

- Determine the boundaries of the business process
- Identify all other possible ends of the process
- Identify all the process steps and map their details
- Complete the events associated with the process states

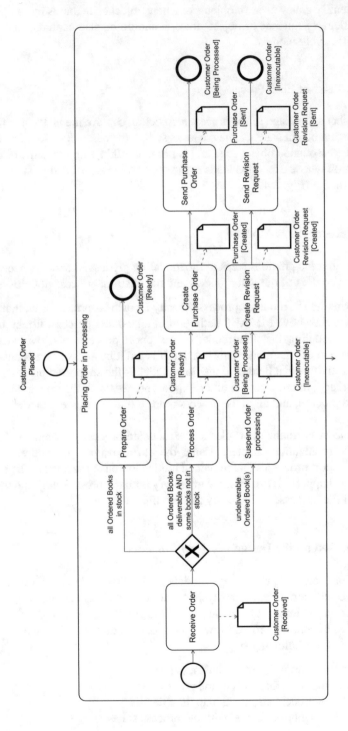

Fig. 2.49 Identifying tasks within a process step

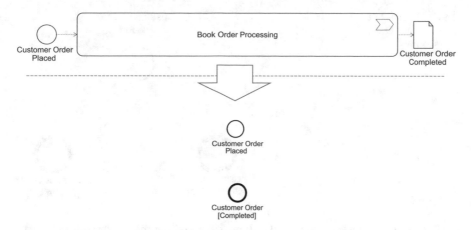

Fig. 2.50 Business process boundaries according to the process map

- Split the flow according to the responses to the identified events
- Capture the entire process flow model step by step
- Review the process flow model

In the following text, we will go through the steps in detail.

A process flow model for each business process is created step by step starting from the process step level of detail. The entire process processing is thus divided into process steps, which are mapped one by one so that each process step is an aggregation of a series of tasks that can be performed one after the other without waiting for any external input (event). Each detail mapping of a business process starts with a process triggering event, and from there, process steps are mapped step by step, and their processing order is recorded in the form of sequential flows and split/join gates until one reaches all the ends of the process.

Determine the Boundaries of the Business Process

First, based on the global process map, capture the triggering events and the target process state for the business process in the process flow model.

In the case of our bookstore, we start with the key process *Book Order Processing*. Based on the process map, we capture one triggering event and one process end (target state) in the process flow model of the *Book Order Processing* process (Fig. 2.50).

Identify All Other Possible Ends of the Process

Try to identify all possible ends of the process. Name each end of the process as the object state that best describes the state of the process at which the execution of the process ends.

Fig. 2.51 Ends of the process Book Order Processing

Customer Order Placed

Customer Order [Completed]

Customer Order [Cancelled]

It may not be possible to identify all possible ends of the processing right from the start. This is to be expected. The aim of this step is a basic awareness of where the modelled process begins and ends, but the detail of this knowledge will of course develop further as the process detail analysis progresses to map the entire flow of the analyzed process.

In the case of our bookstore, we identified only one other end of the process— *Customer Order [Cancelled]* (Fig. 2.51).

Identify All the Process Steps, and Map Their Details

To map process steps, start with the process triggering event that initiates the first process step of the detailed process. Once its details have been mapped, proceed with the next subsequent process steps, using the recommended model creation process steps specified below, to identify them in the step-by-step analysis of the process flow. To map details of each process step, use the following general procedure.

Within the details of each process step, map all the tasks (including the associated states of the objects) as they follow each other. Terminate this series of tasks if one of the following occurs:

- You encounter a synchronization with the process environment [waiting for event(s)]—this is always and only captured outside the process step detail by the process state pattern.
- A process processing flow is merged within a process step, and at least one of the merged flows originates outside the mapped process step.
- If you encounter the end of the process.

Figure 2.52 shows the direction of mapping of the first process step of the process that is triggered by the process triggering event. In this example, we start at the very beginning of the *Book Order Processing* process, and the *Placing Order in Processing* process step is triggered by the process triggering event. We start the

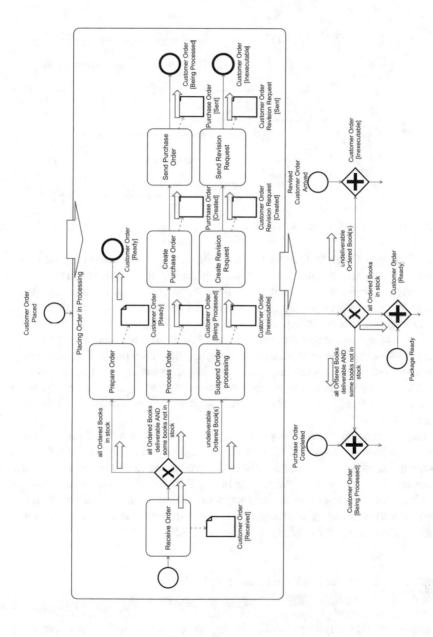

Fig. 2.52 Mapping of the first process step of the Book Order Processing process flow model

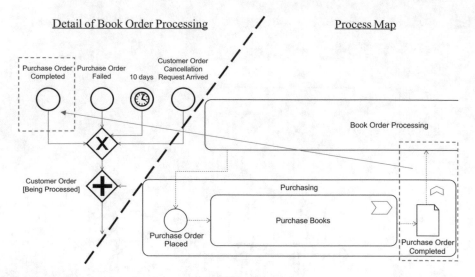

Fig. 2.53 Consistency of process synchronization

detail of *Placing Order in Processing* process step with the process step start element and step-by-step capture each task of the process step until we reach the points in the process flows where the process flow stops and waits for external input (events). We end the process step at these points and capture the waiting for external input through the process state pattern.

All process synchronization points (process states) are identified during process detail modeling, but remember that there are synchronization points that we already know about—the synchronizations with support processes captured in the process map. All these synchronization points need to be captured using the process state pattern in the process flow models and consistent with what is captured in the process map (Fig. 2.53).

It may be that you identify only one task in the process step detail after which a process synchronization occurs. Cancel the process step, and capture only the task with the associated object state directly in the processing flow. For example, if the process step *Placing Order in Processing* in Fig. 2.52 contained only single receive task, after which the process flow stops and waits for confirmation that the customer order is indeed intended for processing, capture the *Receive Order* task without any enclosing process step directly in the model (Fig. 2.54).

Complete the Events Associated with the Process States

Review each identified process state so that the events associated with it capture all relevant events that may occur while waiting for expected inputs. All alternatives need to be captured, e.g., what if the information being waited for never arrives, what if the response is negative, etc. As alternatives are added, alternative processing flows also need to be added. In general, the process model must include all possible

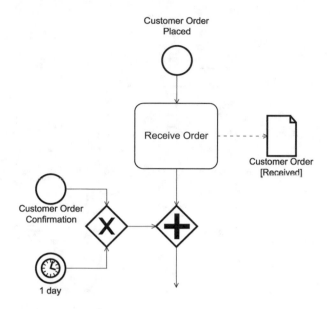

Fig. 2.54 Task instead of a process step

external influences so that a process constructed in this way cannot be caught off guard by a situation to which it will not be able to respond. Timed events are used by default to avoid deadlocks.

In the case of our bookstore, we have identified the highlighted events in (Fig. 2.55). The 10-day timeout is applied in the process states shown to avoid deadlocks. For instance, in the case of waiting for a purchasing support process to complete, the *Purchase Order Completed* event is awaited. If this event does not occur within *10 days* from the start of the process state (and the customer does not cancel the order within that time and purchasing support process does not fail), then the time limit will expire, and the process will react to the inactivity of its support process. This works similarly for waiting for a customer to revise the order. Thus, a timed event represents events such as a statement that someone has not done something ("customer has not responded", etc.).

Split the Flow According to the Responses to the Identified Events

After the process state, divide the processing paths according to the events that occurred, and capture the next steps of the process, mapping them in the same way as described above.

In Fig. 2.56, we divide the processing paths according to the identified events and capture the process steps that react to those events. We then analyze the identified process steps in the same way as described above, with the exception of *Customer Order Cancellation*, which consists of only one task.

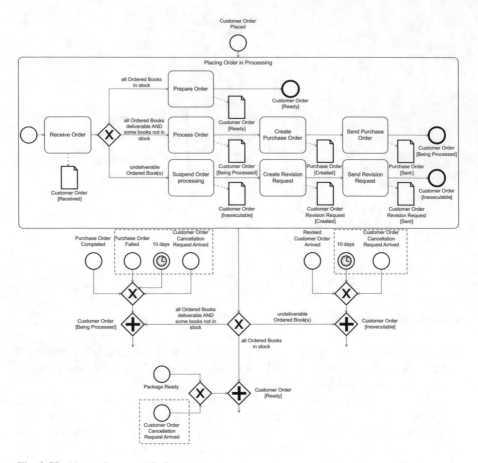

Fig. 2.55 Alternative events in the process state

Capture the Entire Process Flow Model Step by Step

Apply the three steps of the recommended modeling process above iteratively until you reach all the ends of the process in the process flow model. In this way, you will step by step capture the entire detail of the process.

The result of our mapping of the *Book Order Processing* process is shown in Fig. 2.57, where each process step has its detail, as shown for *the Placing Order in Processing* in Fig. 2.52.

Review the Process Flow Model

After completing the previous steps of the modeling process, the model needs to be revised in the context of the other models and the business process definition.

- Decide whether the modeled process is really a business process, i.e., that it corresponds to the above MMABP definition of a business process. It may happen

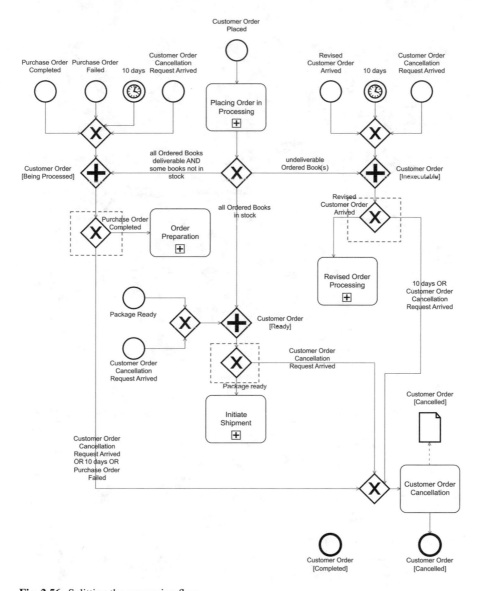

Fig. 2.56 Splitting the processing flow

that after modeling the flow model of a support process, that was identified
within the process map, one finds out that it is not a business process but only a
series of activities that belong to the flow model of the supported process. If it is
the case, merge the flow model of the support process with the flow model of the
supported process, and align the process map so that the process model remains
consistent.

•   Apply process normalization rules to the modeled process flow models (see the
    Process Normalization chapter). Using the normalization procedure, you can

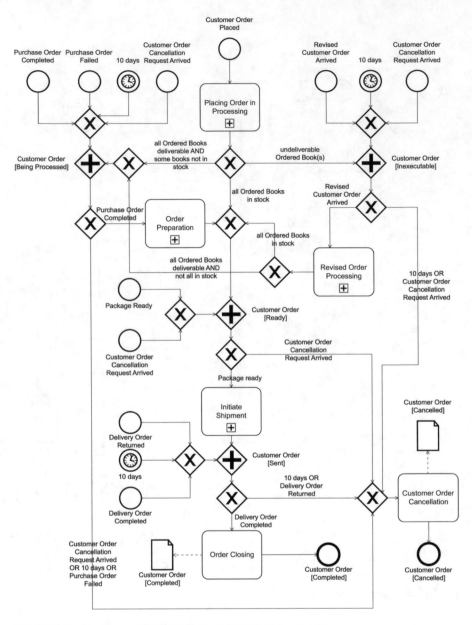

Fig. 2.57 Process flow model of the Book Order Processing process

identify support processes that remained hidden to you at the level of the process map. If this happens, it is necessary to modify both the process map and the flow models of the processes affected by this modification.

2.3.6 Summary of the Basic Rules for Process Flow Modeling

Summary of rules described in the recommended process flow modeling process above:

- The process flow model contains only the purposeful, intentional activities (process steps and tasks) of the modelled business. Activities of customer's will, outsourced processes, etc. are represented only in the form of events (from the modeled process environment) that are the result of these activities.
- Each task is assigned only one object state, which represents the goal that the task achieves. The exception is when a task has alternative goals. Then all alternative object states that the task can achieve must be assigned.
- The synchronization of the process run with events from the process environment is captured according to the desired pattern—as a process state in which the process awaits events with which it synchronizes.
- The interconnection of a business process and its support process is captured in the supported process detail according to the desired pattern—i.e., as a process state in which the supported process synchronizes with the support process through events.
- Rules for the use of AND, OR, and XOR gates based on their meaning in the logic are followed, including rules for possible combinations of these gates to split and merge the processing flows.
- When capturing the synchronization of process processing with the environment, it is taken into account that the awaited ad hoc events may not always occur—the impending deadlock is handled by a time event—a deadline.
- The name of the event briefly and concisely describes a change that occurred outside the modelled process (i.e., from its objective point of view).
- Tasks are named as actions leading to the resulting state of the object associated with the task.
- For each decision, the conditions for each of the possible processing paths are listed.
- Each process flow split and flow merge is modeled using gates only, not otherwise.
- Each process starts with a triggering event (or a logical set of possible events), and all processing flows end with process ends. If there are multiple triggering events, they are always in a direct logical relationship (XOR/AND).
- Each process step detail starts with a start point, and all its processing flows end with the end of the process step.
- The conditions in the decision following the process step correspond to the process step detail.
- The process step detail does not capture synchronization with the environment (a process state awaiting events).

2.4 Further Readings

One of the key factors of the quality of business process models is the author's understanding of the meaning and essence of business process reengineering (BPR) and process-driven management. As a basic source of the idea of process reengineering, we recommend the legendary publications of M. Hammer and J. Champy [1] and T. Davenport [3]. A comprehensive introduction to BPR, more related to process modeling, can be found in Dumas et al. [24].

For a more in-depth look at different approaches to process abstraction and its management, see [6].

In practice, you may encounter a process map in many other forms. For the industry-leading approach, see TOGAF [7] and ArchiMate [25], but you may encounter also process maps used in business process management [24] or ARIS [15] (value chains). The relationship between the process models and enterprise architecture is well explained in [26].

Even if we work with BPMN in a reduced form, it is good to go through the whole standard [11] so that one can understand its breadth and decide for which account what part of BPMN makes sense to use.

BPMN is not the only standard that can be used to diagram a process flow model. The eEPC from the ARIS method [15] remains very popular and is good to know.

For an explanation of the role of intentionality in business processes and its manifestation in the process flow model, see [23].

2.5 Summary

This chapter presents business process analysis and management and why it is an important part of a business system model (architecture). It also provides an overview of the tools and methods needed to create coherent business process model that includes both global and detailed views.

Section 2.1 Introduction to Four Levels of Process Abstraction introduces the reader to concept of process abstraction levels, how the MMABP incorporates it, and how it is reflected in the models that make up the business system model (architecture).

Section 2.2 Process Map introduces the process map and, using the TOGAF event diagram, how it provides an overview of the analyzed business. The process map helps identify business processes and their interrelationships, specify the scope and context of the process analysis, and structure the analysis. When completed, it allows one to determine (with the respect to the purpose of the business analysis) which business processes need to be subjected to a detailed process analysis. This section also provides a detailed step-by-step modeling process on how to systematically create the process map model: which features are important to capture, what to look for when modeling, and what the basic rules are that an analyst should follow when creating the model.

Section 2.3 Process Flow Model presents the process flow model and, using the BPMN diagram, shows how it captures the details of a business process at two consistent levels of detail: process steps and tasks. This model maps the process steps and tasks, outlines their potential sequences, and delineates all possible outcomes. It focuses on analyzing and capturing the points at which business processes synchronize with their environment and on linking the execution of process activities to the object model through object states. This subchapter also provides a detailed step-by-step modeling process on how to systematically create the process flow model: which features are important to capture, what to look for when modeling, and what the basic rules are that an analyst should follow when building the model.

2.6 Exercises

2.6.1 Process Map

1. Choose the correct statements:

   a) Each business process according to the definition has one or more triggering events.
   b) Each business process according to the definition always has multiple triggering events.
   c) Each business process according to the definition has exactly one triggering event.
   d) Each business process according to the definition has always one target state.
   e) Each business process according to the definition has one or more target states.
   f) Each business process according to the definition may have a triggering event.
   g) Each business process according to the definition can have a target state.

2. Which of the following is an appropriate name for a business process?

   a) Accounting
   b) Warehouse Management
   c) Purchasing Goods for Stock
   d) Distributor

3. Which of these is an appropriate name for a business function?

   a) Order
   b) Warehouse Management
   c) Purchasing Goods for Stock
   d) Distributor

4. Choose the correct statement:

   a) Business process belongs to one or more business functions.
   b) Business process belongs always to one business function.
   c) Business process belongs to no business function.
   d) Business process belongs to one or no business function.

5. According to the MMABP, a business process is defined as:

   a) Any series of activities
   b) A series of activities covering complete business case from the expression of a process's customers need to its satisfaction
   c) A series of activities processing inputs into outputs
   d) A series of activities fulfilling all customer's needs in a robotic way by means of modern information technologies, Industry 4.0 principles, and artificial intelligence algorithms

6. Complete the following diagram so that the business process captured in the process map is complete.

7. The process map includes:

   a) Events triggering processes
   b) Outsourced business processes
   c) Internal business processes
   d) Business process target states
   e) Data flows
   f) Data stores
   g) Sequential flows

8. Select which of the following would be an appropriate name for the event:

   a) Expiration of 2 h
   b) Order received
   c) Goods
   d) Purchase of stock

9. Select which of the following would be an appropriate name for the target state:

   a) Order fulfilled
   b) Purchase
   c) Order finalization
   d) Order

10. Which triggering relationships in the process map diagram are inappropriate?

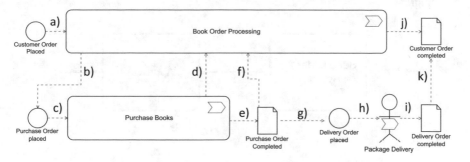

2.6.2   Process Flow Model

1. Activities of the process customer are captured in the detailed process diagram as:

   a) Tasks in which the customer is listed as the actor.
   b) Are not captured at all, only their outcomes in the form of events.
   c) As a separate process with which the enterprise process synchronizes.
   d) There is nothing to capture; the process customer always waits for the outcome of the whole business process.

2. Does every task have to have an associated object state?

   a) Yes
   b) No
   c) Must not

3. Can a task have multiple associated object states?

   a) Yes
   b) No
   c) Yes, but only if only one of them always occurs (they are mutually exclusive)

4. Select the correct capture of order approval by the customer in a detailed process
   diagram.

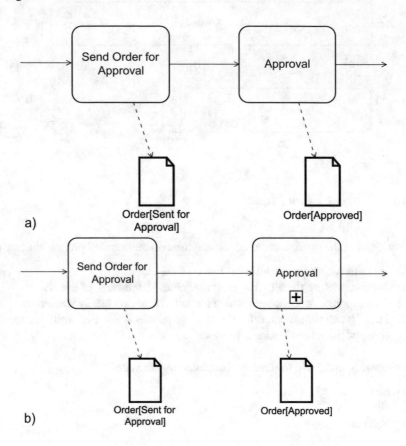

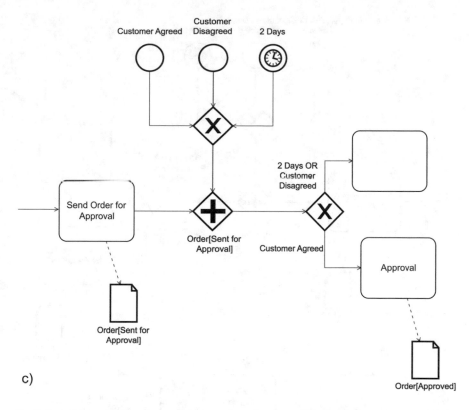

c)

5. Select the correct capture of the synchronization of the business process with its supporting Purchasing process in the detailed process diagram:

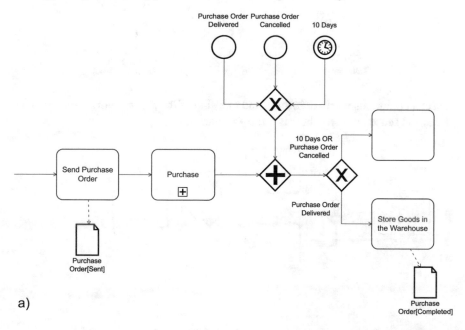

a)

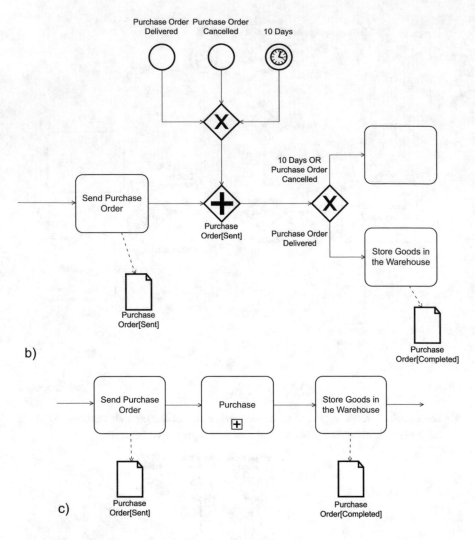

b)

c)

6. Select diagrams where branching and merging of the process flow does not make
   logical sense or where there is a risk of deadlock.

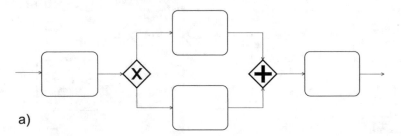

a)

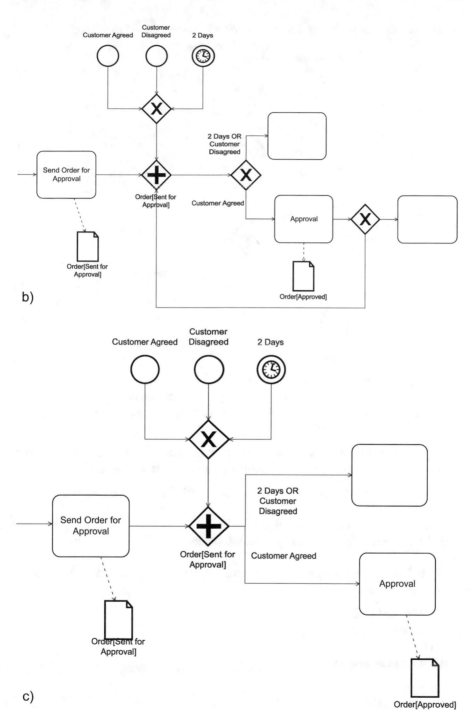

b)

c)

7. Is there something wrong with the provided example of the process state?

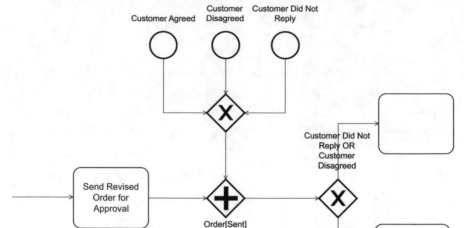

Order[Sent]

a) Nothing—the process state capture is fine.
b) A time event is missing to handle an impending deadlock.
c) The "customer did not reply." Ad hoc event does not make sense. There should be a time event instead.

8. The process state is named as the state of the object that best describes in which state the process processing has stopped. The object state used must:

a) Represent a objects state that is connected with the task in the model that precedes the process state
b) Exist in the life cycle of the object
c) Be the final state in the life cycle of the object

9. Which of the following is the most appropriate name for the task in the detailed process diagram?

a) Order Receival
b) Order Received
c) Orders
d) Order Management

10. Is there anything wrong with this section of the detailed process diagram?

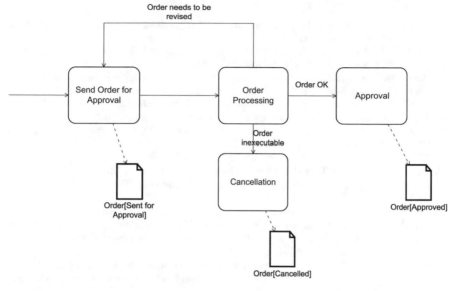

a) Tasks divide and merge process processing flows
b) Not all flows have the specified conditions
c) The diagram is fine
d) Tasks lack data input

11. Each process flow within each detailed process model

a) Must be terminated by a process end or merged with another process flow
b) Must consist of more than one task
c) Must contain a process state
d) Must start with an event or a flow splitting gate

12. Select the correct statement

a) A process step detail always starts with one starting point, and all its processing flows end with one or more process step ends.
b) A process step detail starts with one or more start points, and all its processing flows end with one or more process step ends.
c) A process step detail always starts at one start point, and all its processing flows always end at one process step end.
d) A process step detail always starts with one or more start points, and all its processing flows always end in one process step end.

References

1. Hammer, M., Champy, J.: Reengineering the Corporation: A Manifesto for Business Revolution. Brealey, London (1993)
2. Porter, M.E.: Competitive Advantage: Creating and Sustaining Superior Performance. Free Press/Collier Macmillan, New York/London (1985)
3. Davenport, T.H.: Process Innovation: Reengineering Work Through Information Technology. Harvard Business School Press, Boston, MA (1995)
4. Deming, W.E.: Out of the crisis. The MIT Press, Cambridge, MA (2000)
5. Řepa, V.: Information Modeling of Organizations. Tomáš Bruckner (2012)
6. Svatoš, O., Řepa, V.: Working with process abstraction levels. In: Perspectives in Business Informatics Research: 15th International Conference, BIR 2016, Prague, Czech Republic, 15–16 Sept 2016, Proceedings 15, pp. 65–79. Springer (2016)
7. The Open Group: The TOGAF® Standard, 10th edn. Van Haren (2022)
8. Desfray, P., Raymond, G.: Modeling Enterprise Architecture with TOGAF: A Practical Guide Using UML and BPMN. Morgan Kaufmann (2014)
9. Jung, J., Fraunholz, B.: Masterclass Enterprise Architecture Management. Springer (2021)
10. LeanIX: Business Capabilities. https://www.leanix.net/en/wiki/ea/business-capability (2023)
11. Object Management Group: Business Process Model and Notation (BPMN) Specification Version 2.0.2. http://www.omg.org/spec/BPMN/ (2014)
12. zur Muehlen, M., Recker, J.: How much language is enough? Theoretical and practical use of the business process modeling notation. In: Seminal Contributions to Information Systems Engineering: 25 Years of CAiSE, pp. 429–443 (2013)
13. Rosenblueth, A., Wiener, N., Bigelow, J.: Behavior, purpose and teleology. Phil Sci. **10**, 18–24 (1943)
14. Eriksson, H.-E., Penker, M.: Business Modeling with UML: Business Patterns at Work. Wiley, New York (2000)
15. Software AG: ARIS METHOD MANUAL VERSION 10.0 - SERVICE RELEASE 18 (2022)
16. Codd, E.F.: A relational model of data for large shared data banks. Commun. ACM. **13**(6), 377–387 (1970)
17. Codd, E.F.: Recent Investigations into Relational Data Base Systems. IBM Research Report RJ1385 (1974)
18. Kent, W.: A simple guide to five normal forms in relational database theory. Commun. ACM. **26**(2), 120–125 (1983)
19. Chen, P.P.-S.: The entity-relationship model—toward a unified view of data. ACM Trans. Database Syst. (TODS). **1**(1), 9–36 (1976)
20. Řepa, V.: Business System Modeling Specification. In: Chu, H.-w., Ferrer, J., Nguyen, T., Yongquan, Y. (eds.) Computer, Communication and Control Technologies (CCCT '03), pp. 222–227. IIIS, Orlando (2003) ISBN 980-6560-05-1.
21. Jackson, M.A., Cameron, J.: System Development. Prentice-Hall, Englewood Cliffs, NJ (1983)
22. Jackson, M.A.: Principles of Program Design. Academic Press, London (1975)
23. Řepa, V.: Caring of Intentionality in Business Process Models Using Business Process Patterns. In: ILOG 2014 Information Logistics and Knowledge Supply, pp. 23–34. CEur, Aachen (2014) ISSN 1613-0073. http://ceur-ws.org/Vol-1246/paper-03.pdf
24. Dumas, M., et al.: Fundamentals of Business Process Management. Springer (2018)
25. The Open Group: ArchiMate® 3.2 Specification. Van Haren (2023)
26. Weske, M.: Business Process Management: Concepts, Languages, Architectures. Springer, Berlin (2019). https://doi.org/10.1007/978-3-662-59432-2

Chapter 3
Causality and Business Objects

Abstract Analysis of business objects focuses on mapping of classes of business objects and the business rules that describe causality and modality that is inherent to them. For their capturing, we use two models. Model of concepts allows one in a systematic way to establish business glossary in the form of a UML class diagram for the analyzed business and so to get an overview of concepts used by the business, understand the business concepts and their relationships, and specify detailed properties of the business concepts. An object life cycle model allows one to specify business rules in relation to relevant class of business objects (business concept) in a systematic way and so in the form of a UML state machine diagram to specify what life phases an object of a particular class may go through during its lifetime, what events are essential for an object in particular life phase, what the response is to relevant events when they occur when the object is in a particular life stage, and at what moments the life of an object ends. For both models, we specify a step-by-step modeling process for their creation.

Effectively managing an organization's efficacy and future development necessitates a precise understanding of all essential facets and their interconnections. In this regard, informatics provides a semiformal technique known as *conceptual modeling*, initially developed in data management theory as a subset of information systems development. As real-world systems, often referred to as *business systems*, attain a certain level of complexity, accurate and comprehensive representation within the *information system* becomes imperative. The model of concepts serves this purpose by articulating the *real world as a system of objects and their relationships*, outlining how this can be accurately depicted through data in the information system.

The term *conceptual* originated in the realm of *data modeling*, a lineage still evident in its common interpretation in the context of *object-oriented modeling*, specifically through tools like the *Unified Modeling Language* [1]. Object-oriented analysis and design materials, such as those crafted by Craig Larman, provide the following description of conceptual modeling [2]:

© The Author(s), under exclusive license to Springer Nature
Switzerland AG 2024
V. Řepa, O. Svatoš, *Fundamentals of Business Architecture Modeling*, The
Enterprise Engineering Series, https://doi.org/10.1007/978-3-031-59035-1_3

- Classes representing concepts from the real-world domain.
- Binary associations describe relationships between two concepts.
- The concepts can have attributes but no operations.
- General associations indicate that the specialized concepts are subsets of a more general concept. The specialized concepts have associations or attributes that are not in the general concept.
- Each association conclusion can have graphical adornments indicating their end name, multiplicity, and much more.

Cris Kobryn [3], the Co-Chair of the UML Revision Task Force, incorporates the conceptual model when defining the "Structural Model" as a system view that accentuates the structure of objects, encompassing their classifiers, relationships, attributes, and operations. The primary aim of this model is to illustrate the *static structure of the system*, including the *entities* in existence, *internal structure*, and *relationships* with other entities.

Additionally, Kobryn offers several recommendations for *structural modeling*:

- Establish a "skeleton" (or "backbone") that allows for extension and refinement as domain knowledge expands.
- Prioritize the effective use of basic constructs; introduce advanced constructs or notations only when necessary.
- Postpone considerations of implementation details until later stages in the modeling process.
- Structural diagrams should:

  – Highlight specific facets of the structural model
  – Contain classifiers at the same level of abstraction
  – Organize large numbers of classifiers into packages

Roni Weisman [4] from Softera provides further insights into the *Conceptual System Model*. He distinguishes three types of objects:

- Entity (objects that hold the system's data)
- Boundary Object (interface objects directly interacting with the external world, i.e., actors)
- Control Object (objects managing system operations)

As evident from the preceding paragraphs, various approaches exist in the realm of object-oriented methods for conceptual modeling. Each of these approaches simplifies the Object Model (depicted by the Class Diagram) to the model of objects and their relationships, emphasizing attributes over methods. Roni Weisman's approach, as discussed earlier, also follows this reduction, even when considering *Entities* and *Control Objects*. The distinction between *static* and *dynamics ensuring* objects serves as a clear illustration of this reduction, aligning the common understanding of *conceptual* with the synonym for *static*.

In MMABP, we advocate for a *genuinely object-oriented conceptual modeling* approach. This entails not only modeling the static facets of the real world but also capturing its dynamics. The existence of an object, comprising both *data (attributes)* and *functions (operations)*, should justify the control of data processing operations. Moreover, adopting a conceptual standpoint in line with object-oriented principles requires moving beyond viewing an object's operations merely as a set of procedures for communicating with other objects. Instead, one should explore their broader conceptual significance—the essence of their synergy. This essential sense of an object's operations is encapsulated in the *object life cycle*.

To describe the life cycle of an object, MMABP uses *UML State Machine Diagram*. State Chart, also known as a *State Machine Diagram*, originally served as a graphical representation for modeling the behavior of a system or software application in response to various events or changes in its environment. The origins of State Chart can be traced back to the 1940s and 1950s when John von Neumann introduced the notion of a "finite state machine" as a theoretical model of computation [5]. This concept aimed to describe a system capable of existing in a finite number of states, transitioning between these states based on inputs. In the 1970s, David Harel extended von Neumann's work and introduced the concept of state charts [6], which used the graphical notations to represent the states and transitions of a system. State Charts gained significant traction in the 1980s and 1990s, particularly in the field of software engineering. They were widely adopted as a modeling technique for object-oriented software design, and the *Unified Modeling Language* [1] included a notation for state diagrams. Today, State Charts continue to be used in a variety of domains, including software engineering, control engineering, and system design. They provide a visual means of representing complex behavior that helps designers understand system behavior, identify potential issues, and refine designs.

Figure 3.1 presents the object life cycle model as a complement to the model of concepts. It is evident that all operations of the conceptual object should be organized into a single algorithm that outlines each operation's role in the overall process of the object's life. This positioning defines the conceptual significance of each operation. From this perspective, popular object operations like *give_list* or *send_status* appear nonsensical, as does the notion of *sending messages* between objects, as exemplified by the human-like interaction between *Order* and *Goods* in this example. While such a viewpoint might be suitable for modeling objects in a program system, it is apparently inappropriate for conceptual objects.

The figure also highlights the existence of dependencies between operations of different objects, corresponding not only to the association between objects in terms of existence (e.g., the *Delivery* method in this example) but also in a "structural sense"—in the context of the life cycle structure. For instance, the fact that *goods do not need to be ordered* (indicated by the partiality of the association between *Goods* and *Order*) aligns with the possibility of direct transition from *Created* to *Exempted* phase of *Goods*. Similarly, the fact that *goods may be reordered* (as seen in the cardinality n of the association) corresponds to the iteration of the *Filled* phase in the life of the *Order*. For a more comprehensive understanding of structural dependencies, crucial for precisely defining object-oriented conceptual modeling principles, one can refer to Jackson's JSD [7][1] and Chap. 5.

---

[1] It appears that in the realm of conceptual modeling, there is an opportunity for the "renaissance" of clearly correct and unambiguous general principles akin to structured programming, as advocated by Jackson already in his basic work [8]. The influence of Jackson's theory is discussed also in Chap. 5 as a topic of so-called structural consistency.

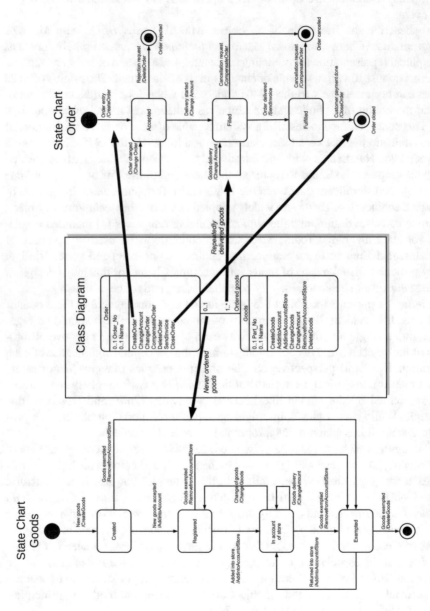

Fig. 3.1 Object life cycles versus object model using UML State Machine Diagram

While State Charts are primarily used to describe states and transitions in technical systems, MMABP uses them to express the causality of changes in the Real World. This application of the diagram is closer to the ontology modeling perspective than the engineering perspective. Therefore, it is crucial to recognize the difference between the life cycle of an object, which represents causality, and the behavior of the system, which represents intentional actions. This distinction may not be obvious from a technological (engineering) point of view and is related to the often-discussed difference between State Charts and Petri Nets [9, 10]. Despite their distinct origins and approaches, state charts and Petri nets share similarities in their structure and concepts. Both employ graphical notations to depict system behavior, relying on the fundamental concepts of states, transitions, and events. Technologically, state charts can be viewed as a specialized case of Petri nets, where states and transitions are explicitly represented, and concurrency and synchronization aspects are implicit. There have been attempts to integrate state charts and Petri nets into a unified modeling language, aiming to leverage their complementary strengths. David Harel is recognized for proposing such integration. In [11], he advocated for extending the State charts formalism to model the behavior of reactive systems. In [12], the authors further expanded the State charts formalism with features like hierarchical state machines, concurrency, and real-time constraints. In this conceptualization, State charts are diagrams comprising elements that enhance the visual modeling of reactive system behaviors. They go beyond traditional state diagrams by incorporating notions of hierarchy, concurrency, and communication.

From the MMABP perspective, a natural embodiment of a reactive system in the Real World is a business process. In the context of Harel's definition [13], reactive systems are those that continuously interact with their environment, sensing and responding to events and other inputs. Business processes encapsulate a sequence of actions and interactions among various entities (such as customers, employees, systems) that respond to events or inputs from the environment (such as customer requests, system failures, regulatory changes). The state of a business process changes as a result of these interactions and inputs, and the process must respond to these changes in order to meet its objectives. In this light, business processes can be viewed as reactive systems that respond to events and inputs to achieve their goals.

Because the business process is about achieving goals, its description shouldn't be seen as a representation of causality, a natural logical facet of the real world. Therefore, it is critical to distinguish between the business process and the system of ontological objects represented as concepts in the model of concepts. The use of State Charts in conceptual modeling should never be interpreted as a description of the business process or its infrastructure (machine, IT system) but only as an *articulation of the logic inherent in the real world*. MMABP supports this distinction through *rules* governing the use of state diagrams:

1. *Life Cycle General Completeness* The object's life cycle model must encompass its entire existence. It should begin with an event that signifies the creation of the object (class instance) and cover all potential terminations in the object's life— various scenarios marking the end of the instance, including various death events.

2. *Algorithmic Correctness* The life cycle model should embody fundamental algorithmic properties, in particular unambiguousness, discreteness, and finiteness. In practical terms, this means that states should not overlap in meaning or time and that any conceivable combination of transitions should avoid leading to a deadlock.

3. *General Information Richness* Each internal state in the object's life cycle should have at least two output transitions. This requirement ensures that each state represents alternative responses, a necessary condition because the life cycle model embodies the definition of modal logic. Without multiple output transitions, there would be no distinction between the state and its only possible successor, and there would be no "modal" information associated with the state.

4. *Contextual Consistency* The object's life cycle should align with its context as specified in the Class Diagram. This consistency is grounded in several principles:
   - Each transition between the object's states means a change in the relationship(s) with another object(s) or the transformation of the object's attribute(s).
   - If the class described by the life cycle is generic, and if this generalization is "dynamic" in the sense of OntoUML terminology [14], then the individual life cycle states should correspond to the subtypes of this generalization structure.
   - If the class described by the life cycle is decomposed into multiple dynamic generalization structures, each should be defined with a separate life cycle model.

The meaning of the conceptual model discussed above in the context of MMABP is in accordance with the OntoUML concept, which is based on the idea that the conceptual model actually expresses the real-world ontology [14]. MMABP aims to be consistent with OntoUML, but with respect to its principle of "minimality," it reduces the use of OntoUML concepts to the minimum necessary to satisfy the MMABP principles. OntoUML enhances the expressiveness of UML by extending the language (namely, the Class Diagram) with special stereotypes for specific constructions and associated additional rules that guide the modeler to respect the basic ontological distinctions, thus dramatically increasing the precision and potential accuracy of the class model. With respect to the MMABP principle of minimality, depending on the specific situation in the analysis, only certain stereotypes need to be used. Since one of the basic MMABP models is the object life cycle model, it is important to distinguish between static and dynamic generalization structures as defined in [14]. According to OntoUML, MMABP marks the subtypes of the dynamic generalization structure with the stereotype «*phase*», which means that the particular subtypes represent life phases of their generic class. In MMABP, certain «*phase*» classes must 1:1 correspond to certain states in the State Chart of the particular class. MMABP further extends OntoUML with an additional stereotype «*end*». Such a subtype represents the end of the life cycle. The end of the life cycle cannot be regarded as a state (life phase) of the object, since it represents the situation, when the object does not longer exist. On the other hand, it should belong to the generalization structure since it is excluded with the other states in the life of

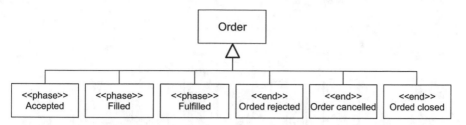

Fig. 3.2 Dynamic generalization of the class Order

the object. This is why we call the end of the life cycle a "pseudo-state," just as we call the start of the life cycle.

Figure 3.2 shows the generalization structure of the class *Order* from the example in Fig. 3.1.

Figures 3.1 and 3.2 show an essential difference between the stereotypes ≪*phase*≫ and ≪*end*≫:

- ≪*phase*≫ stereotype represents an internal phase in the life of the object, which has a limited duration and changes according to the life cycle model.
- ≪*end*≫ stereotype represents the moment of the object's demise, which has near-zero duration[2] and thus can never be changed.

Despite its minimalism, MMABP is fully open to the use of OntoUML, since many other OntoUML extensions of UML may be useful depending on the particular content and purpose of modeling, which is generally allowed due to the full compatibility of MMABP and UntoUML in the area of modeling of concepts.

3.1 Model of Concepts

Model of concepts is a model that allows one in a systematic way to establish business glossary in form of a UML class diagram for the analyzed business and so to:

- Get an overview of concepts used by the business
- Define and structure the business concepts
- Understand the business concepts and their relationships
- Specify detailed properties of the business concepts
- Systematically manage business concepts and their definitions over time as the reality of the business changes

We use the UML Class Diagram [1] (Fig. 3.3) as a tool to capture the model of concepts.

---

[2] By "near-zero duration," we mean a logical (functional) zero, a period of time during which the object cannot change in any way. It can be implemented in an infrastructure technology as an arbitrarily long period of time that ends only with the physical demise of the object.

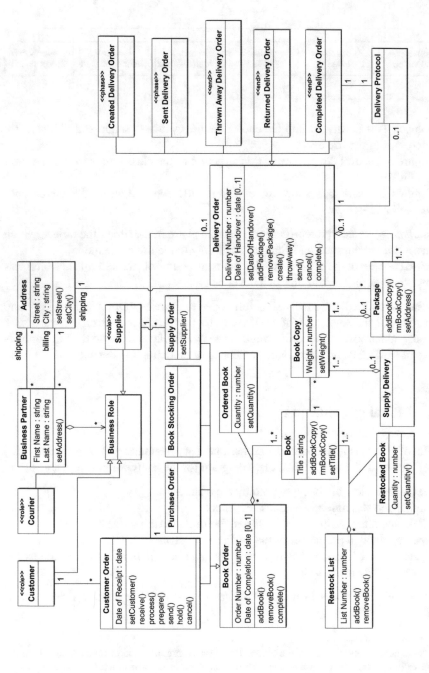

Fig. 3.3 Example of model of concepts in UML class diagram

Table 3.1 Overview of the key elements needed to capture the model of concepts in UML class diagram

Element	Description
Class Attribute 1 : string Attribute 2 : string [0..1] Operation 1() Operation 2()	A *class* is a concept that represents a set of objects (possible instances of a class) that have the same meaning and share the same properties (attributes and operations)
————————▷	*Generalization* represents the relationship between a more general and a more specific class. It is the basic classification of object classes
employer * employee *	An *association* represents the possibility of a general relationship between objects of two different classes or even of the same class. The meaning of the relationship is characterized by the multiplicities and possible roles that a class of objects has in the relationship
◇————————— ◆—————————	*Aggregation* and *composition* are special cases of association, which means "consisting of" and differs in the strength of its bond

In the minimal business architecture, we use the following key elements listed in Table 3.1 to capture the model of concepts in UML class diagram.

3.1.1   Model of Concepts Introduction

The model of concepts is the second global model (Fig. 3.4) and is used to capture the structure of reality. It captures the classes of business objects of the real world and their basic (essential) relationships. Although the model of concepts represents a global view of the modelled system, it is also affected by how the detailed view is being developed later in the process. The model of concepts should then capture not only the classes of business objects identified at the global level but also those classes of business objects identified in the detailed analysis.

The primary goal of creating a model of concepts from a business analysis perspective is to understand the reality of the business and the concepts used by the people who form the business.

3.1.2   Capturing Classes and Their Relationships in a Model of Concepts

When we consider the object model, we have to start with the objects. An object is an entity with clearly defined boundaries and identity that carries state and potential dynamics. The state is represented by values of attributes and relationships and the dynamics by the operations, methods, and life cycle of the object.

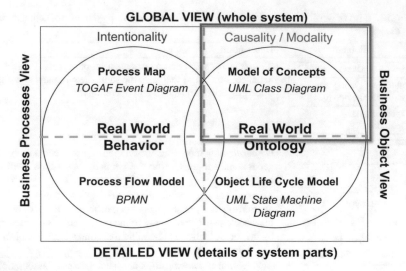

Fig. 3.4 Position of the model of concepts within the business system model

We depict the object model as abstract/generalizing at the level of classes of objects. A class is a concept that describes a set of objects that have the same meaning and share the same properties (attributes and operations). Thus, a class is a generalization of a particular set of objects, and all its properties should capture all possible properties that can occur for objects of a particular class. It is also possible to look at this relationship from the other side—objects are instances of their classes.

An attribute is a property of a class that represents an essential characteristic of the class. For attributes without an explicit specification of obligation, it is assumed that their values are populated by the constructor when the object is created, i.e., that they are mandatory. If this is not the case, it is necessary to specify (in UML using multiplicity) whether an attribute can (0..1) or must (1..1) contain a value.

An operation is a property of a class that describes the potential dynamics of objects of the class. An operation is often confused with a so-called method, but the latter is already a specific implementation of an operation that specifies a particular algorithm or procedure tied to the operation.

A model of concepts consists not only of object abstractions but also of class abstractions. Within the model of concepts, we use two types of hierarchical abstraction: generalization and aggregation. These two types of hierarchical abstraction have their own special way of being captured through relationships in the model of concepts. For the regular relationships we use the associations.

Generalization

Generalization is the relationship between a generic and specific classes. This relationship can be viewed from two directions (Fig. 3.5):

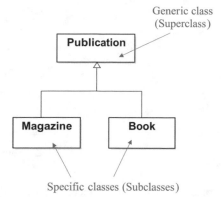

Fig. 3.5 Generalization

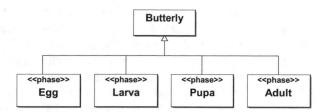

Fig. 3.6 Dynamic specialization example

- In the direction from the more specific class to the more general class, we speak of generalization.
- In the direction from the more general class to the more specific class, we speak of specialization.

In general, wherever there is a proposal to use the attribute "type of ...", it signals specialization. This has a practical dimension as well. It is important that the model captures all that is relevant, so that the reader does not have to scroll through additional lists to find what values the attribute "type of ..." can take on.

Specializations can also refer to phases of development of one entity that may be very different in attributes and operations but have a single common identity (Fig. 3.6). The different specific types here show how the same object changes over time. In ontology engineering, such specialization is therefore called "dynamic" and stereotyped as ≪*phase*≫ [14]. The dynamic specialization can also contain final stages stereotyped as ≪*end*≫ as illustrated in Fig. 3.2.

The way of capturing generalization has undergone a long evolution in UML. The original meaning of generalization, which we also adhere to in this book, was that the specializations are disjunctive with each other. This was later reconsidered, the generalization is overlapping by default, and using constraints, one can specify, precisely, a group of specializations and whether the group is disjunctive or not [1]. In OntoUML, for this, the stereotypes ≪*disjoint*≫ and ≪*joint*≫ are used [14]. We find relying on constraints (which are hard to

Fig. 3.7 Overlapping
specializations pattern

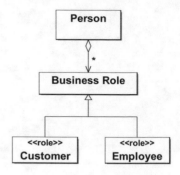

understand for the average business user) unnecessary when this distinction can be
captured using existing elements.

As mentioned above, we consider the generalization/specialization relation to be
disjunctive (i.e., mutually exclusive) by default. If we want to capture that specializations are not disjunctive, i.e., as Fig. 3.7 shows that one person can act in multiple
roles within a business at the same time, we use the pattern below that combines
aggregation and generalization together. This way we capture that a Business
Partner can be from the Business Role perspective (generalization set) a Customer
and/or an Employee. In other words, an employee can be also a customer of the
business. This way of capturing does not need any additional comments or constraints in the diagram, and it is easy to interpret for the ordinary user. In alignment
with OntoUML, we use the stereotype «*role*» for classes that represent roles.[3]

UML calls generalization "inheritance." MMABP rejects this name as confusing
due to the essential difference between the two concepts and strongly recommends
that this name not be used. The concept of "inheritance" naturally assumes that the
"generalization" relationship is a relationship between two different objects (such
as the relationship between child and parent), which is a fatal misunderstanding of
the nature of this relationship.

Generalization should not be considered a relation between objects, since it
describes only a single object (instance) that is represented by both the generic and
specific concepts. It is only a relation between concepts. The specific concept represents a (specific) kind of the generic one.[4]

---

[3] The reason for considering generalization to be disjunctive is actually a matter of principle. While
in traditional conceptual modeling the use of overlapping sub-kinds of the class may make sense
in special situations, once we bring object life cycles into the picture, it is generally unacceptable.
Overlap of the class sub-kinds in dynamic generalization structure means the overlap of object life
cycles, which contradicts the algorithmic nature of the life cycle. Life phases of the same object
simply cannot overlap. For more information about object life cycle modeling, see Sect. 3.2.

[4] The unfortunate name "inheritance" reflects a superficial perception of hierarchy between concepts, based on the inessential fact that all subconcepts share the attributes (including operations)
of the generic concept. In generalization, however, concepts "share" not only attributes but even
identity, which is a fatal distinction.

Fig. 3.8 Aggregation

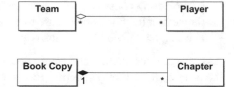

Fig. 3.9 Composition

In conceptual modeling, the generalization structure is traditionally called an "ISA hierarchy," meaning that the specific class *is a* (special kind of) generic class. MMABP recommends calling and understanding generalization in this way, rather than perceiving it as inheritance, since we understand things the way we call them. Perceiving the generalization as an "IS A hierarchy" naturally prevents understanding it as a relationship between two different objects.

In the object-oriented view, generalization dominates the second basic type of hierarchy: aggregation. In practice, this means that generalization should be regarded as the main general meta-quality of an object, while aggregation is just one of the possible types of relationships between object classes.[5]

Aggregation or Composition

In the case of aggregation, an abstract class represents a concept that is composed of other classes. In a model of concepts, we distinguish between two types of aggregations: aggregation and composition.

Aggregation in a model of concepts represents a weak relationship, where grouped objects can exist independently without an aggregating object (also called a "container" in this context), and a single object can be the constituent of multiple groupings at any one time. As an example, consider Fig. 3.8. The relationship between a team and its players is captured as an aggregation, since the following applies:

- A team consists of players. If the team is disbanded, the individual players of the team continue to exist.
- A player can be a member of multiple different teams.

Composition in a model of concepts represents a strong relationship, where grouped objects can only exist in a particular composition, not without it. Thus, a component object can be part of only one composition at any given time. As an example, consider Fig. 3.9. The relationship between a book copy and its chapters is captured as a composition, since the following applies:

---

[5] In contrast, in processes, the aggregation type of hierarchy dominates generalization. Consequently, aggregation should be viewed as a general meta-quality of a process, while generalization is represented by the relationships between processes. A "generic" process model expresses the common general structure of steps and uses the services of specialized support processes for specific situations in particular steps.

- A book copy consists of chapters. If the book copy is destroyed, the individual chapters of the book copy cease to exist.
- The chapters of which the book copy consists are part of this one book copy only.

Aggregation and composition are special cases of association, and for capturing them in a model of concepts, the general rules for association (multiplicity, roles) apply.

Association

We capture general relationships between classes using associations. An association represents the possibility of a relationship between objects of two different classes (*Company <-> Person*) or of the same class (*Person <-> Person*) (Fig. 3.10).

Both ends of an association must have a specified multiplicity, which allows to express the number of objects involved in the association. In UML, an interval is used for this. A 0, * or 1 in the left part of the interval specifies the partiality of the relationship [(non)obligation], and a 1 or * in the right part of the interval specifies the cardinality of the relationship. In this way, multiplicity allows specifying business rules that are bound to objects and their relationships.

The roles of each class in the association are a way to give meaning to the relationships between classes. Thus, we can indicate the role that an object of one class plays for objects of another class (*employee <-> employer*) or that an object of one class plays for objects of the same class (*subordinate <-> supervisor*) (see Fig. 3.10).

If an association has its own attributes, operations, or even specific relationships to classes other than the two class it associates, an association class must be used to capture it. In Fig. 3.11, this is illustrated by the classes *Ordered Book* and *Restocked Book*. These classes will then contain the specific attributes for the relationship, such as the quantity of the title (*Book*).

Distinguishing the Essence of What the Class of Objects Represents

When analyzing and capturing individual classes of objects and their associations, we must always distinguish the essence of what the class of objects represents. In everyday language, we often treat many terms as synonyms, but they actually mean something else.

Fig. 3.10 Examples of associations between classes

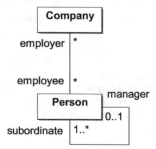

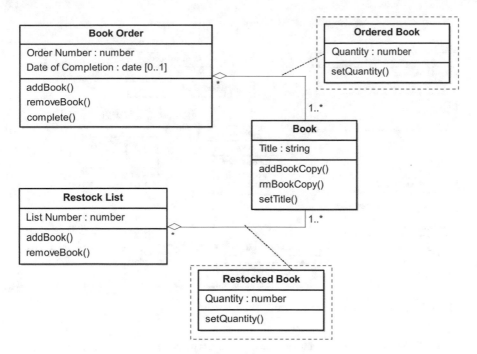

Fig. 3.11 Association class

We can take a book as an example, which is one of the basic concepts of our book-store example. Although the customer orders the books, we buy the books from the suppliers, we stock the books, and we send the books in packages to customers, we don't always actually work correctly with the term book.

In the analysis, we must distinguish between the book as a catalogue item (descriptive item) and the actual physical book (book copy) (Fig. 3.12). *Book Orders* work generally with titles (*Book*), but the supplier supplies specific copies (*Book Copy*), and so the customer is supplied with specific copies (*Book Copy*). This has practical implications. For example, how the number of books is recorded. In the case of the *Book Orders*, the quantity is an attribute of the *Ordered Book* association class, but in a package, for example, the quantity of books in it is the quantity of instances of the *Book Copy* class (no attribute).

3.1.3   Capturing Inputs and Outputs of Individual Class Operations

If the analysis also needs to analyze the inputs and outputs of the operations, the analysis of the inputs and outputs of each identified operation described below should be carried out.

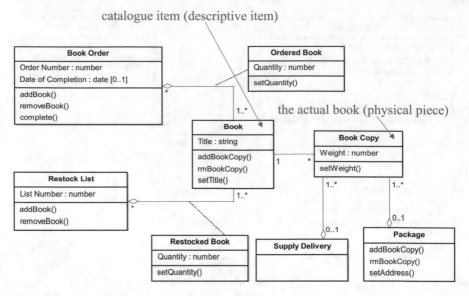

Fig. 3.12 Catalogue item vs. actual piece

Table 3.2 Example of table capturing inputs and outputs of individual class operations

#	Class	Operation	Description	Input/ output	Data reference	Source/target
1.	Supply Delivery	Accept()	Order acceptance	Input	Supply Delivery. Number	Warehouseman
2.	Supply Delivery	Accept()	Order acceptance	Output	Supply Delivery. State	Supply Delivery
3.						

The operations identified for each class of objects require inputs for their execution, and these always have their source. Furthermore, operations are also a source of output that either someone is waiting for or that needs to be stored somewhere. Since these are properties of particular operations, there is no need to capture these properties in the class diagram in the form of particular symbols. If the CASE modeling tool, one is using, allows one to capture this in the properties of the operations, use it. If not, Table 3.2 can be used to capture these properties.

The examples in Table 3.2 illustrate its possible use. Since an operation can have multiple inputs and outputs, an auxiliary column "Input/Output" is used, the resolution of which allows everything to be captured in one table. In the process of populating the table, it is important to remember that we are describing an object world, and so all the information listed must also exist within the object model.

The above table may not only serve to define the inputs and outputs of each identified operation, but it also can be the basis for analyzing the inputs and outputs of each task in the process flow model. As already discussed in Sect. 2.3.3, the analysis of inputs and outputs must be done at the level of individual operations, where we can link what inputs are transformed into what outputs. Process tasks, within which multiple operations can be performed, are already more abstract, and the link between input and output is lost at this level of detail.

3.1.4 How to Create a Model of Concepts

The model of concepts within the business system model must be clear and understandable to the reader without having to know the class attribute values. The model and the reasoning within it must remain at a conceptual level that primarily addresses what classes of objects the business system consists of, not how it would be implemented in, for example, a database.

It usually makes sense to start capturing the model of concepts in parallel with the process map and continuously develop it. When capturing a process map, we encounter business customers, events, target states, etc., and these are always related to objects, except for time events. The basic difference between a process map and a model of concepts is that a model of concepts describes the logic of the particular business environment (how things are), while a process map expresses the concept of the business (how we want to act in this environment). These two positions must complement each other consistently, which is why it is already natural to create both models in parallel.

By following the recommended modeling process, you get:

- Overview of concepts used by the business including their properties and relationships
- Real model of concepts and not only a "data model"
- Model in generally accepted standard notation (UML class diagram)

The development of the model of concepts is never ending. It needs to be continuously maintained and developed both during the global and detailed analysis as the whole business system model is being developed. The basic consistency rules presented in Chap. 4 are a good help in finding related changes.

The step-by-step process of creating a model of concepts is illustrated with an example model of a bookstore business system described in Sect. 2.2.5. This example of a bookstore is interwoven throughout the whole process of creating a business system model (minimal business architecture). The examples build on each other as the chapters on process and object model and their consistency progress. The illustrative examples are provided for the purpose of demonstrating a particular step in the modeling process, and therefore, it should always be kept in mind that these are simplified excerpts from an otherwise complex model.

The process of creating a model of concepts consists of the following steps:

- Identify objects
- Identify the classes of objects
- Identify generalizations
- Complete the generalizations

- Identify associations
- Determine the multiplicity of the identified associations
- Specify aggregations and compositions
- Identify the classes that represent roles
- Complete sets of roles
- Specify roles in associations
- Specify class attributes
- Specify class operations
- Specify dynamic generalizations

In the following text, we will go through the steps in detail.

Identify Objects

Based on the information found within the process model, identify objects related to:

- Events, target process states in the process map
- Business partners to which need the processes in the process map respond
- Resources used by business processes in the process map
- Events and process states in the business process flow models
- Object states associated with tasks in the business process flow models
- Branching conditions in the business process flow models

In our bookstore example, we stay at the global view and base our analysis on the process map. We can find many references to objects (Fig. 3.13) in the process

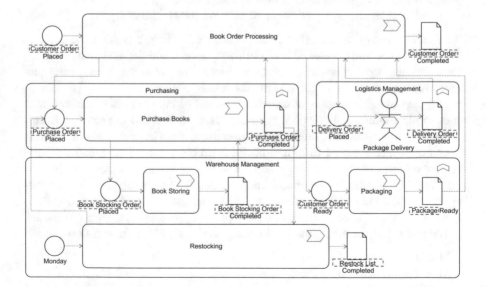

Fig. 3.13 References to objects in the process map

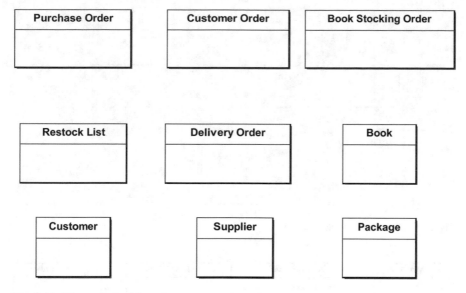

Fig. 3.14   Classes derived from the process map

map. At first glance, there are only objects bound to events and target states, but there are also indirectly mentioned objects such as retail customers, books, or book suppliers.

Identify the Classes of Objects

Based on the identified objects, determine the classes of objects and capture them in the model of concepts.

In the case of our bookstore, the classes shown in Fig. 3.14 can be identified based on the information in the process map (Fig. 3.13).

Identify Generalizations

Identify groups of classes that have a common substance. For these classes, define generalizations in the form of more generic classes that will carry common attributes and relationships. Capture the generalizations (class and the relationships) in the model of concepts.

In the case of our bookstore, it is clear from Fig. 3.14 that some of the identified classes are similar in nature and are likely to have common properties. As an example, consider the different types of orders. Their common properties will then be carried by the newly identified generic class *Book Order* (Fig. 3.15).

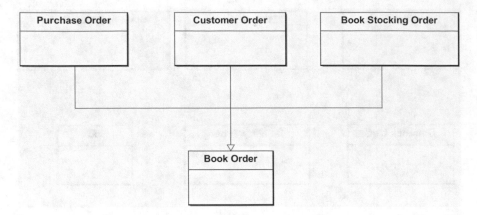

Fig. 3.15 Generalization identification

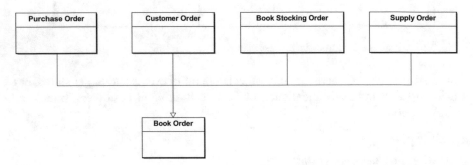

Fig. 3.16 Completion of specializations

Complete the Generalizations

For identified generalizations (identified generic classes), check that all their respective specializations are identified (complete). If not, identify the missing specializations. Capture the identified specializations in the model of concepts.

In the case of our bookstore and the identified generic class *Book Order*, there may be other types of orders used in the business that are not visible at the process map level. As part of the analysis of other possible specializations, we identified another specialization of *the Book Order*—the *Supply Order*, by which the bookstore orders books from its suppliers (Fig. 3.16).

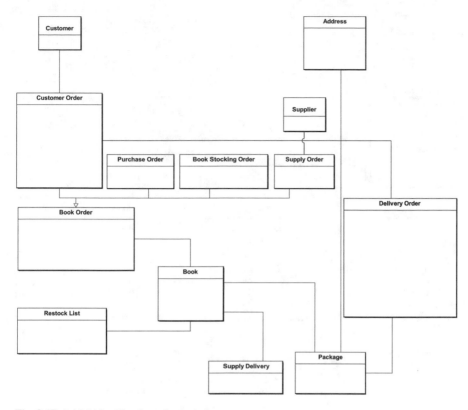

Fig. 3.17 Initial identification of associations

Identify Associations

Identify associations between classes, and capture them in the model of concepts. Start with the already identified classes, and check the possible associations for each of them. If you find a new class with which an existing class has an association, capture it in the model.

For example, in the case of our bookstore, we have identified associations between *Customer Order* and the *Customer*, *Supplier Order* and the *Supplier*, and *Book* and other relevant classes including a new one, the *Supply Delivery*, which represents the list of supplied books by the supplier (Fig. 3.17).

Looking at these associations, it is clear that for some of the associations identified, there will be attributes (like the quantity of books attribute) that are purely association-specific. We create a place holder for them in form of an association classes (Fig. 3.18).

Last but not least, we have to take into account the difference between the descriptive items and the actual pieces. For this reason, we are adding the *Book Copy* class, which, unlike the *Book* class, represents physical copies of a book (Fig. 3.19).

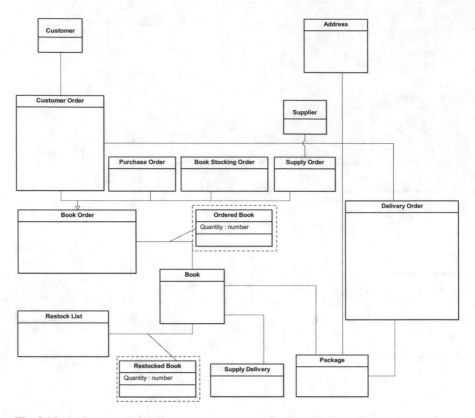

Fig. 3.18 Adding association classes

Determine the Multiplicity of the Identified Associations

Using multiplicity, specify the mandatory and optional nature of the associations for each class.

For our bookstore example, we show the addition of multiplicities in Fig. 3.20. For example, the association between *Book* and *Book Copy*. That multiplicity implies that there can be book catalog items for which there is either no copy or one or more copies, but conversely each copy must always be related to a specific single book catalog item.

Specify Aggregations and Compositions

Examine each association, and distinguish simple associations from aggregations. Analyze the individual aggregating classes, and determine all the classes that they may consist of. Distinguish whether instances of the classes that make up the aggregations can exist independently or not. For those that can exist independently,

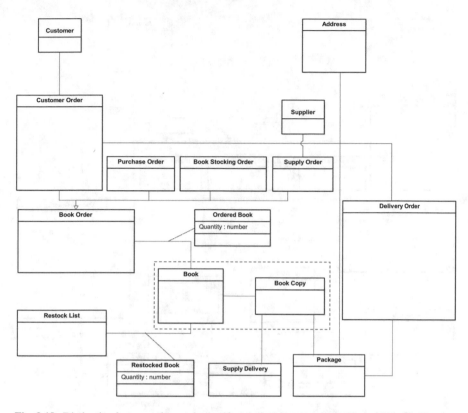

Fig. 3.19 Distinction between the catalogue (descriptive) items and specific copies of books

capture the relationship with them as aggregations; for those that cannot, capture the relationship as compositions.

For our bookshop example, we have differentiated the aggregations from regular association in the Fig. 3.21. For example, the relationship between *Book Order* and *Book*. A *Book Order* is an abstract concept that brings together (aggregates), among other things, the items of a particular order (it is their container). Since the *Books* can exist outside the particular order, a weak relationship "aggregation" is used.

Identify the Classes That Represent Roles

Decide which of the identified classes represent roles of another class and stereo-type them as ≪role≫. Always distinguish between role and actor. An actor (class) can act in different roles. If, when analyzing roles, you come across classes representing actors that are not yet captured in the model of concepts, add them to the model.

Capture the relationship between the actor class and the class representing its role in the model of concepts using the overlapping specializations pattern (Fig. 3.7).

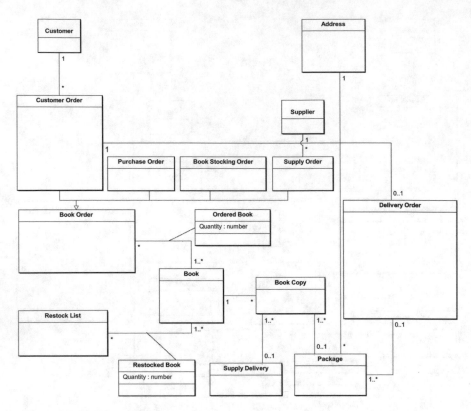

Fig. 3.20 Multiplicity of associations

Remember that one class can have different role sets. So name the class representing the role set to best represent that role set (two role sets, *Business Role* and *User Role*, are shown in Fig. 3.22).

In this way, we capture in the model of concepts that a particular *Person* can act in multiple roles at once. Each role can have (and usually does have) its own attributes, and even so, we keep the identity of the person acting in those roles in one place (the *Person* class); thus, there is no duplication of actor's details.

In the case of our bookstore, we have two classes that represent roles (Fig. 3.23)—*Customer* and *Supplier*.

The actor, in this example, is captured as the *Business Partner* and can act in both the roles of *Customer* and *Supplier* (our supplier can also buy books from us), and therefore, we use the overlapping specializations pattern (Fig. 3.24) and use the stereotype ≪roles≫ for classes that represent roles.

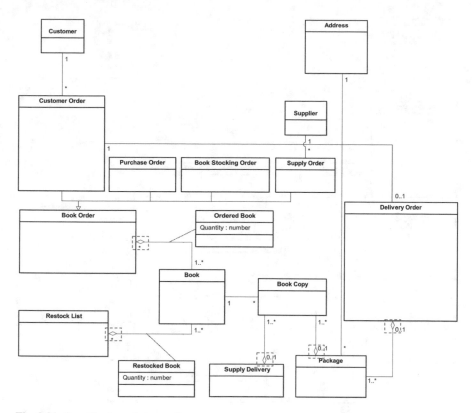

Fig. 3.21 Specification of aggregations

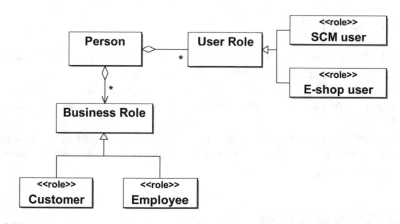

Fig. 3.22 Role capture pattern for the model of concepts

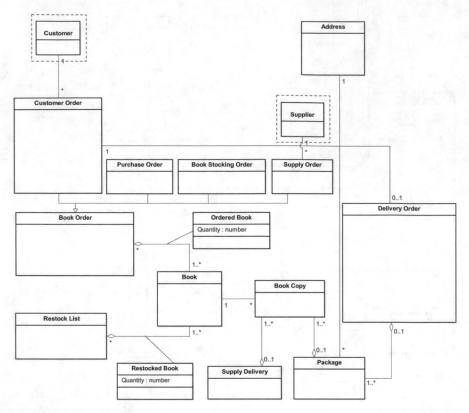

Fig. 3.23 Identifying classes that represent roles

Complete Sets of Roles

For each identified role set, check that the list of roles is complete. If not, identify the missing roles, and add them to the model of concepts.

After analyzing the roles already identified, it is a good idea to look again at the specializations of each set of roles and check whether all the essential roles have been identified.

In the case of our bookstore, we discovered during our review that we were missing the role of a courier who picks up packages from us and takes them to customers (Fig. 3.25).

Specify Roles in Associations

Add roles to the classes in those associations where you find that the classes have different roles.

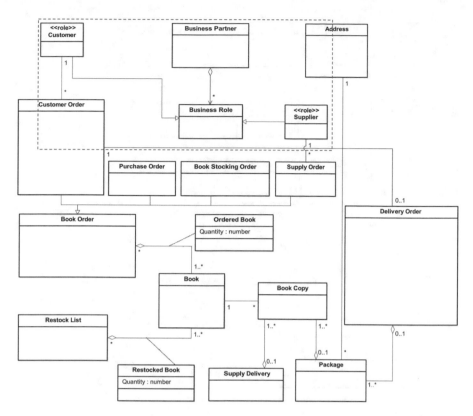

Fig. 3.24 Capturing the overlapping roles

Often, when looking for associations between classes, an analyst may find that the classes act in different roles in the associations. Examples are the employee and his supervisor in Fig. 3.10 or the different roles of the address in Fig. 3.26. To distinguish the roles, the role specification on the association should be used. If you find that the specified role has its own attributes, you need to capture it using the class (see above).

In the case of our bookstore, we record shipping and billing addresses for our individual partners. Addresses can differ not only in the value of their attributes (specific address) but also in how many addresses in each role a business partner can have. This is captured by the multiplicity and role specifications of the associations, as illustrated in the Fig. 3.26.

Specify Class Attributes

For all classes, specify the relevant attributes and whether they are mandatory or optional.

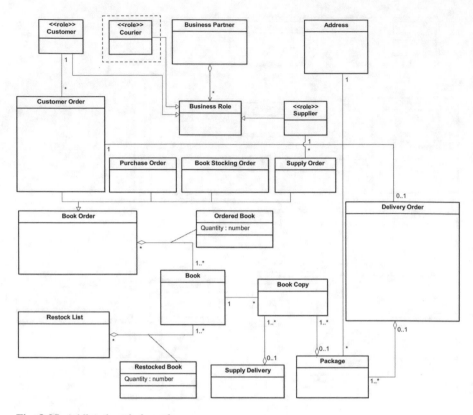

Fig. 3.25 Adding the missing role

All attributes representing the essential characteristics of the class for the business being modelled should be captured. Attribute obligation is captured through multiplicity: 1..1 indicates a mandatory attribute and 0..1 an optional one. It is not necessary to specify the data type at the conceptual level.

In the case of our example bookstore model of concepts, we have specified the relevant class attributes in Fig. 3.27. Let's take a *Customer Order* as an example. First, we need to consider that *Customer Order* is a specialization of *Book Order*, and thus all attributes common to all book orders will be listed as properties of this generic class. Thus, in this example, of the three attributes identified for *Customer Order*, two are properties of *Book Order*, and one is specific to *Customer Order*.

In Fig. 3.27, one can also see that the obligation of the attribute values was considered. In the example shown, all attributes are mandatory, except for *the Date of Completion* and *Date of Handover* attributes.

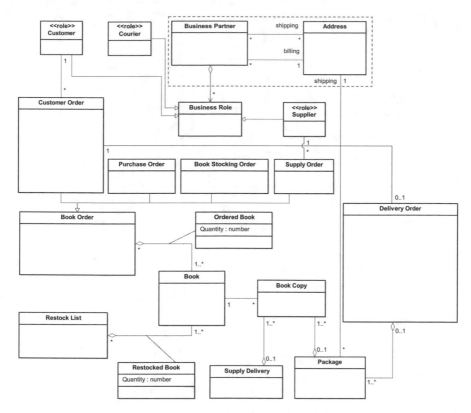

Fig. 3.26 An address and its roles

Specify Class Operations

Examine the individual attributes and associations (including aggregations and compositions) of each class, and specify the operations that change their value. Capture them in the model of concepts. For each class of objects, determine whether it has a corresponding object life cycle model associated with it. If so, examine that model, and capture the operations listed in the state transitions as operations of that class in the model of concepts.

Class operations need to be specified based on some evidence, not just intuitively. The basic sources for specifying class operations are two models: the object life cycle model of the particular class and the model of the concepts itself. The process for specifying operations step by step during the creation of the object life cycle model is presented in Sect. 3.2.3. In the case of the model of concepts itself, the basic sources for identifying operations are all the possible associations (including aggregations and compositions) that the class of objects can establish and all its attributes whose values need to be set.

In the case of our example bookstore model of concepts, we have specified the relevant class operations in Fig. 3.28.

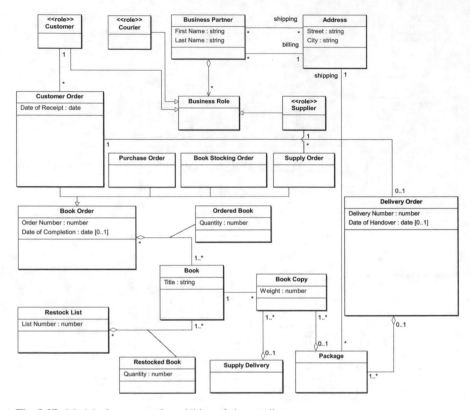

Fig. 3.27 Model of concepts after addition of class attributes

Let's take the *Delivery Order* as an example. Based on the relationship of the *Delivery Order* and the *Package*, we have specified operations *addPackage()* and *removePackage()*. The reason why there are two operations is because it is a 1:N relationship, and thus there must be operations that allow iterative addition and removal of container items.

Based on the attributes of the *Delivery Order*, we have identified operation *set-DateOfHandover()*. The *Delivery Number* attribute is a mandatory attribute in this case, and its setting is performed (as with all mandatory attributes) at the time of object creation (performed by the *create()* operation).

All the other operations specified for *Delivery Order* are based on the object life cycle model associated with it (Fig. 3.38).

Specify Dynamic Generalizations

Based on the object life cycle models, capture the object states in the model of concepts as specializations of the classes to which the object life cycle states belong (Fig. 3.29). Label such sub-types with the stereotype ≪phase≫ for object states and ≪end≫ for pseudo final states to indicate that it is a dynamic generalization structure.

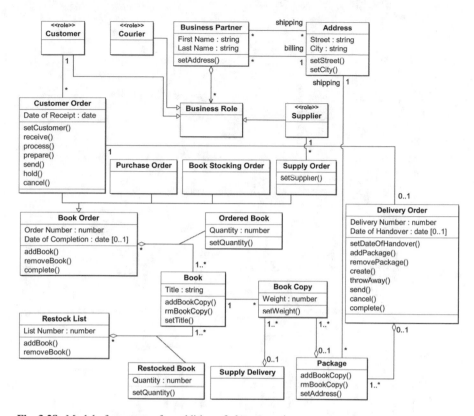

Fig. 3.28 Model of concepts after addition of class operations

The modeled object life cycles allow us to enrich the model of concepts with a temporal dimension. This then makes it possible to define how the structural constraints change over time—for each object's stage (specialization), the obligations of associations and attributes can be defined individually.

Thus, in our bookstore example in Fig. 3.29, capturing the stages of an object's life in the model of concepts allows capturing the fact that the *Delivery Order* has a relationship with the *Delivery Protocol*, but only if the *Delivery Order* is *Completed* is this association mandatory for the *Delivery Order*.

3.1.5   Summary of Basic Rules for Modeling Concepts

Summary of rules described above in the recommended process for creating model of concepts:

- All classes are named so that their name corresponds to what they represent. For example, classes are named either as generalizations of specific objects that have the same properties (class) or generalizations of specific classes, capturing properties they have in common (super class).

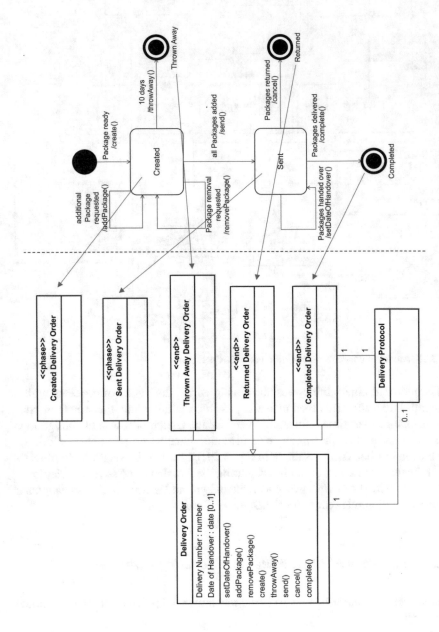

Fig. 3.29 Dynamic generalization in the model of concepts according to the Delivery Order object life cycle model

- Aggregation or composition is exclusively used only where some aggregation occurs. That is, the relation can be read: an object of class X is composed of objects of class Y.
- The classification of objects into types is handled through specializations/roles not through the attribute "type ...".
- Each class is characterized by attributes and operations, and these properties represent the content relevant to that class. The class does not contain any artificial identifiers/keys as attributes.
- If one instance of a class (object) can act in multiple roles at the same time (e.g., customer, supplier, employee, etc.) and these roles have no attributes, this is captured by using the role names for the associations representing each role. If they have attributes, the aggregation of specializations pattern is to be used.
- Capturing that some classes have a common essence and thus properties is handled by generalization not by duplication of attributes, operations, or associations.

3.2   Object Life Cycle Model

An object life cycle model is a model that allows one to specify business rules in relation to relevant class of business objects (business concept) in a systematic way. An object life cycle model allows one to specify:

- The life phases that an object of a particular class may go through during its lifetime
- What events are essential for an object in particular life phase
- What the response is to relevant events when they occur when the object is in a particular life stage
- At what moments the life of an object ends

We capture the object life cycle in a state chart in the form of a standard UML State Machine Diagram [1] (Fig. 3.30).

In the minimal business architecture, we use the following key elements listed in Table 3.3 to capture the object life cycle model in UML state machine diagram.

3.2.1   Object Life Cycle Introduction

The object life cycle model is a detailed model of the business object view (Fig. 3.31) and is used to describe business system causality (system of business rules) relevant to objects of a particular class through capturing the essential states of objects for a particular business and the reasons for transitions between them. Unlike detailed business process model, this is a description of generally applicable rules that apply to each class of objects, not a description of intentional behavior aimed at a

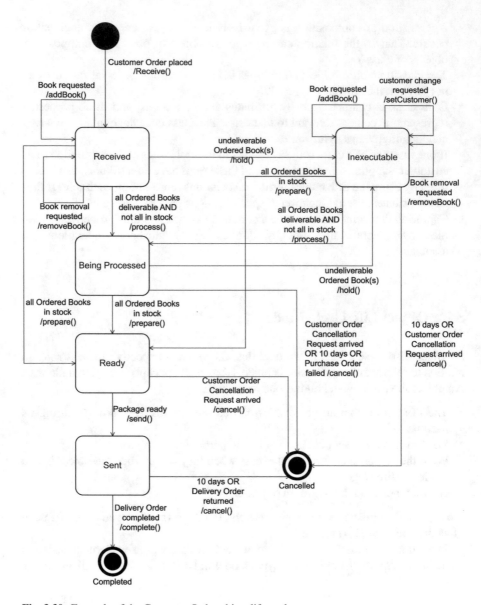

Fig. 3.30 Example of the Customer Order object life cycle

particular goal. The life cycle model describes the causal logic of possible changes during the life of the object.

There should be modelled the life cycles of objects of those classes that are relevant to the modelled business system and for which it makes sense to map the life cycle of the object. At a minimum, these are classes of objects whose states affect which tasks in the process will be executed (objects associated with events and branching conditions in business process models) or whose states are associated with the individual tasks in the process flow model.

Table 3.3 Overview of the key elements needed to capture the object life cycle model in UML state machine diagram

Element	Description
●	*The starting point* represents the point in time at which the cause of the creation of the object occurred
State ⊙	*The state* of an object represents achievement of such a milestone in the life of the object that is relevant to the modelled business system. An object remains in a particular state until there occurs a reason (event) to change from the current state to another state A special case is the final pseudo state, in which the life of an object ends
reason / operation() →	*The transition* between object states specifies the reason (event) for the object in the particular state that must occur to perform the specified operation and change the object state from the current state to the target state. The reason in form of an event can be of two kinds: an occurrence of an ad hoc change in other object or objects (change of object state or state of affairs[a]) or the passing of time (absolute or relative)

[a]Occurrence of a particular attribute value or association instance

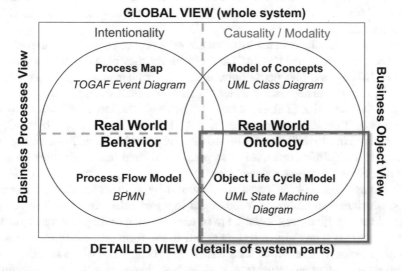

Fig. 3.31 The position of object life cycle modeling within the business system model

3.2.2   Capturing the Life Cycle of an Object in Object Life Cycle Model

We always try to capture the entire life cycle of an object in the object life cycle model—from its creation to its termination.

The basic building block of the model is the state of an object. The object state represents the achievement of a milestone in the life of the object that is relevant to the business system being modelled. An object remains in a particular state until

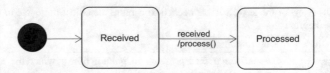

Fig. 3.32 Wrong definition of the reason for the state transition

there is a reason to move from the current state to another state. A special case is the
final pseudo state, in which the life of an object ends. Since this model does not
express an intention, there is no "target state," only possible ends of the object's life.
Object states are linked by transitions between states. A transition between states
occurs if the expected reason for the transition occurs. Thus, transitions between
states can never be parallel—the transition whose reason occurs first always acti-
vates first. Thus, an object is always in one state within its one life cycle.[6]

The object life cycle focuses only on the significant states of the object for a
particular business and the reasons for transitions between them. Usually, it is about
changes in object properties that the business considers significant and has named
states for it and regularly works with them under these names. From a principled
point of view, it is characteristic of a significant state of an object that there are
transitions from each such object state (other than the final pseudo state) to at least
two other states of the object.

The states of an object in reality often are not to captured explicitly in some specific object property named "state." On the contrary, they may take the form of various filled dates, existing constraints, etc., whose change is significant for the
business. The way to approach the identification of object states is then that as soon
as one feels the need to think about object states and therefore have such a property
of an object, it implies a certain need to model the life cycle of the object. Object
states do not have to indicate only the completed state, i.e., in addition to, e.g., created, approved, fulfilled order, it is also possible to have states indicating progress,
i.e., order being processed, delivered, etc.

The transitions between states are captured by an oriented flow between the
states, which defines a reason for the object in a particular state that must occur in
order for the specified class operation to be executed and the object's state to change
from the current state to the target state [all in the form of a relation description:
reason/operation()]. The reason for a transition is occurrence of the specified event
that represents either an occurrence of an ad hoc change in other object or objects
(change of object state or state of affairs) or the passing of time (absolute or relative).

Note the correct definition of the reason. The change in the essential state must
be a response to an external stimulus to which the object is reacting. If it were not,
as in Fig. 3.32, for example, it would make the Received state redundant, since the
reason of the state transition to the Processed state would then be immediately satisfied once the object entered the Received state, and the object would then go immediately from one state transition to another without stopping in the Received state.

---

[6] This means, by the way, that the object life cycle model is determined by the rules for algorithmic
correctness.

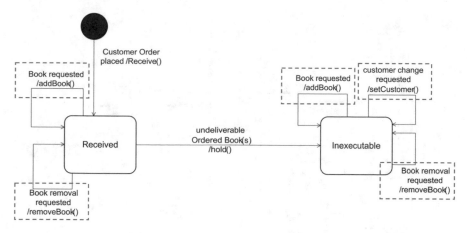

Fig. 3.33 Transitions between states that do not change the state of the Customer Order object

Transitions between states do not always change the state of an object; there are usually many operations of the object that do not change its state—for example, they change attribute values and create links, but the state of the object remains the same. However, the change made is recorded as a transition in the life cycle as a transition that starts and ends with the same object state (Fig. 3.33).

For each object state (except final pseudo states), it must be ensured that at least one of the transitions from that state to another state occurs. It is also important to remember that at least one of the transitions from a particular state must always occur for the life cycle to make sense. This can often be solved, for example, by using a reason for the transition based on the time event.

The life cycles of different objects may interact, but this should not lead to the life cycles of objects from different classes being merged together into a single life cycle.[7] On the contrary, the relationships between life cycles should be captured by reference in the transition reason (Fig. 3.34) and the corresponding object associations (e.g., here the association between the two order types, given by the fact that *Delivery Order* always belongs to a certain *Customer Order*).

Object state names should not, as a rule, unless there is an explicit reason for doing so, combine the reason for transitioning between states with the object state name. It is sufficient that they are given next to the arrows representing transitions between states.

---

[7] Because such a life cycle would contradict the definition of algorithm. The algorithmic correctness of the life cycle can be used to uncover the existing not yet uncovered classes in the situation where we need to include in the life cycle the state that would overlap some other state(s). M. Jackson in his Jackson System Development methodology [ref] calls such an entity a "marsupial entity," which signalizes that we are considering several objects in one body.

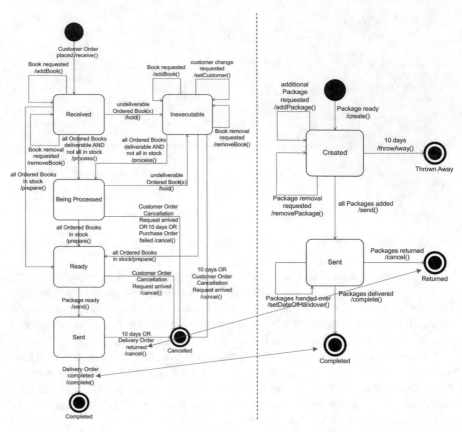

Fig. 3.34 References to object states in the state transition reason of Customer Order (left) to Delivery Order (right)

3.2.3   How to Create an Object Life Cycle Model

Looking at the basic MMABP scheme (Fig. 3.31), it is clear that the detailed analysis can be approached from two directions. We have the option to start with either process flow models or object life cycle models. When creating a detailed model, of course, there is inevitably a simultaneous development of both detailed views (process and object) and their interlinking, but one has to start somewhere.

The initial situation can be distinguished according to the state of the business whose business system model is being created. If the business being analyzed has well-established and well-articulated business rules, then it makes sense to start with object life cycle models, focusing primarily on the business rules of the existing business, and then add process flow models. On the contrary, if the business being analyzed is new, usually yet to be designed and implemented, the analysis will primarily focus on the design of a new business that does not exist yet, so it makes sense to start with process flow models and then add object life cycle models.

By following the recommended modeling process, you get:

- A complete and clear object life cycle models
- Models with an appropriate level of detail that can be understood by regular business stakeholders
- UML state machine compliant diagram

When modeling a business system model, it is important to remember that its creation process, even if described sequentially, is iterative. While modeling the individual models that MMABP business system model consists of, new information is often identified that affects not only the currently modelled model but often also other models related to this model. In this case, it is therefore necessary to make changes, resulting from this new information, in all relevant models so that they remain consistent. The basic consistency rules presented in Chap. 4 are a good help in finding related changes.

The step-by-step object life cycle model creation process is illustrated below with a specific example of a small bookstore described in Sect. 2.2.5. This example of a bookstore is interwoven throughout the whole process of creating a business system model (minimal business architecture). The examples build on each other as the chapters on process and object model and their consistency progress. The illustrative examples are provided for the purpose of demonstrating a particular step in the modeling process, and therefore, it should always be kept in mind that these are simplified excerpts from an otherwise complex model.

As mentioned above, there are two starting points, depending on the state of the business whose business system model is being created. If the business to be analyzed has well-established and well-articulated business rules, follow the steps outlined below in the section Analysis Based on Business Rules of Existing Business. If the business to be analyzed is new, usually yet to be designed and implemented, go to page 158 and follow the steps outlined in the section Analysis Focused on the Design of a New Business.

Analysis Based on Business Rules of Existing Business

We start the detailed analysis by capturing the life cycles of important objects. Thus, we assume that there are no initial inputs resulting from the process flow models.

The process of creating object life cycle models, based on business rules of existing business, consists of the following steps:

- Identify the essential classes of objects
- Determine when objects of the essential classes are created
- Map the object's response to events
- Complete the state transitions related to the structure of the object

In the following text, we will go through the steps in detail.

The creation of object life cycle models starts with identification of essential classes of objects. Then for each essential class of objects, we model step by step its object life cycle model—starting from object's creation to its termination.

Identify the Essential Classes of Objects

Identify the classes of objects that the business considers essential to achieve the business process goals. Start with objects referenced in the process map that represent either explicit or implicit expressions of the customer need for the process or objects that track the progress of satisfying the customer need.

In general, it is necessary to model all object life cycles whose states have been mentioned in the process model, but it may be that some objects are not essential to the overall focus of the analysis and can be abstracted from. The basic criterion for the need to model a life cycle is nontrivial causality,[8] tied to the existence of the object.

For the case of our bookstore, for which we created a process map, we can see the identified essential classes in Fig. 3.35.

Determine When Objects of the Essential Classes Are Created

For each essential class of objects, map what causes these objects to be created and what is the initial state of the object in which the object is born from the mapped business perspective.

In the case of our bookstore, the example focuses on the key object *Customer Order*. This object is already created by the customer outside the modelled business, and therefore for the business we are modeling it, it is created when the business becomes aware of it—at the time the *Customer Order* is received (Fig. 3.36).

Map the Object's Response to Events

For each object state, determine what all changes can occur in this phase of the object's life, that is, what all possible events need to be responded to and what object operation (operation of the object whose life cycle is modeled) will perform that response. Consider both events that cause the object to transition from the current object state to another state and events that cause the object to execute an operation and leave the object in the same state. For those events that initiate change of

---

[8]Trivial causality means that we need to know no more about the object's life cycle than the circumstances of its creation and death. Other changes during its life manifest themselves only as changes in its attributes and/or relationships with other objects, which are not determined by any special rules.

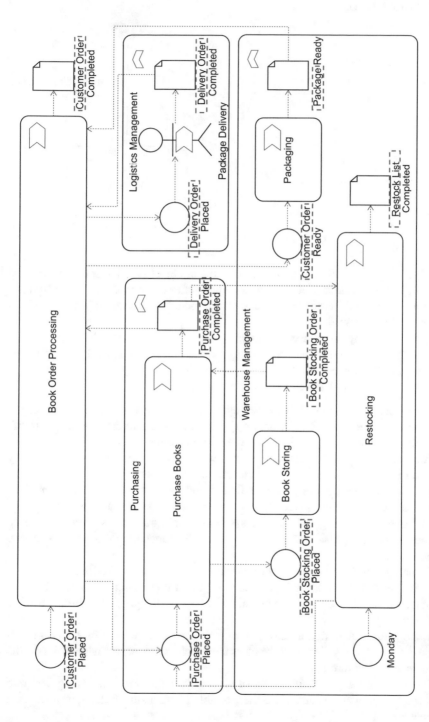

Fig. 3.35 Identification of essential classes of objects

Fig. 3.36 Customer Order
creation

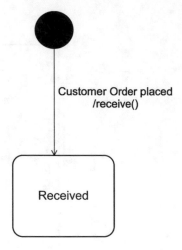

the object state to another, specify the subsequent object states. Capture everything in the object life cycle model—newly specified states and transitions between states (whether between different or the same state), including the reason (event) and the corresponding operation.

Iteratively apply the above (as indicated for our example of Customer Order in Fig. 3.37) until you have determined all possible object states, final pseudo states, and transitions between them.

When capturing the life cycle of an object:

- For IT people: Do not limit the life cycle of a particular class of objects to the context of an electronic information system; the goal is to capture the entire life cycle of an entity, not just its reflection in digital data.
- For each state of an object, always try to identify all possible events that may occur and to which the object in that state must respond.
- For each object state, other than the final pseudo state, ensure that there are alternative state transitions so that at least one of them is guaranteed to occur.
- Do not use branching and merging symbols to split transitions from one state to another (even if UML allows this); use only direct transitions between two object states.
- Remember that the reason for the state transition must be in the form of an event, which represents either an occurrence of an ad hoc change in other object or objects (change of object state or state of affairs) or the passing of time (absolute or relative).
- The operation specified in the state transition must be an existing operation that can be found as a property of the class (in the class model) for whose objects the life cycle is captured.
- Do not try to merge the life cycles of objects from different classes together into a single life cycle; instead, use the possible parallelism of states to uncover a new object.

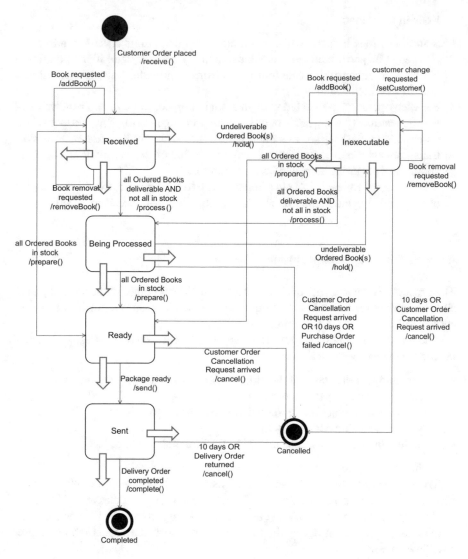

Fig. 3.37   Object life cycle model creation

Complete the State Transitions Related to the Structure of the Object

Look at object life cycles from the perspective of the model of concepts. For each object life cycle model, check that it contains all the operations listed for the class of objects to which the life cycle belongs, and add transitions to the object life cycle model with operations that are missing from the object life cycle model. These are usually the attribute and association changing operations—see Sect. 3.1.4 for more information.

Keep in mind that:

- State transitions indicate when and under what conditions class operations are allowed to be performed when an object is in a particular state. If an operation is not listed at either of the state transitions from a particular state, its execution is not allowed in that state.
- For each operation associated with an association, consider whether the value of the association (the object it points to) may change during the lifetime of the object of the class. If so, this must be accounted for by the existence of state transitions whose execution may change the value of the association. The same applies to operations associated with attributes.
- It is necessary for each 1:N class relationship to have an iterative representation of a transition cycle in the life cycle of an object of that class (Fig. 3.38).

Analysis Focusing on New Business Design

The process of capturing life cycles of important objects comes in the second phase, and the analyst therefore has the outputs of the detailed analysis of business processes available to him right from the start.

The process of creating object life cycle models, focused on the design of a new business, consists of the following steps:

- Collect and sort the states of the objects identified in the process flow models
- Determine which object life cycles will be modeled
- Determine when objects of essential classes come into existence
- Map the object's response to events
- Complete the state transitions related to the structure of the object

In the following text, we will go through the steps in detail.

The creation of object life cycle models starts with review of the object states identified in the process flow models. Then for each essential class of objects, we model step by step its object life cycle model—starting from object's creation to its termination, always considering the succession of object states specified in the process flow models.

Collect and Sort the States of the Objects Identified in the Process Flow Models

Collect the individual states of the objects listed in the process flow models (in the event names, associated with tasks, process states, or in the conditions listed for decisions), and sort them according to the classes of objects to which they belong. Since the names of the associated elements in different models can be very different, it is important to examine their content first. Remember that multiple processes often work with a single object, and so the information on the individual object life cycles is fragmented.

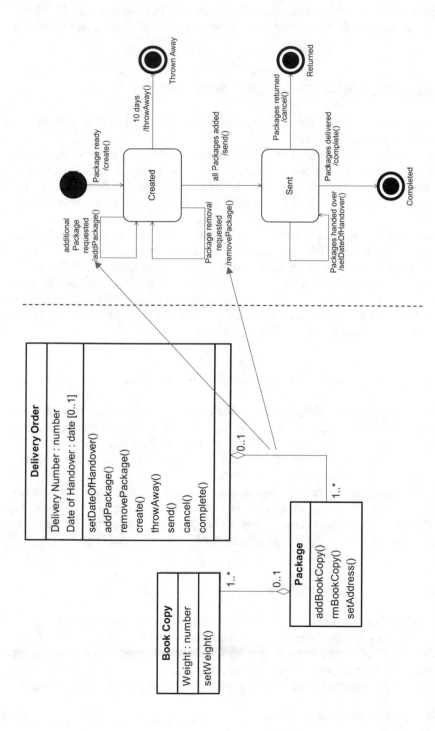

Fig. 3.38 Iterative transition between states for Delivery Order

In the case of our bookstore, references to object states can be found, for example, in the details of the *Book Order Processing* process in the cases shown in Fig. 3.39.

Determine Which Object Life Cycles Will Be Modeled

Based on the sorted object states, determine which object life cycles are essential to the business and need to be captured.

In general, it is necessary to model all object life cycles whose states have been mentioned in the process model, but it may be that some objects are not essential to the overall focus of the analysis and can be abstracted from. The basic criterion for the need to model a life cycle is nontrivial causality,[9] tied to the existence of the object.

In the case of the example Book Order Processing process in Fig. 3.39, it is quite straightforward as it contains key classes of objects like Customer Order or Delivery Order, and these are definitely objects that need to have their object life cycles defined as their complexity is rising from the nature what all can happen to such orders during their lifetime. On the other hand, we can also find the Ordered Books object here, and we may assume that is an association class with trivial life cycle. So, we would not create a life cycle for such class of objects.

Determine When Objects of Essential Classes Come into Existence

For each essential class of objects, map what causes these objects to be created and what the initial state of the object is in which the object is born from the mapped business perspective. If the initial state of an object is missing from the process flow models, consider whether there is a factual reason for this. If not, add it with the corresponding task to the process flow model.

In the case of our bookstore, the example focuses on the key object Customer Order. This object is already created by the customer outside the modeled business, and therefore for the business we are modeling it, it is created when the business becomes aware of it—at the time the Customer Order is received (Fig. 3.40).

Map the Object's Response to Events

Add the object states derived from the process flow model to the started life cycle model, infer the possible transitions between states from the way the object states follow each other in the process flow model, and create the first skeleton of the life cycle model. Then apply the standard procedure for creating an object life cycle model, and go through the entire life cycle from initial state to all final pseudo

---

[9] See footnote 8.

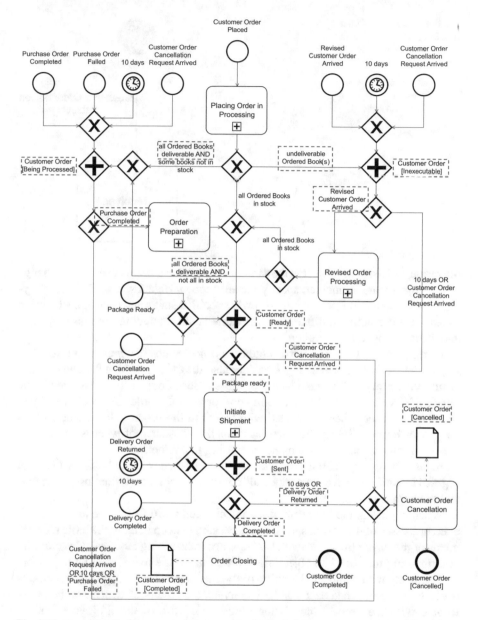

Fig. 3.39 Example of references to object states in the Book Order Processing process flow model

states. For each object state, determine what all changes can occur in this phase of the object's life, that is, what all possible events need to be responded to and what object operation (operation of the object whose life cycle is modeled) will perform that response. Consider both events that cause the object to transition from the current object state to another state and events that cause the object to execute an

Fig. 3.40 Customer Order creation

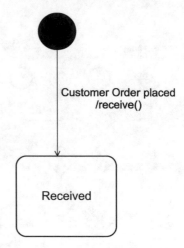

Customer Order placed
/receive()

Received

operation and leave the object in the same state. For those events that initiate change of the object state to another, specify the subsequent object states. Capture everything in the object life cycle model—newly specified states and transitions between states (whether between different or the same state), including the reason (event) and the corresponding operation.

During the analysis, take into account the object states that were identified during the detailed process mapping. Consider also the order in which the object states occur in the process flow model—the possible order of object states captured in the object life cycle model must not be in conflict with the order in which the object states follow each other (associated with tasks) in the process flow model. When correcting for consistency, take into account the substance of what is captured—correct what is wrong, not one model according to another.

Iteratively apply the above (as indicated for our example of Customer Order in Fig. 3.41) until you have determined all possible object states, final pseudo states, and transitions between them.

When capturing the life cycle of an object, even if we follow the already modelled processes of the new business, it is necessary to keep in mind the basic requirements of the object life cycle model. We are not transcribing business rules partially described in processes into object life cycles, but we are really creating object life cycle models with complete definition of the business rules for each object and this needs to be approached as a standard analysis, the results of which are then confronted with the process model (the derived skeleton of the life cycle model). Remember that the process flow models do not contain all the information needed to create a life cycle model of an object. They lack information on operations (both those that change states and those that do not) and often even on the reasons for triggering operations. Multiple processes often work with a single object, and so the information on the individual object life cycles is fragmented.

So, when modeling the object life cycle, keep in mind the following:

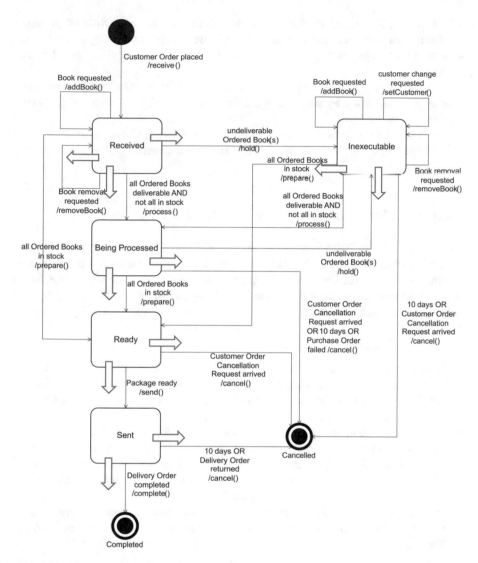

Fig. 3.41 Object life cycle model creation

- For IT people: Do not limit the life cycle of a particular class of objects to the context of an electronic information system; the goal is to capture the entire life cycle of an entity, not just its reflection in digital data.
- For each state of an object, always try to identify all possible events that may occur and to which the object in that state must respond.
- For each object state, other than the final pseudo state, ensure that there are alternative state transitions so that at least one of them is guaranteed to occur.
- Do not use branching and merging symbols to split transitions from one state to another (even if UML allows this); use only direct transitions between two object states.

- Remember that the reason for the state transition must be in the form of an event that represents either an occurrence of an ad hoc change in other object or objects (change of object state or state of affairs) or the passing of time (absolute or relative).
- The operation specified in the state transition must be an existing operation that can be found as a property of the class (in the class model) for whose objects the life cycle is captured.
- Do not try to merge the life cycles of objects from different classes together into a single life cycle; instead, use the possible parallelism of states to uncover a new object.

Complete the State Transitions Related to the Structure of the Object

Look at object life cycles from the perspective of the model of concepts. For each object life cycle model, check that it contains all the operations listed for the class of objects to which the life cycle belongs, and add transitions to the object life cycle model with operations that are missing from the object life cycle model. These are usually the attribute and association changing operations—see Sect. 3.1.4 for more information.

Keep in mind that:

- State transitions indicate when and under what conditions class operations are allowed to be performed when an object is in a particular state. If an operation is not listed at either of the state transitions from a particular state, its execution is not allowed in that state.
- For each operation associated with an association, consider whether the value of the association (the object it points to) may change during the lifetime of the object of the class. If so, this must be accounted for by the existence of state transitions whose execution may change the value of the association. The same applies to operations associated with attributes.
- It is necessary for each 1:N class relationship to have an iterative representation of a transition cycle in the life cycle of an object of that class (see Fig. 3.38).

3.2.4   Summary of Basic Rules for Object Life Cycle Modeling

Summary of rules described above in the recommended object life cycle model creation process:

- The object life cycle model covers all variations of the entire life cycle of an object—from its creation to its termination.
- The model captures all the relevant object states that an object from a particular class of objects may go through during its lifetime.

- The states are named as the specific states of the single object whose life cycle the model captures, so that the states of different objects are not intermixed within the same life cycle.
- All transitions between object states are captured and have a description in the form of a transition reason and an operation, which is a property of the object, that performs the transition between the object states.
- The reason for the transition is an event or a combination of events in the form of a logical expression.
- The life cycle of an object has one beginning.
- The life cycle of an object has at least one final pseudo state.
- From each object state, other than the final pseudo state, there are at least two outgoing state transitions.
- For each state of the object, other than the final pseudo state, at least one of the transitions from that state to another state is guaranteed to occur.

3.3   Further Reading

The field of object modeling is quite broad and very detailed. The beginning business analyst/architect is advised to read thoroughly the UML standard [1] (in the context of MMABP, mainly focus on class diagram and state machine diagram), which summarizes the best practices of several decades of object modeling in terms of analysis focused on information systems analysis and design and whose diagrams are the basic standard in the field of object modeling.

MMABP also works with the specific field of conceptual modeling. Although if it was originally developed in the context of relational databases, its logical foundation is the modal logic, introduced by Lewis in [15] and developed for informatics by Kripke in [16]. The main source for conceptual modeling is the work of P. Chen, namely, [17]. For an introduction to conceptual modeling in the context of UML, we recommend [3, 4]. UML can also be used to capture ontologies, and how to approach this in full complexity can be found in OntoUML [14]. If you want to get into the detail of the enterprise ontology modeling, then look into Enterprise Engineering [18].

To analyze the inputs and outputs of operations, in addition to the options presented in Sect. 3.1.3, the structured analysis tools, specifically the data flow diagram (DFD), can be used to perform this analysis using a diagram. For a description of the DFD and the analysis technique using it, we recommend the methodology of Yourdon [19].

3.4   Summary

This chapter presents analysis of business objects that is focused on the mapping of business object classes and the corresponding business rules that articulate causality and modality inherent to them and why it is an important part of a business system model (architecture). It also provides an overview of the tools and methods needed for creation of coherent business object model that includes global and detailed views.

Section 3.1 Model of Concepts introduces the reader to the model of concepts, which allows one in a systematic way to establish business glossary in form of a UML class diagram for the analyzed business and so to get an overview of concepts used by the business, understand the business concepts and their relationships, and specify detailed properties of the business concepts. This section provides also a detailed step-by-step modeling process on how to systematically create the model of concepts: which features are important to capture, what to look for when modeling, and what basic rules an analyst should follow when creating the model.

Section 3.2 Object Life Cycle Model introduces the reader to the object life cycle model that allows one to specify business rules in relation to relevant class of business objects (business concept) in a systematic way and so in the form of a UML state machine diagram to specify what life phases an object of a particular class may go through during its lifetime, what events are essential for an object in particular life phase, what the response is to relevant events when they occur when the object is in a particular life stage, and at what moments the life of an object ends. This subchapter provides also a detailed step-by-step modeling process on how to systematically create the object life cycle model: which features are important to capture, what to look for when modeling, and what the basic rules are that an analyst should follow when creating the model.

3.5   Exercises

3.5.1   Model of Concepts

1. For objects in a composition type relationship, the following applies:
   a) An object of a particular class is composed of objects of the associated class.
   b) The objects of which a particular object is composed are part of that object only.
   c) The objects of which a particular object is composed may be part of more than one object.
   d) The objects of which a particular object is composed cease to exist when the object that is composed of them ceases to exist.
   e) The objects of which a particular object is composed continue to exist even if the object that is composed of them ceases to exist.

2. For objects in an aggregation-type relationship, the following applies:
   a) An object of a particular class is composed of objects of the associated class.

    b) The objects of which a particular object is composed are part of that object only.

    c) The objects of which a particular object is composed may be part of more than one object.

    d) The objects of which a particular object is composed cease to exist when the object that is composed of them ceases to exist.

    e) The objects of which a particular object is composed continue to exist even if the object that is composed of them ceases to exist.

3. What kinds of hierarchical abstraction can we encounter?

    a) Aggregation

    b) Generalization

    c) Association

    d) Realization

4. Which of the expressions describe a generalization:

    a) car → (wheel, steering wheel)

    b) car → (truck, passenger car)

    c) invoice → (invoice item)

    d) person → (child, young person, old person)

    e) commodity → (milk, meat)

5. Which of these associations is captured correctly?

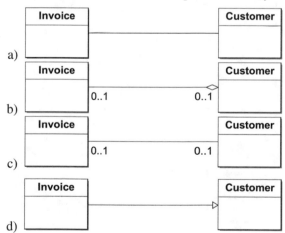

6. Each class is characterized by

    a) Attributes

    b) Operations

    c) Functions

    d) Variables

7. If a customer can have multiple addresses (permanent, temporary, or correspondence) that are no different, this is captured in the model of concepts as:
   a) There is one class for each type of address.
   b) The classes Address and Customer have three different associations with
      each other, and in each class Address has a different role.
   c) These are all attributes of the Customer class.

8. Which of the diagrams most clearly captures the fact that a Person can act in
   multiple roles simultaneously:

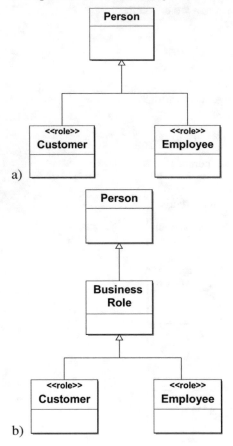

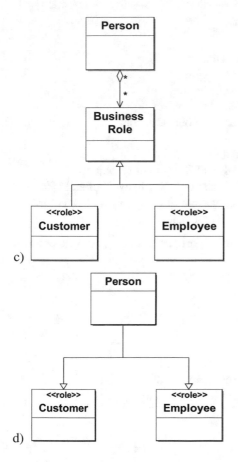

c)

d)

9. If classes of objects that are similar in nature, such as customer, employee, or supplier, have some of the same attributes, is it necessary to capture this in the model of concepts?

   a) No, each class of objects has its own attributes.
   b) Yes, using generalization, where the more general class will carry common attributes.
   c) Yes, you need to create a special class (e.g., Personal Data) for the same attributes so that there is no duplication and associate the other classes with this class using association.

3.5.2 Object Life Cycle Model

1. An object life cycle model is a model that
   a) Always starts with the creation of an object
   b) Always ends with the termination of the object
   c) Usually ends with the termination of the object
   d) Always ends with the achievement of a business goal

2. An object life cycle model is a model that
   a) Captures all possible variations of the life cycle of an object
   b) Captures only the most common variant of the life cycle of an object
   c) Captures only the desired/targeted variant of the life cycle of an object
   d) Captures the life cycle of one particular object

3. Which of these object state names are inappropriate for the life cycle of an Order class object?
   a) Sent
   b) Shipment delivered
   c) Processing
   d) Customer unreachable

4. An event represents
   a) Occurrence of change of an object state
   b) Occurrence of change of an object attribute value
   c) Occurrence of change of an object link (association) value
   d) Passing of time
   e) Execution of an operation

5. Object life cycle
   a) Always has one start point
   b) May have multiple start points
   c) May not have a start point
   d) Always has one final state

6. Object life cycle
   a) May have multiple start points
   b) May have multiple final states
   c) May not have a final state
   d) May not have a start point
   e) Always has one final state

7. Which states in the diagram are redundant?

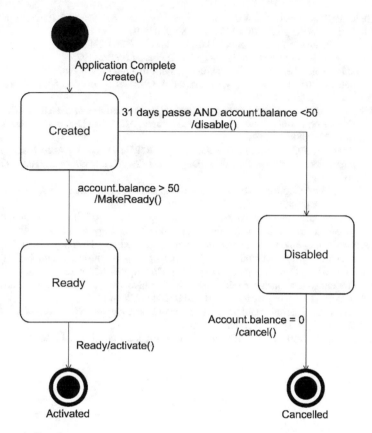

a) Ready
b) Disabled
c) Activated
d) Cancelled
e) Created

References

1. Object Management Group: Unified modelling Language (UML) specification v2.5.1. https://www.omg.org/spec/UML/ (2017)
2. Larman, C.: Applying UML and Patterns: An Introduction to Object Oriented Analysis and Design and Iterative Development. Prentice Hall PTR, Upper Saddle River, NJ (2010)
3. Kobryn, C. (2000) Introduction to UML: Structural Modelling and Use Cases. Object Modelling with OMG – UML Tutorial Series. www.omg.org
4. Weisman, R.: Introduction to UML Based SW Development Process. www.softera.com (1999)
5. Von Neumann, J.: Theory of self-reproducing automata. University of Illinois Press, Urbana, IL (1966)

6. Harel, D.: Statecharts: a visual formalism for complex systems. Sci Comput Program. **8**, 231–274 (1987). https://doi.org/10.1016/0167-6423(87)90035-9
7. Jackson, M.A.: System development. Prentice/Hall, Englewood Cliffs, NJ (1983)
8. Jackson, M.A.: Principles of Program Design. Academic Press, London (1975)
9. Petri, C.A.: Fundamentals of a Theory of Asynchronous Information Flow. (1962)
10. Petri, C.A.: Introduction to general net theory. In: Brauer, W. (ed.) Net Theory and Applications, pp. 1–19. Springer, Berlin (1980)
11. Harel, D.: Statecharts in the making: a personal account. In: Proceedings of the Third ACM SIGPLAN Conference on History of Programming Languages. ACM, San Diego, CA (2007). https://doi.org/10.1145/1238844.1238849
12. Ramos, M.A., Masiero, P.C., Penteado, R.A.D., Braga, R.T.V.: Extending statecharts to model system interactions. J. Softw. Eng. Res. Dev. **3**(12) (2015). https://doi.org/10.1186/s40411-015-0026-x
13. Harel, D., Politi, M.: Modeling Reactive Systems with Statecharts: The Statemate Approach. McGraw-Hill, New York (1998)
14. Guizzardi, G.: Ontological Foundations for Structural Conceptual Models. Telematics Instituut/University of Twente. Centre for Telematics and Information Technology, Enschede (2005)
15. Lewis, C.I.: A Survey of Symbolic Logic. University of California Press, Berkeley, CA (1918)
16. Kripke, S.A.: Semantical analysis of modal logic I normal modal propositional calculi. MLQ – Math. Log. Quart. **9**, 67–96 (1963). https://doi.org/10.1002/malq.19630090502
17. Chen, P.P.-S.: The entity-relationship model – toward a unified view of data. ACM Trans. Database Syst. **1**, 9–36 (1976). https://doi.org/10.1145/320434.320440
18. Dietz, J.L., Mulder, H.B.: Enterprise Ontology: A Human-Centric Approach to Understanding the Essence of Organisation. Springer Nature (2020)
19. Yourdon, E.: Modern Structured Analysis. Yourdon Press, Englewood Cliffs, NJ (1989)

Chapter 4
Integrating the Objects-Oriented and Processes-Oriented Models

Abstract Evaluation of the consistency of the business system model (architecture) is a tool for identification of errors and inconsistencies in the models, the business system model consists of, that may arise in the process of abstraction and subsequent capture (typos, shifts in meaning, omissions, etc.). In addition, evaluating consistency and making corrections to ensure it is an important and effective tool to achieve the quality of the model of the whole business system, not only in terms of correctness but also in terms of relative completeness. The issue of consistency thus represents not only a risk of error but also an opportunity to achieve a high internal quality of the business system model that the individual models together form. Therefore, this chapter presents procedures for evaluating the consistency of the business system model and what to focus on, including practical examples illustrated by models whose creation process was described in the previous chapters.

Consistency of the business system model (architecture) means *the absence of any contradiction between different expressions of the same fact in different models the business system model consists of.* By the contradiction, we mean not only a contradiction between two existing elements of different models but also the situation when a particular element, whose necessity follows from another model, is missing in the particular model. Therefore, MMABP distinguishes between two basic criteria of consistency: *correctness* and *completeness*.

In order to comprehensively capture all conceivable variations of model consistency, MMABP has the *Business System Consistency Specification* [1]. This framework builds on the basic tenet of the *Philosophical Framework for Business System Modeling* [2] as explained in Chap. 2. It encapsulates the notion that a business system model includes business objects that embody the environment, facts, and rules to which all activities must conform. In addition, it includes business processes that delineate activities and approaches for achieving goals.

As evident from the aforementioned definition of consistency, the same fact can be represented in diverse ways across various models. Consequently, we must

© The Author(s), under exclusive license to Springer Nature
Switzerland AG 2024
V. Řepa, O. Svatoš, *Fundamentals of Business Architecture Modeling*, The
Enterprise Engineering Series, https://doi.org/10.1007/978-3-031-59035-1_4

173

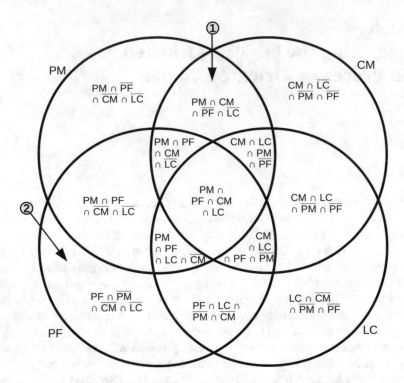

Fig. 4.1 Simplified picture of the business system sets using Venn diagram [3]

scrutinize how a general fact may manifest itself in distinct manners within specific combinations of particular models. The framework delineates all conceivable combinations of four fundamental types of models within the business system, established by two essential dimensions and two principal categories defined in the *Philosophical Framework for Business System Modeling* [4]. To systematically explore all conceivable model combinations, we employ the language of set theory. Each specific model is epitomized in the framework by the set of facts it expresses. The intersections of these sets then signify particular combinations of models.

Figure 4.1 provides a deliberately simplified depiction of the business system sets using John Venn's diagram, recommended in his renowned article [3]. The illustration encompasses all 13 relevant conjunction subsets of the four sets,[1] where:

---

[1] The complete combination of the four sets using the ellipse diagram recommended by John Venn in [3] actually contains 15 compartments (the 16th article of the 4×4 combination represents the disjunction of all sets, which is irrelevant for the consistency, since as a disjunction it does not mean any specific combination). For the purpose of understanding the consistency, we lightly simplify the whole picture by omitting the sub-sets which are not relevant for this purpose:

(a) $CM \cap PF \cap \overline{PM} \cap \overline{LC}$

(b) $PM \cap LC \cap \overline{CM} \cap \overline{PF}$

With respect to the purpose of the business system, these intersections represent meaningless diagonal combinations of models, where the necessary information is missing. For example, the

- PM represents the set of facts expressed in the *process map* of the particular business system
- PF represents the set of facts expressed in all *process flow* models specifying the flow of certain business processes from the process map of the particular business system
- CM represents the set of facts expressed in the *model of concepts* of the particular business system
- LC represents the set of facts expressed in all *object life cycle* models specifying the life cycles of some objects from the model of concepts of the particular business system

Each intersection signifies the logical conjunction of all facts expressed in the involved models, which are then the subjects of a consistency evaluation in this context in terms of the two criteria mentioned above: model correctness and completeness. For example, arrow 1 denotes the set of facts expressed in both the process map and model of concepts, excluding any expressed in process flow models or object life cycle Models. Similarly, arrow 2 denotes the set of facts expressed solely in process flow models, without inclusion from any other model.

Figures 4.2 and 4.3 provide insight into interpretation of specific sets within the framework and outline the contextual relationship to the Philosophical Framework of Business System Modeling [4]. The top two models represent the system view, while the bottom two models represent the detail view. The left pair of models (process map and process flow models) elucidate facts about "acting," while the right pair (model of concepts and object life cycle models) describe facts about "being." In Fig. 4.2, the emphasis is on all four bilateral intersections, each of which represents either the process-oriented or object-oriented set of models (i.e., left or right side of the framework) or only the system of detailed models (i.e., the top or bottom of the framework).

- The combination of the process map with process flow models represents the *general model of acting*. Consistency evaluation in this context focuses on the completeness and correctness of the intentional aspects of the business without considering the general, process-independent rules of the business system.
- The combination of the model of concepts with object life cycle models forms the *general model of being*. Consistency evaluation in this context focuses on the completeness and correctness of the captured general, process-independent rules

---

consistency of model of concepts and process flow models always includes even the relationships between processes, i.e., the information from the process map. Similarly, the consistency of process map and object life cycle models must always include even the relationships between objects, i.e., the information from the model of concepts. In other words, there are no common consistency issues of model of concepts and process flow models without process map [see the missing intersection (a)], just as there are no common consistency issues of process map and object life cycle models without model of concepts [see the missing intersection (b)]. Thus, these sets are both empty by definition and can be omitted from the framework. This omission allows us to use circles instead of Venn's ellipses, which makes the model more readable.

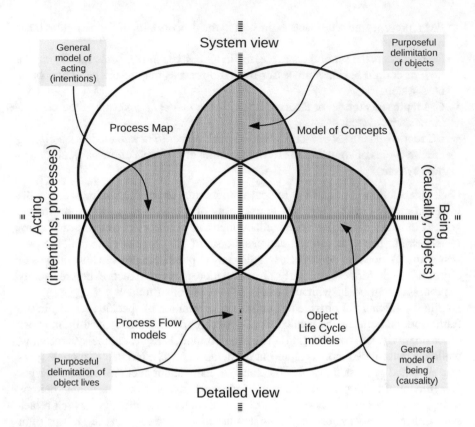

Fig. 4.2 Interpretation of business system sets, part I

of the business system without regard to specific business processes, i.e., individual business goals and their methods of achievement.

- The combination of the two global models (process map and model of concepts) represents the *purposeful delimitation of objects*. The process map defines which objects and relationships within the business system are significant and must be taken into account for the accurate design of business processes. Consistency evaluation in this context focuses on the completeness and correctness of respecting the general modality of the business system within the framework of business processes.
- The combination of all detailed models (process flow and object life cycle models) embodies the *purposeful delimitation of object lives*. Life cycles articulate the relevant general causality of the business system, which is crucial for the detailed conception of business processes involving the specified object. The consistency in this context focuses on the completeness and correctness of maintaining the general business system causality within the algorithmic structures of specific business processes.

In Fig. 4.3, all four trilateral intersections are highlighted, including the total (quadrilateral) intersection of all four model types.

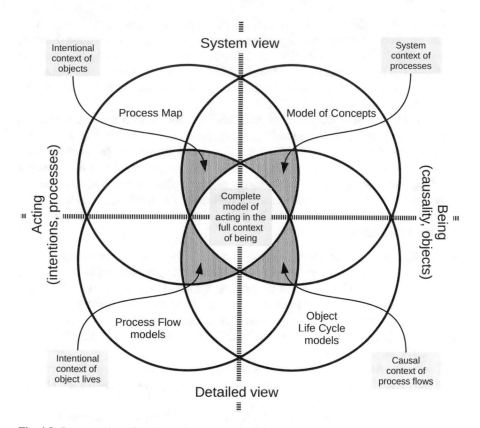

Fig. 4.3 Interpretation of business system sets, part II

- The combination of the process map and all process flow models with the model of concepts represents the comprehensive *intentional context of business objects*. Consistency evaluation in this context focuses on the completeness and correctness of the model of concepts with respect to business processes. This includes ensuring the existence of all relevant objects handled in business processes, along with their relevant classifications and associations.
- The combination of the model of concepts and all object life cycle models with the process map represents the complete *system context of business processes*. Consistency evaluation in this context focuses on the completeness and correctness of the process map with respect to the modality and causality of the business system. This includes confirming the existence of all relevant business processes and their associations in the process map that are necessary to handle all relevant objects in their full life cycle context and corresponding associations with other objects.
- The combination of the process map and all process flow models with the object life cycle models embodies the comprehensive *intentional context of object lives*. Consistency evaluation in this context focuses on the completeness and correct-

ness of object life cycle models with respect to business processes. This includes the existence of all relevant object states and proper transitions between them for each object managed in business processes. The relevance of object states and transitions is determined by the focus of the business processes, where states and their relationships (potential transitions) represent business rules to be considered in the processes.

- The combination of the model of concepts and all object life cycle models with the process flow models represents the complete *causal context of business process flows*. Consistency evaluation in this context focuses on the completeness and correctness of the process flow models from the perspective of the causality of the business system. This includes ensuring the existence of all relevant actions in business processes in a relevant order (structures), according to the business rules expressed in the life cycles of relevant objects and their associations with other objects.

In Fig. 4.3, the overall intersection of all four model types symbolizes *the complete model of acting in the full context of being*. Consistency evaluation in this context focuses on the completeness and correctness of the shared meanings of specific phenomena that occur in different models, especially the events (representing the modality/causality of the business system) and actions (representing business intentions). This includes maintaining a balance between a business system logic and intended business actions.

Table 4.1 succinctly outlines all 13 compartments of the framework, providing their interpretations in terms of meaning and the type of consistency invoked by the particular combination of models.

There are first four rows of Table 4.1 left that we have not addressed yet. For this, we have to distinguish between consistency and conformance.

- *Consistency* refers to the *absence of contradictions between different representations of the same fact in different models*, emphasizing a relationship between phenomena without establishing a hierarchical order.
- *Conformance*, on the other hand, is the relationship between two representations of the same fact that are at different levels within a hierarchy. The lower-level representation must conform to and adhere to the higher-level representation.

In our approach to ensuring consistency in business system models, what we call the "internal" consistency within individual models (see the first four rows in Table 4.1) essentially means alignment (conformance) with a fact that has a superior position to the model. This alignment serves as a measure for the overall accuracy of the model. In the context of business system models, this superior benchmark is the Real World. Since all four models of the business system provide specific representations of the modal logic inherent in the Real World, their conformance with the Real World relies on the principles of Kripke semantics [5]. Conformance of each specific model with the Real World typically requires the fact's validity *in all possible worlds*.

Table 4.1 Interpretation of the framework compartments

#	Compartment	Represents	Type of consistency	Meaning
1	$PM \cap \overline{PF} \cap \overline{CM} \cap \overline{LC}$	Process Map only	Internal consistency of the process system	Collaboration
2	$PF \cap \overline{PM} \cap \overline{CM} \cap \overline{LC}$	Process Flow only	Internal consistency of the process flow	Acting
3	$CM \cap \overline{LC} \cap \overline{PF} \cap \overline{PM}$	Model of Concepts only	Internal consistency of the conceptual model	Real-World structure (general modality)
4	$LC \cap \overline{CM} \cap \overline{PF} \cap \overline{PM}$	Object Life Cycle models only	Internal consistency of the object life cycle	Real-World objects causality (temporal modality)
5	$PM \cap PF \cap \overline{CM} \cap \overline{LC}$	Process models only	Consistency of process relations	General model of acting (business goals and processes)
6	$CM \cap LC \cap \overline{PF} \cap \overline{PM}$	Object models only	Consistency of object relations	General model of being (Real-World modality and causality)
7	$PM \cap CM \cap \overline{PF} \cap \overline{LC}$	Complete system view only	Global consistency of the business system structure	Purposeful delimitation of objects
8	$PF \cap LC \cap \overline{PM} \cap \overline{CM}$	Complete details only	Temporal consistency of the business system	Purposeful delimitation of object lives
9	$PM \cap PF \cap CM \cap \overline{LC}$	Complete process model with conceptual model	Consistency of processes with general business system structure	Intentional context of objects
10	$CM \cap LC \cap \overline{PF} \cap PM$	Complete object model with Process Map	General consistency of the process system structure	System context of processes
11	$PM \cap PF \cap \overline{CM} \cap LC$	Complete process model with object life cycles	Consistency of processes with business system causality	Intentional context of object lives
12	$CM \cap LC \cap \overline{PF} \cap PM$	Complete object model with Process flow models	General consistency of process actions	Causal context of process flows
13	$PM \cap PF \cap CM \cap LC$	Issues of all four models together	Overall consistency of events with business actions	Complete model of acting in the full context of being

4.1   Conformance Evaluation

Conformance evaluation is a specific discipline that focuses on evaluation of the alignment of models with the real world. It is particularly relevant in situations involving a single model, where the influence of other models is abstracted, making *adherence to the Real World* a primary criterion for assessing the overall correctness and completeness of the model. There are four areas of conformance evaluation, outlined in the first four rows of Table 4.1.

For these areas, we list the basic rules that should be satisfied so that the model is aligned with the real world. If this is not the case, the model should be adjusted to match how the fact is present in the real world in all its possible occurrences (all possible worlds in terms of temporal logic).

- *Internal consistency of the process system (process map)*
  - *Completeness* The business process model includes all specified products, and each recognized event is used in at least one business process model as a trigger for some action.
  - *General correctness* Each business process fulfills its main target, and its properties and relationships to other processes are valid for all possible instances of the process.
- *Internal consistency of the process flow (process flow model)*
  - *Completeness* The process flow model begins with the triggering event(s) and covers all possible ends of the process that are relevant to the process target.
  - *General correctness* The process flow model exhibits essential algorithmic properties such as correctness, uniqueness, finiteness, openness, and generality. In addition, it is valid for all possible instances of the process.
- *Internal consistency of the concepts (model of concepts)*
  - *Completeness* There is at least one way between any two classes in the model of concepts.
  - *General Correctness* Each class of objects corresponds to real and existing objects and each relationship to other class of objects models existing possible relationship. The described classes of objects and their relationships are valid for all possible instances of each class of objects.
- *Internal consistency of the object life cycle (object life cycle model)*
  - *Completeness* The description of the object life cycle covers the entire life of the object, including three mandatory types of object methods: constructor, destructor, and transformer (the first two stereotypes are defined in the UML standard [6]; MMABP adds the third).
  - *General Correctness* The object life cycle model corresponds to real and objective actions and their sequences in the life of the object. It applies to all possible instances of the class of objects (all possible worlds in terms of temporal logic).

4.2 Consistency Evaluation

MMABP works with three basic types of consistency, depending on the focus of consistency, which can be the meaning of the modeled fact, the structure of the modeled facts, or temporal order of the modeled facts. Therefore, a distinction is made between *factual*, *structural*, and *temporal* consistency.

1. *Factual Consistency* Factual consistency is the basic type of consistency, involving rules that deal directly with the facts represented in the models. The range of conceivable facts expressed in models is, of course, unlimited. This type of consistency emphasizes ensuring that the facts represented in different models are consistent with each other in terms of their intended meaning.
2. *Temporal Consistency* Temporal consistency is a specific type of consistency of temporal models (process flow and object life cycle models). This type of consistency emphasizes ensuring that the temporal models are not inconsistent in their temporal sequence of facts.
3. *Structural Consistency* Structural consistency introduces a different approach, working with several abstractions related to the ordering of facts, called structure types. In this mode, the focus shifts from the specific facts to abstracted representations, emphasizing the structural organization of the facts. This mode is inspired by the work of M. A. Jackson [7], who demonstrated that structure can serve as a common basis for ordering both data and algorithmic elements. MMABP extends Jackson's concept of structure by using it as a universal basis for aligning corresponding elements in different real-world models. The core principle is that different representations of the structure of identical facts in different models should imply the same underlying structure. Structural consistency revolves around the different representations of structure types in different models, ensuring coherent alignment.

For the above types, we provide basic consistency rules that describe the basic rules that must hold across the intersections of the models in order for the models to be consistent with each other. The basic consistency rules are always described only between two models, but related models must always be considered when evaluating them, as indicated by the intersections in Fig. 4.1.

When evaluating, it is important to remember that we are often working not only with a model, but also with natural language. Not everything in a model is formal notation, especially the naming of events, the specification of process flow splitting conditions, etc. Thus, consistency checking in these cases is not about having the same words everywhere but about having the same meaning and using accurate terms that are consistent with the content of the model.

Each rule should be evaluated on the basis of two criteria: correctness and completeness, i.e., evaluating not only the contradiction between two existing elements of different models (correctness) but also the situation when a certain element, whose necessity follows from another model, is missing in the particular model (completeness).

If an inconsistency is found, it should be corrected to ensure the consistency of the business system model. It should be remembered here that the consistency is not conformance. It is not a matter of aligning one model to the other (since both models may be incorrect), but to correct, one must first determine what are the facts (reality) and how they should be captured correctly and then correct the models accordingly.

The consistency rules are illustrated below with a specific example of a small bookstore described in Sect. 2.2.5. This example of a bookstore is interwoven throughout the whole process of creating a business system model (minimal business architecture). The examples build on each other as the chapters on process and object model and their consistency progress. The illustrative examples are provided for the purpose of demonstrating a particular step in the modeling process, and therefore, it should always be kept in mind that these are simplified excerpts from an otherwise complex model.

4.3 Basic Factual Consistency Rules

When evaluating the factual consistency of the business system model, it is important to consider that the business system model consists of four different types of models, i.e., four different views (diagrams) of the business system being modeled.

Figure 4.4 presents a metamodel that shows how the elements of the diagrams described in Chaps. 2 and 3 that are used to capture a particular model are interrelated. For the purpose of evaluating factual consistency, the metamodel focuses primarily on the relationships between the elements used in the diagrams to capture the models. Because of this, it allows for misinterpretations, e.g., that there may be a business process that contains only an event and a process end, and therefore, it is always necessary to base the development of individual models on the rules and modeling process given in Chaps. 2 and 3 and the rules given by the standard for the particular diagram.

When evaluating the factual consistency of the individual models (represented by particular diagrams) against each other, begin with the following rules, which have their basis in the metamodel in Fig. 4.4, and the idea that the model of the business system (architecture) is complete. Many inconsistencies of this type can be prevented by using CASE tools that allow you to model the business system in defined models and link them together. Full support for MMABP is provided by Enterprise Assistant [8], but tools such as Modelio [9] also allow the required models to be created and linked to some extent.

4.3.1 Process Map and Model of Concepts Consistency

Rule: *Objects referenced by event names and process target states must correspond to classes of objects in the model of concepts.*

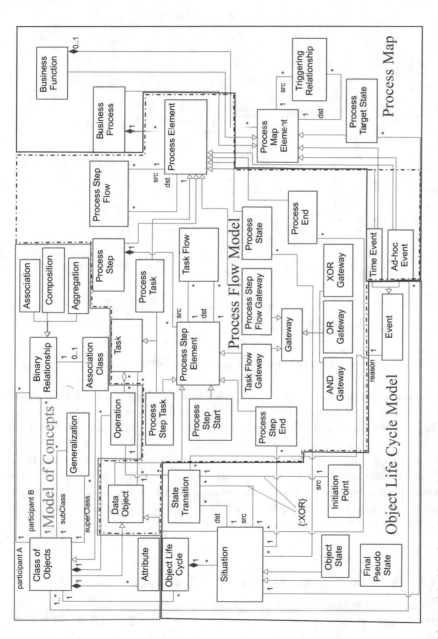

Fig. 4.4 Metamodel addressing relations of elements used in the diagrams that capture the models that make up the business system model (architecture)

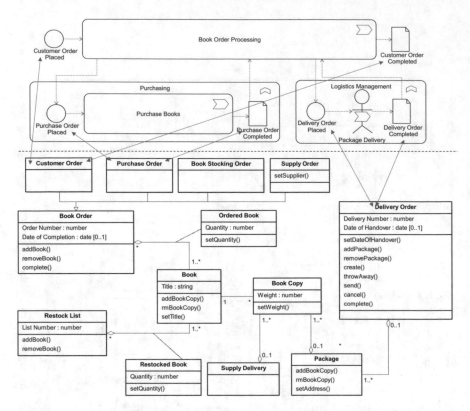

Fig. 4.5 Example of process map and model of concepts consistency

The process map and its elements exist within the ontology defined by the object model (Fig. 4.5), i.e., in the model of the real world (ontology) within which we try to capture the intentional behavior—individual business processes and their relationships. It must not happen that in the process model, we refer in the names of events and target states to objects that we do not have within the object model. In practice, these inconsistencies usually occur when the model of concepts is not developed simultaneously with the process model. The referenced objects in the process map then do not match the concepts in the model of concepts or they are even missing in the model of concepts.

4.3.2   Process Map and the Process Flow Models Consistency

Rule #1: *The triggering events of each business process are identical in both models.*

The triggering events of business processes captured in the process map must also be the triggering events of the processes in their process flow models (Fig. 4.6).

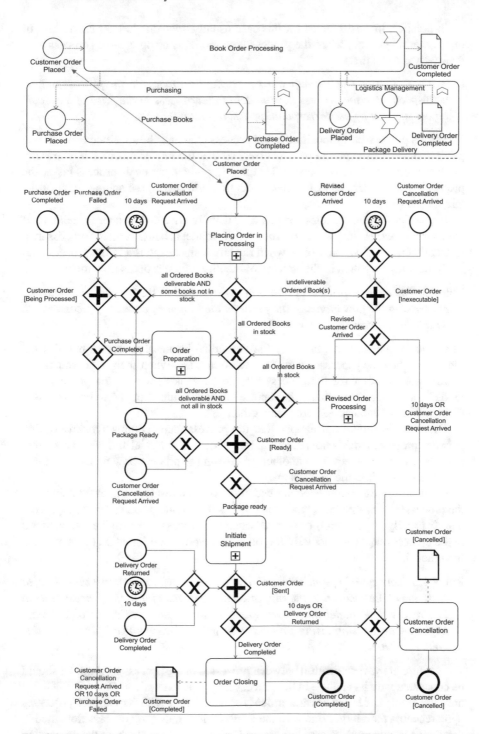

Fig. 4.6 Example of triggering event consistency of process map and Book Order Processing process flow model

In practice, inconsistencies for this case usually arise due to later refinement of the triggering event(s) when the process flow model is being created (process map is usually created first).

Rule #2: *The target state specified for a particular process in the process map is also specified in the process flow model of that process in the form of a specific object state set by the corresponding task of that process.*

The target process states specified in the process map must be specified in a detailed process model of the particular processes, so that the model specifies how exactly the target process state will occur. That is, after which series of process tasks, the processing will reach the task whose execution will realize the achievement of the target state (Fig. 4.7).

In practice, inconsistencies for this case usually arise due to later refinement of the process's target state when its process flow model is being created (process map is usually created first) or, worse, when the target state captured in the process map is accidentally forgotten in the process of creation of the process flow model.

Rule #3: *The support processes of a process captured in the process map must be captured in the flow model of the process, they support, as those processes with which this process synchronizes.*

The process map captures not only the individual business processes but also the moments when the processes wait for each other, i.e., when their synchronization takes place. In order for the process map to be consistent with the process flow models, it is necessary that this capture of synchronization between processes (Fig. 4.8) is not inconsistent with each other.

Therefore, it should not happen that the process map captures synchronization between processes that is not present in the process flow model and, vice versa, that the process synchronizes with another process in the process flow model, but there is no mention of it in the process map.

In practice, these inconsistencies usually occur as a result of a later refinement of the process synchronizations when the process flow model is being created (process map is usually created first) or, worse, when the process synchronization captured in the process map is accidentally forgotten in the process of creation of the process flow model.

Rule #4: *When capturing synchronization of a process with its support processes, at least one of the events that the supported process waits for in the process state in its process flow model must correspond to the occurrence of an object state triggered by the supporting process with which the supported process at this point synchronizes in the process map.*

The capture of synchronization between processes in the process flow model should be consistent with its capture in the process map. The example in Fig. 4.9 illustrates how the Book Order Processing process synchronizes with its support processes upon reaching their target states. In the Book Order Processing process flow model, these synchronizations have to be captured as process states at which the processing

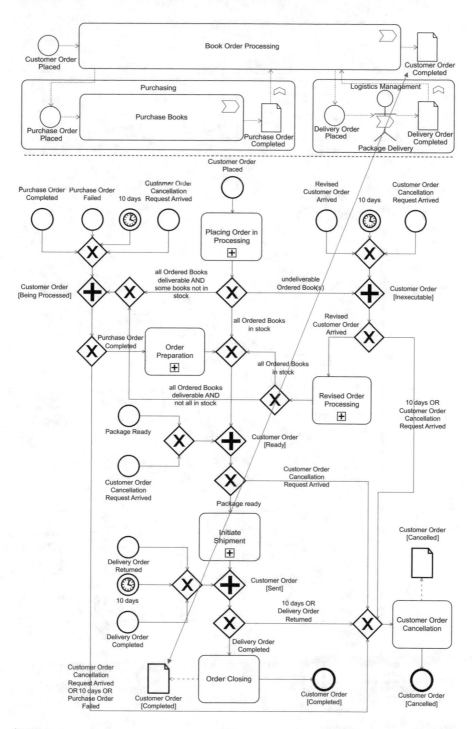

Fig. 4.7 Example of target state consistency of process map and Book Order Processing process flow model

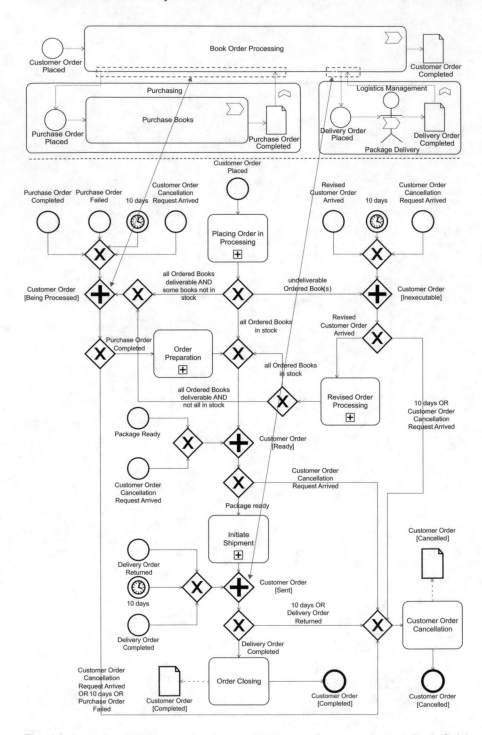

Fig. 4.8 Example of process synchronization consistency of process map and Book Order Processing process flow model 1

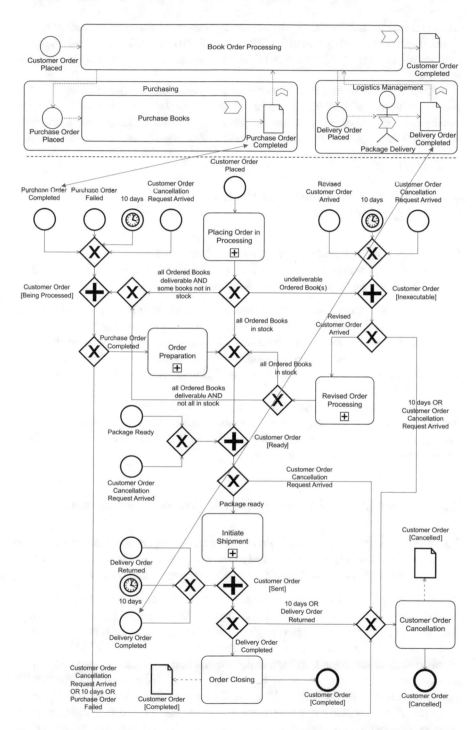

Fig. 4.9 Example of process synchronization consistency of process map and Book Order Processing process flow model 2

waits (among others) for the events corresponding to the achievement of the target states (representing object states) of the support processes. These events have to correspond to target process states of the support processes captured in the process map.

In practice, inconsistencies for this case usually arise due to later refinement of the process synchronizations when the process flow model is being created (process map is usually created first) or, worse, when the process synchronization captured in the process map is accidentally forgotten in the process of creation of the process flow model.

4.3.3 Model of Concepts and Process Flow Models Consistency

Rule: *Objects referenced by events, process states, task-associated object states, and process flow splitting conditions in process flow models must correspond to existing classes of objects in the model of concepts.*

The process flow model and its elements exist within the ontology defined by the object model (Fig. 4.10), i.e., in the model of the real world (ontology) within which we try to capture the intentional behavior—business processes and their detail. It must not happen that in the process model, we refer in the names of events, process states, object states, and inflow splitting conditions to objects that we do not have within the object model.

In practice, these inconsistencies usually occur when the model of concepts is not developed simultaneously with the process model. The referenced objects in the process flow model then do not match the concepts in the model of concepts or they are even missing in the model of concepts.

4.3.4 Consistency Between Different Process Flow Models

Rule #1: *If a process initiates its support process, the triggering event that initiates the support process must correspond to the occurrence of the object state (associated with the task) specified in the supported process flow model.*

Flow models of processes that synchronize with each other should have this synchronization captured accordingly in both process flow models. If one process triggers another process (as its support process), this fact should be captured by elements that correspond with each other across the process flow models (Fig. 4.11). That is, in this case, that the event Purchase Order Placed that initiates the Purchase Books support process corresponds to the occurrence of the object state Purchase Order [Sent] associated with the task in the Book Order Processing process flow model.

In practice, inconsistencies for this case usually arise due to later refinement of process flow within individual process flow models, without this update being

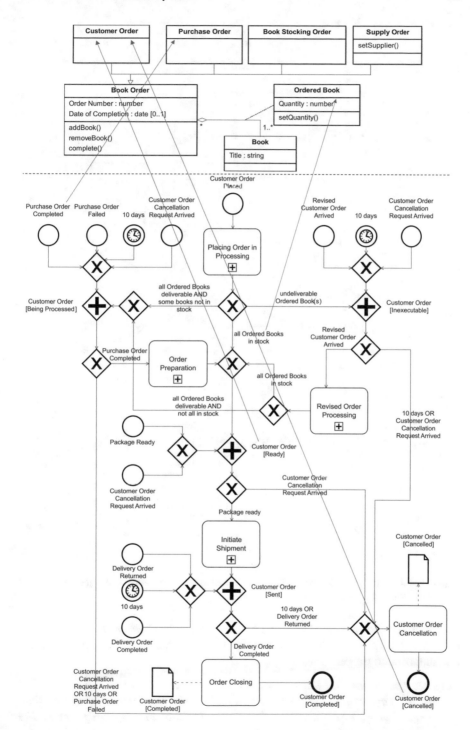

Fig. 4.10 Example of Book Order Processing process flow model and model of concepts consistency

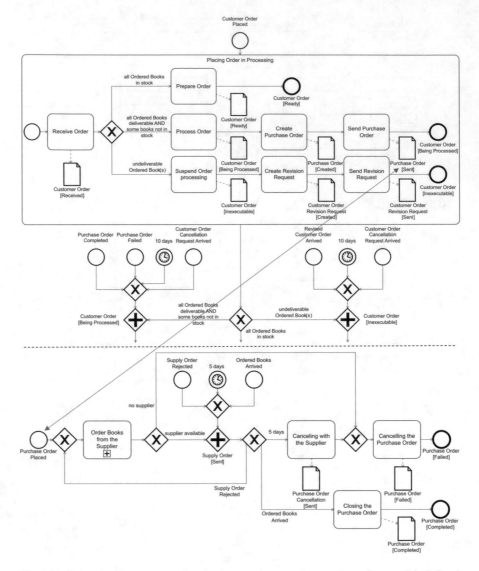

Fig. 4.11 Example of process synchronization consistency of two process flow models 1 (Book Order Processing and Purchase Books processes)

passed on to other models. Occurrence of the particular object state in the process flow model may then no longer correspond to the support process triggering event it is supposed to trigger.

Rule #2: *The events that the supported process is waiting for in synchronization with its support process shall correspond to the occurrence of object state changes, which are result of tasks executed within the support process. The exceptions to this are time events and events originating outside the support process.*

A process that is supported by a support process should capture the synchronization with the support process in its process flow model so it takes into consideration all possible events that may during the synchronization(s) with the support process occur.

Thus, the process state pattern that captures the synchronization of a process with its support process in the process flow model should capture all events (occurrence of object state changes) relevant to the supported process that are the result of tasks executed within the support process and that may occur during the synchronization with the support process (Fig. 4.12).

In practice, inconsistencies for this case usually arise due to later refinement of the process flow or synchronizations (events awaited in the process states) within individual process flow models, without this update being passed on to other models. In the process state in the supported process flow model then, there may be captured events that no longer exist, have been renamed, or should have existed, but no one has added the corresponding task (with the corresponding object state) to the support process flow model, or there may be even missing relevant events for the synchronization of the process with its support process.

4.3.5 Process Flow Models and Object Life Cycle Models Consistency

Rule #1: Each event that initiates the execution of a process task corresponds to a reason of state transition between the states of the object whose resulting state is associated with that process task.

The reason for the transition between states in the object life cycle model is an event. It is necessary that the events and the subsequent state of the object specified in the process flow model are consistent with the particular state transition from the relevant object life cycle model, for example, the end state cancelled of Customer Order in Fig. 4.13. Transitions to the cancelled state in the Customer Order life cycle have events captured as the reason. Similarly, in the process flow model, a task that takes Customer Order to the cancelled state (the object state associated with the task) is triggered by the same events as those captured in the Customer Order object life cycle model.

In practice, inconsistencies in this case usually arise due to later refinement within the individual process flow and object life cycle models, without this update being passed on to other models. Events that initiate the execution of process tasks may be then different than events in reasons of state transitions between the states of the objects whose resulting states are associated with the corresponding process tasks.

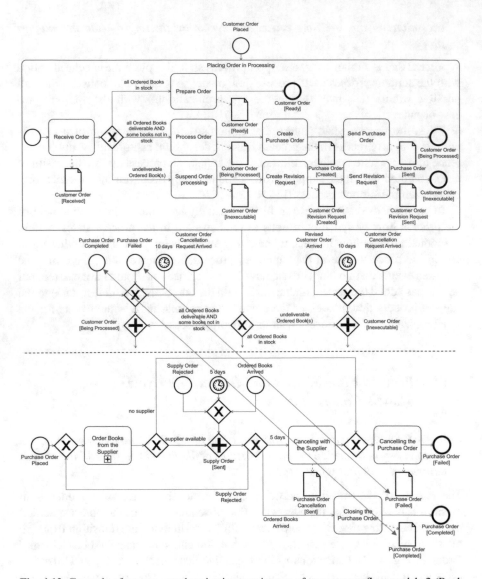

Fig. 4.12 Example of process synchronization consistency of two process flow models 2 (Book Order Processing and Purchase Books processes)

Rule #2: *The states of the objects specified in the process flow splitting conditions correspond to the object states in the object life cycle models.*

Object states referenced by flow splitting conditions in process flow models must reference existing object states captured in relevant object life cycles (Fig. 4.14). Again, the process model operates in the world whose ontology is defined by the object model, and therefore, the referenced object names and states names must also come from this world.

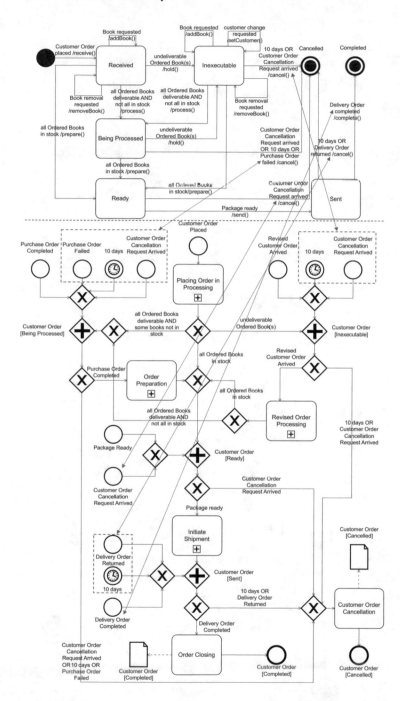

Fig. 4.13 Example of consistency of events in Book Order Processing process flow model with Customer Order object life cycle model

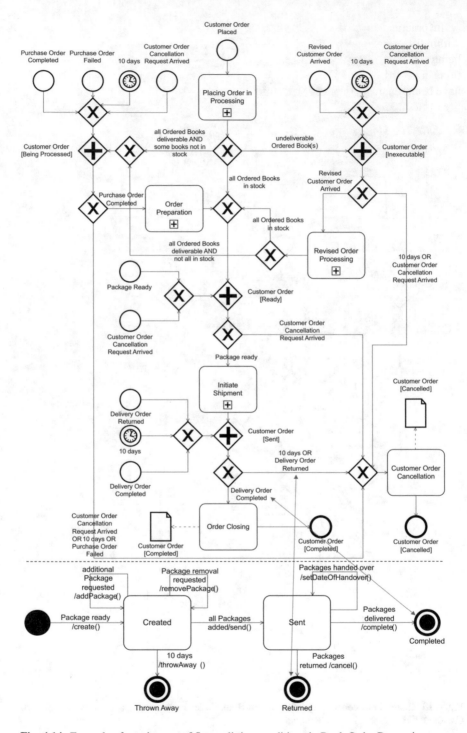

Fig. 4.14 Example of consistency of flow splitting conditions in Book Order Processing process flow model with Delivery Order object life cycle model

In practice, inconsistencies in this case usually arise due to later refinement within the individual process flow and object life cycle models, without this update being passed on to other models. Object states referenced by flow splitting conditions in process flow models then may refer to object states that may no longer exist, have been renamed, or should have existed, but no one has added them to the object life cycle model.

Rule #3: *The object states that are associated with tasks in the process flow models correspond to existing states in the object life cycle models.*

The object states represented by the data object elements associated with tasks in process flow models must exist in relevant object life cycle models (Fig. 4.15). Again, the process model operates in the world whose ontology is defined by the object model, and therefore, the referenced object names and states names must also come from this world.

In practice, inconsistencies in this case usually arise due to later refinement within the individual process flow and object life cycle models, without these updates being passed on to other models. Data objects associated with tasks in process flow models then may represent object states that may no longer exist, have been renamed, or should have existed, but no one has added them to the object life cycle model.

4.3.6   Object Life Cycle Models and Model of Concepts Consistency

Rule #1: *The operations captured in the state transitions in the object life cycle model correspond to the operations of the class of the object.*

In accordance with UML standard, operations that are specified in the object life cycle model must also be specified as a property of the corresponding class of objects in the model of concepts (Fig. 4.16).

In practice, inconsistencies in this case usually arise due to later refinement within the individual model of concepts and object life cycle models, without these updates being passed on to other models. Operations in state transitions in an object life cycle model then may refer to operations that may no longer exist, have been renamed, or should have existed, but no one has added them to the model of concepts.

Rule #2: *The attributes and relationships of the object referenced in the state transition reason shall correspond to existing attributes and relationships of the class of objects concerned.*

In the reason of transition between two object states, one can refer to an event that represents occurrence of change of object attribute value, relationships between objects, etc. In order for this reason to be valid, it needs to refer to attributes and

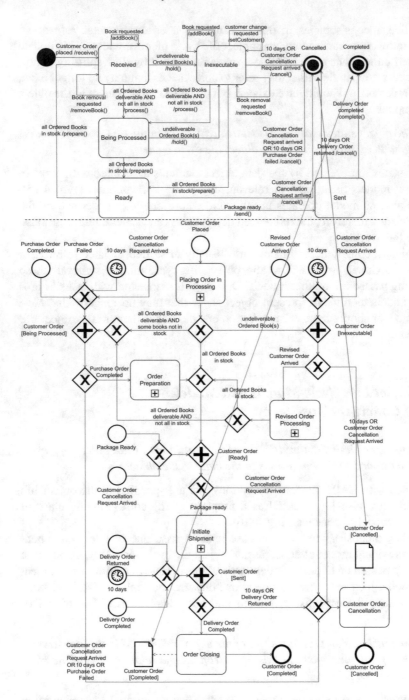

Fig. 4.15 Example of consistency of object states referenced in the detailed Book Order Processing process model with Customer Order object life cycle model

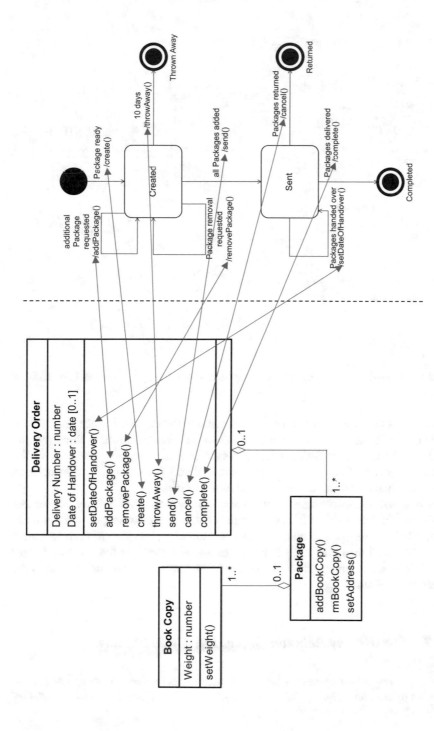

Fig. 4.16 Example of operation consistency of model of concepts and Delivery Order object life cycle model

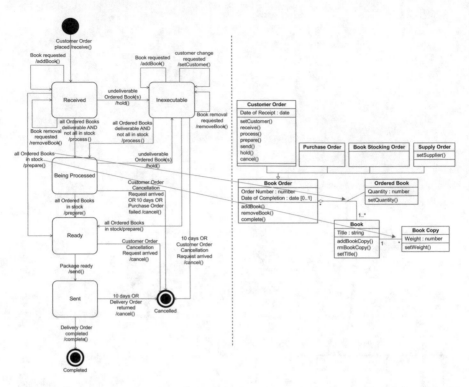

Fig. 4.17 Example of consistency of Customer Order object life cycle model and the model of concepts

relationships that actually exist, i.e., are captured in the model of concepts. Take for an example Fig. 4.17. The reason of state transition between the states Received and Ready of the Customer Order object life cycle refers to existing relations in the model of concepts that capture the fact that Ordered Book may or may not be in stock, i.e., there are Book Copies of that Book available.

In practice, inconsistencies in this case usually arise due to later refinement within the individual object life cycle models and model of concepts, without these updates being passed on to other models. Reason of a state transition in an object life cycle model then may refer to attributes and relationships that may no longer exist, have been renamed, or should have existed, but no one has added them to the model of concepts.

4.3.7   *Consistency Between Object Life Cycle Models*

Rule: *If the reason for transition between object states is given as occurrence of the state of another object, this state must exist in object life cycle model of that object.*

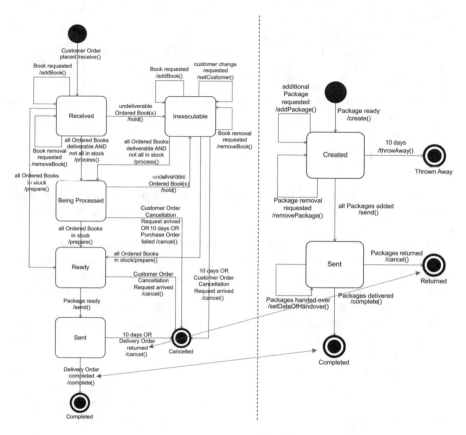

Fig. 4.18 Example of consistency between Customer Order and Delivery Order object life cycle models

In a life cycle model of an object, it is possible to refer to occurrence of object states of other objects in the reason of transition between object states. For such a reason to be valid, it must refer to object states that can actually occur, i.e., are specified in the life cycle model of the referenced object (Fig. 4.18).

In practice, inconsistencies in this case usually arise due to later refinement within the individual object life cycle models, without these updates being passed on to other models. Reason of a state transition in an object life cycle model then may refer to object states that longer exist, have been renamed, or should have existed, but no one added them to the corresponding object life cycle model.

4.4   Basic Temporal Consistency Rules

Temporal consistency emphasizes ensuring that the temporal models are consistent in their temporal sequence of facts, especially the sequences of object states. It must not happen that the sequence in which the object states follow each other in

Table 4.2 Consistency table for business system model

#	Event/reason ⟶ In process flow (BPMN)	In object life cycle (UML SMD)	Action ⟶ In process flow (BPMN)	In object life cycle (UML SMD)	State In process flow (BPMN)	In object life cycle (UML SMD)
1						
2						
3						
4						
5						

the process flow (associated with tasks) in the process flow model is in conflict with the sequence in which the object states follow each other in the object life cycle models.

Temporal consistency evaluation can be done intuitively by going through all the process flow models and the individual sequences of tasks with associated object states and comparing them with the corresponding object life cycles to see if the sequences of object states in the process flow models are consistent with the sequences defined in the individual object life cycle models. If they are inconsistent, models need to be aligned, and it needs to be determined which sequence is the correct one. This is very difficult to do if a CASE tool, like the Enterprise Assistant [8], does not support this at least to some basic extent.

The other option is to do this evaluation is using so called consistency table, which structurally compares how consistently the temporal models (process flow models and object life cycle models) capture the succession (event/reason → action → resulting state) and whether they match each other (Table 4.2). If not, the models need to be adjusted to avoid inconsistencies.

Table 4.2, in effect, not only allows checking the abovementioned succession consistency but also partly the structure by putting elements, which should be of the same type and meaning, from different models next to each other, (event, action, state) and thus also allows evaluation whether the elements from different models correspond to each other.

Let us illustrate how such consistency table is filled row by row. The example is an excerpt from the bookstore example, and the figures bellow illustrate the two cases that may occur: when the mapped action is started by an event from the environment of the evaluated business process and by an event that occurs within the evaluated business process.

To systematically complete the consistency table, it is a good idea to take process flow models as a basis and to always trace the corresponding sequence from the corresponding object life cycle model to the mapped process model elements.

Figure 4.19 illustrates the filling of a table row when the initiator of the action is an event from the environment of the evaluated business process. The arrows in the illustration indicate what sequences of elements to look for in each model and then how to record them in the consistency table.

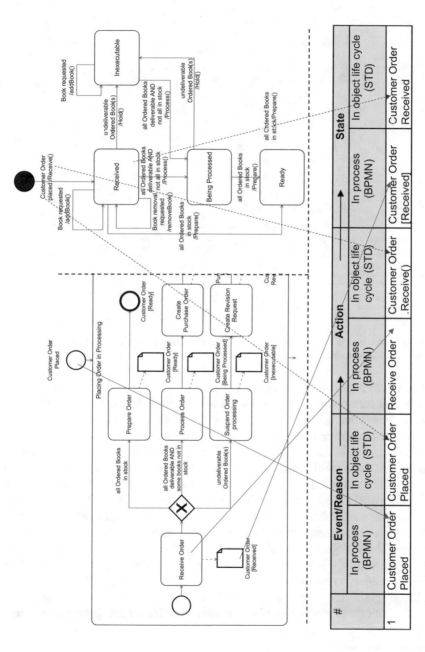

Fig. 4.19 Example row in consistency table capturing action triggered by an event from the environment of the evaluated business process

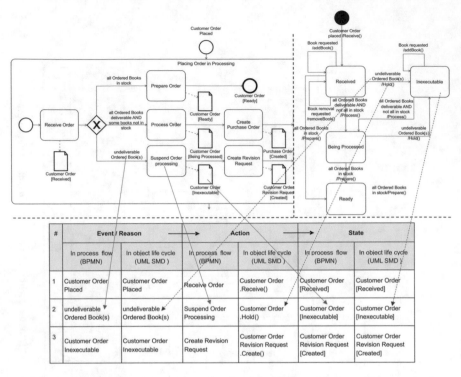

Fig. 4.20 Example row in consistency table capturing action triggered by an event that occurs within the evaluated business process

Figure 4.20 illustrates the filling of a table row when the initiator of the action is an event that occurs within the evaluated business process. The arrows in the illustration indicate what sequences of elements to look for in each model and then how to record them in the consistency table in the second row.

In the third row in the consistency table in Fig. 4.20 is the action also initiated by the event that occurs within the evaluated business process. In this case, it is not the Customer Order object that is responding to the event[2] but the Customer Order Revision Request object (its life cycle model is not in the Fig. 4.20). Business processes usually work with many different objects, so when evaluating the temporal consistency of a business process using a consistency table, we encounter many different relevant object life cycle models. This also applies in reverse; there are objects whose life is affected by different processes—different life stages of an object are subject to different business processes. This is the power of temporal consistency evaluation: with the help of different temporal views, which should map the same reality, one is able to evaluate whether one reality is captured in different

---

[2] Actually, it cannot since it is its internal event.

models. If not, it is immediately clear which parts of which models need to be reviewed and corrected.

Other rows of the consistency table are then further filled row by row as indicated in Figs. 4.19 and 4.20, with each row taking into consideration the distinction of how the recorded action was initiated.

If any of the recorded rows shows an inconsistency in the sequence event/reason → action → state, it is necessary to review the models and decide which model is right (if any) and which has to be changed so that the sequence is consistent in both models.

4.5 Basic Structural Consistency Rules

Structural consistency rules are based on the recognizing different manifestations of the type of structure in different aspects of different models. Recognized correspondences of structures can then be used to create the rules for both the structural consistency of individual models and structural consistency in combinations of different models, such as:

- Consistency of the constructions in the process flow model and corresponding transitions in the object life cycle model, etc.
- Consistency of the class relationship multiplicity and corresponding transitions in the object life cycle model

In the following section, we provide the reader with several examples of the application of selected structural consistency rules. The list of structural consistency rules should be considered permanently open for future contributions, just like any other type of consistency rules.

4.5.1 Process Flow and Object Life Cycle Models Consistency

Rule: *For objects whose states are captured as alternatives in the process model, it is true that these states are also alternatives in their life cycle.*

If the states of an object within a particular object life cycle model are alternative, these states need to be alternative in the process flow model too (Fig. 4.21). If this is not the case, it is necessary to find out which variant of the business rule is true and to adapt both models to it.

In practice, these inconsistencies usually occur when process flow models and object life cycle models are developed independently (by different teams of analysts). Process flow models are then in conflict with the relevant object life cycle models.

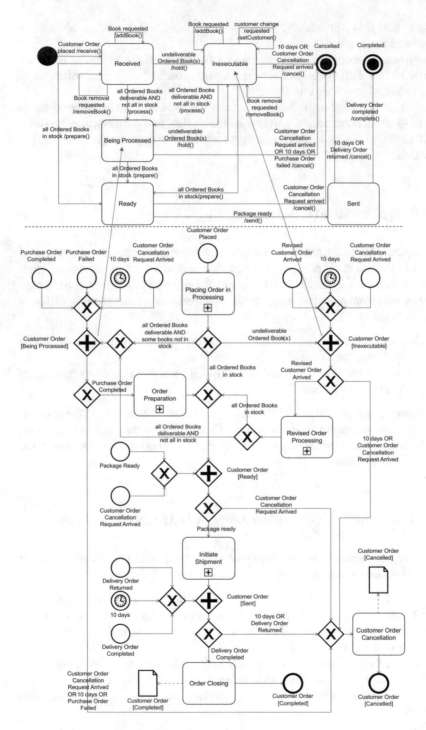

Fig. 4.21 Example of structural consistency of alternatives in Book Order Processing process flow model and Customer Order object life cycle model

4.5.2   Object Life Cycle Models and Model of Concepts Consistency

Rule #1: *The attributes and relationships of a class are reflected in the object life cycle model in the corresponding state transitions that the relationships and attributes change.*

The attributes of a class of objects and its possible relationships with other classes of objects captured in the model of concepts must be set in the case of instances of this class using the particular operations of the class. Thus, it is necessary that the operations specified for a particular class of objects make this possible, i.e., that the operations of the class cover all changes to the relationships and attributes that are relevant to the class and that its object life cycle model also includes these operations.

As an example, consider the example given in Fig. 4.22. Objects of the Delivery Order class must have operations to create and change relationships with objects of the Package class and operations to set the values of the Delivery Number and Date of Handover attributes, and these operations must also be included in the Delivery Order object life cycle model, which specifies when (at what object life cycle phases) these operations can be performed.

In practice, inconsistencies in this case usually arise as a result of later refinements within each of the object life cycle models and the model of concepts without these updates being propagated to the other models or as a result of omitting the information captured in the model of concepts when creating the life cycle models.

Rule #2: *Each 1:N association in the model of concepts is reflected in an iterative cycle in the life cycle model of an object of that class.*

The creation and modification of a possible 1:N class relationship captured in the model of concepts must be captured in the object life cycle model of that class as state transitions that can be performed iteratively (Fig. 4.23). As an example, consider the example given in Fig. 4.23. The 1:N relationship between the Delivery Order class and the Package class captured in the model of concepts is reflected in state transitions of the Delivery Order object life cycle model in the state Created. These state transitions then allow iterations that realize the 1:N relationship between the Delivery Order class and the Package class, while the Delivery Order object is in the Created state.

In practice, inconsistencies in this case usually arise as a result of later refinements within each of the object life cycle models and the model of concepts without these updates being propagated to the other models or as a result of omitting the information captured in the model of concepts when creating the life cycle models.

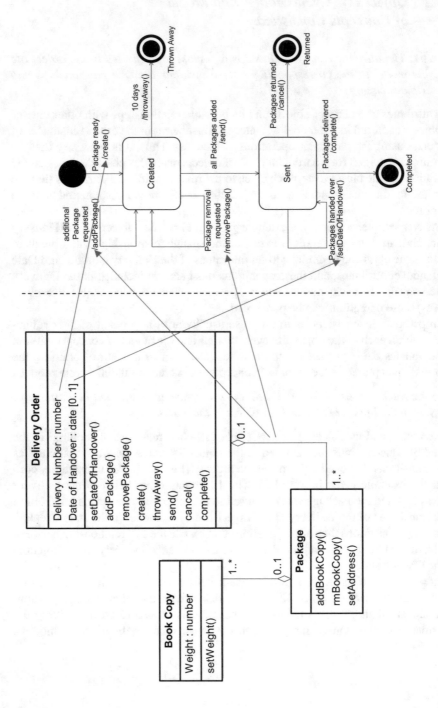

Fig. 4.22 Example of structural consistency of model of concepts and Delivery Order object life cycle model 1

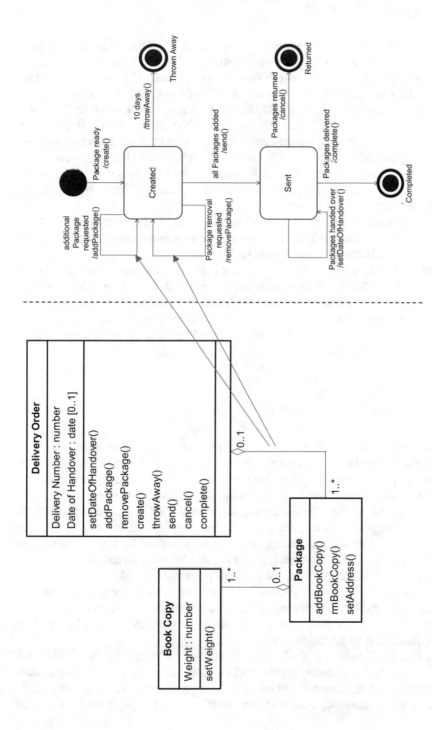

Fig. 4.23 Example of structural consistency of model of concepts and Delivery Order object life cycle model 2

4.6   Further Reading

The concept of consistency should be understood in a broader sense than just a technical issue. Models should be consistent not only with each other but also with the facts related to them in terms of their broader context. For example, their business context can be borrowed from the other levels of Enterprise Architecture, the general characteristics of which, including consistency, best describe the ArchiMate metamodel published in [10] and specifically with respect to MMABP in [11]. As an essential resource for a logical context of the model of concepts, we recommend [5], whose extension with object life cycles is explained in [12]. Technical aspects of the consistency of object-oriented models generally follow from the UML metamodel, described in [6]; its ontological aspects are best covered by the OntoUML methodology [13].

A broader context of the consistency of models regarding also process-oriented models can be found in [4]. Some basic ideas of an internal consistency of the process flow models can be found also in [14].

MMABP consistency rules are generally based on its Philosophical Framework published in [2]. The basic ideas on which the special structural consistency is based were originally described by Jackson in [7] and later generalized in [15].

As an example of a well-known modeling tool that pays attention to the consistency of models, we refer to [9]; a more comprehensive support for consistency in the style of the MMABP is in [8].

4.7   Summary

This chapter presents how the objects-oriented and processes-oriented models are interconnected and what it means for consistency of the business system model that consists of these models. It shows that evaluation of the consistency of the business system model (architecture) is not only a tool for identification of errors and inconsistencies in the business system model, which may arise in the process of abstraction and subsequent capture (typos, shifts in meaning, omissions, etc.), but also that evaluating consistency and making corrections to ensure it is an important and effective tool to achieve the quality of the model of the whole business system, not only in terms of correctness but also in terms of relative completeness.

Section 4.1 Conformance Evaluation introduces conformance, i.e., absence of contradictions between the representation of a fact in a model and the same fact in reality. It goes on to explain how to evaluate it and gives the basic rules by which conformance can be evaluated.

Section 4.2 Consistency Evaluation introduces consistency, i.e., absence of contradictions between different representations of the same fact in different models. There are presented three types of consistency: factual, structural, and temporal. All three types are presented, and how their evaluation should be performed is described.

Section 4.3 Basic Factual Consistency Rules presents basic factual consistency rules that emphasize ensuring that the facts represented in different models are consistent with each other in terms of their intended meaning. The presentation includes practical examples illustrated by models whose creation process was described in the previous chapters.

Section 4.4 Basic Temporal Consistency Rules presents basic temporal consistency rules that emphasizes ensuring that the temporal models are not inconsistent in their temporal sequence of facts. The presentation includes practical examples illustrated by models whose creation process was described in the previous chapters.

Section 4.5 Basic Structural Consistency Rules presents basic structural consistency rules that revolve around the different representations of structure types in different models, ensuring coherent alignment. The presentation includes practical examples illustrated by models whose creation process was described in the previous chapters.

4.8 Exercises

1. For a consistent (business) process flow model with the process map, the following must apply:
   a) The triggering event(s) for the business process are identical in both models.
   b) At least one of the triggering event(s) for the business process is captured in both models as an event that initiates the process.
   c) All the triggering event(s) for the business process are captured in both models as events that initiate the process.
   d) The triggering event(s) for the business process are different in both models.

2. For a consistent (business) process flow model with the process map, the following must apply:
   a) Every target state specified for the business process in the process map is also specified in the process flow model of that process in the form of process end.
   b) Every target state specified for the business process in the process map is also specified in the process flow model of that process in the form of a particular data object element associated with the corresponding task of that process.
   c) Every target state specified for the business process in the process map is also specified in the process flow model of that process in the form of process state.

3. For a consistent (business) process flow model with the process map, the following must apply:
   a) The support processes of a business process captured in the process map are captured in its process flow model as sub-processes of the process.
   b) The support processes of a business process captured in the process map are captured in its process flow model of the process as those processes with which the process synchronizes.

   c) The support processes of a business process captured in the process map are not captured in the process flow model of the process they support. Their relation is only captured in the process map.

4. For mutually consistent process flow models, the following must apply for capturing the synchronization of processes:
   a) If a process initiates its support process, the triggering event that initiates the support process corresponds to the occurrence of the object state (associated with the task) specified in the supported process flow model.
   b) If a process initiates its support process, the triggering event that initiates the support process corresponds to the occurrence of the process state specified in the supported process flow model.
   c) If a process initiates its support process, the triggering event that initiates the support process corresponds to the occurrence of the process end specified in the supported process flow model.

5. For mutually consistent process flow models, the following must apply for capturing the synchronization of processes:
   a) At least one of the events that the supported process is waiting for in its process state corresponds to the end of the support process with which it synchronizes.
   b) The events that the supported process is waiting for in synchronization with its support process correspond to the object states associated with tasks in process flow model of the support process. The exceptions to this are time events and events with origins outside the support process.
   c) The events that the supported process is waiting for in synchronization with its support process correspond to the process states in process flow model of the support process. The exceptions to this are time events and events with origins outside the support process.

6. For consistent process flow models with object life cycle models, the following must apply:
   a) For objects whose states are captured as alternatives in the process flow models, these states are also alternatives in their object life cycle models.
   b) For objects whose states are captured as alternatives in the process flow models, these states are not captured as alternatives in their object life cycle models.
   c) For objects whose states are captured as alternatives their object life cycle models, these states are also captured as alternatives in the process flow models.

7. For consistent process flow models with object life cycle models, the following must apply:
   a) Each event that triggers the processing of a process task corresponds to an object state.
   b) Each process state that triggers the processing of a process task corresponds to a transition reason between the states of the object whose resulting state is associated with the process state.

c) Each event that triggers the processing of a process task corresponds to a transition reason between the states of the object whose resulting state is associated with the process task.

8. For consistent process flow models with object life cycle models, the following must apply:
   a) All states of the objects specified in the process flow splitting conditions correspond to the states (including final pseudo states) in the object life cycle models.
   b) All states of the objects specified in the process flow splitting conditions correspond to the process states in the object life cycle models.
   c) All states of the objects specified in the process flow splitting conditions correspond to the final pseudo states in the object life cycles.

9. For consistent process flow models with object life cycle models, the following must apply:
   a) All states of objects that are associated with tasks correspond to the reasons in state transitions in the life cycle models of the objects.
   b) All states of objects that are associated with tasks correspond to the object states (including final pseudo states) in the life cycle models of the objects.
   c) All states of objects that are associated with tasks correspond to the object final pseudo states in the life cycle models of the objects.

10. For object life cycle models to be consistent with model of concepts, the following must apply:
    a) Multiple life cycles of an object of a single class correspond to the fact that an object from that class can act in multiple roles according to the model of concepts.
    b) Each 1:N relationship in a model of concepts is reflected in an iterative cycle in the life cycle model of an object of that class.
    c) The attributes and relationships of a class are reflected in the object life cycle model in the corresponding transitions between the states of the object that the relationships and attributes change.
    d) The operations captured in the state transitions in the object life cycle model correspond to the operations of the class of the object.
    e) The attributes and relationships of an object specified in the state transition reason correspond to the attributes and relationships of the classes of object concerned.

References

1. Řepa, V.: Business system modeling specification. In: Chu, H.-w., Ferrer, J., Nguyen, T., Yongquan, Y. (eds.) Computer, Communication and Control Technologies (CCCT '03), pp. 222–227. IIIS, Orlando (2003) ISBN 980-6560-05-1

2. Řepa, V.: Philosophical framework for business system modeling. In: 2023 IEEE 25th Conference on Business Informatics (CBI), pp. 1–6. IEEE, Prague (2023). https://doi.org/10.1109/CBI58679.2023.10187427

3. Venn, J.: I. On the diagrammatic and mechanical representation of propositions and reasonings. London, Edinburgh, and Dublin Phil. Magaz. J. Sci. **10**, 1–18 (1880). https://doi.org/10.1080/14786448008626877

4. Řepa, V.: Essential challenges in business systems modeling. In: Information Systems: Research, Development, Applications, Education, pp. 99–110. Springer International Publishing AG, Cham (2017) ISBN 978-3-319-66995-3

5. Kripke, S.: Semantical Considerations on Modal Logic. Acta Philosophica Fennica. **16**, 83–94 (1963)

6. Object Management Group: Unified modelling Language (UML) specification v2.5.1. https://www.omg.org/spec/UML/ (2017)

7. Jackson, M.A.: Principles of Program Design. Academic Press, London (1975)

8. Neit Consulting: Enterprise Assistant. https://www.popisto.online/

9. Modelio: https://www.modelio.org/

10. ArchiMate® 3.1 Specification. Van Haren Publishing, 's-Hertogenbosch (2019)

11. Řepa, V., Svatoš, O.: Alignment of business and application layers of ArchiMate. In: 17th International Conference Perspectives in Business Informatics Research (BIR 2018), pp. 57–69. CEUR-WS, Stockholm (2018) ISSN 1613-0073. http://ceur-ws.org/Vol-2218/paper6.pdf

12. Řepa, V.: Extending conceptual model with object life cycles. In: Hinkelmann, K., López-Pellicer, F.J., Polini, A. (eds.) Perspectives in Business Informatics Research, pp. 275–288. Springer Nature Switzerland, Cham (2023). https://doi.org/10.1007/978-3-031-43126-5_20

13. Guizzardi, G.: Ontological Foundations for Structural Conceptual Models. Telematics Instituut/University of Twente. Centre for Telematics and Information Technology, Enschede (2005)

14. Dumas, M., La Rosa, M., Mendling, J., Reijers, H.A.: Fundamentals of Business Process Management. Springer Berlin Heidelberg, Berlin (2013). https://doi.org/10.1007/978-3-642-33143-5

15. Jackson, M.A.: System Development. Prentice Hall, Englewood Cliffs, NJ (1983)

Chapter 5
Implementation of Business System Model in an Organization

Abstract To realize the benefits of process-driven management, a process-driven organization must be implemented in a real environment. It involves organizing and supporting actors, whether human or machine, through an appropriate infrastructure. The core infrastructure is a unified process-driven information system that differs from traditional systems in that it not only supports actors but also executes and monitors business processes in real time while facilitating continuous development. At its core is a Workflow Management System that is central to the creation, evolution, and real-time execution of process models. This ensures the information services of a highly flexible system that adapts to real situations—a key aspect of process-driven organization.

Implementing a process-driven system requires a foundational organizational concept, aligning actor competencies with business processes.

The MMABP technique involves analytical steps, refining the process system and constructing competencies from process relationships. Treating communication between processes as services establishes mutual competencies that inherit the flexibility of the system. This complex process and the ongoing evolution of process-driven management require the adoption of organizational maturity concepts and Michael Hammer's PEMM model. This mature model considers both process and organizational maturity and provides the basis for developing a process-driven organization according to its maturity level.

5.1 Introduction

In Chap. 2, we explain the way in which process-oriented management of the organization can overcome the limitations of the hierarchical organizational structure and establish a more sophisticated way of exploiting the effect of specialization as a primary tool for increasing effectiveness and efficiency, based on the collaboration of processes. It is based on the distinction between two basic functional types of processes: *key processes*, which are directly linked to the customer and cover the

© The Author(s), under exclusive license to Springer Nature   215
Switzerland AG 2024
V. Řepa, O. Svatoš, *Fundamentals of Business Architecture Modeling*, The
Enterprise Engineering Series, https://doi.org/10.1007/978-3-031-59035-1_5

entire business cycle from the identification of the customer's needs to his full satisfaction with the product/service, and *support processes*, which are indirectly linked to the customer through key processes. While the key processes ensure the complete service to the customer, the support processes support other process(es) with specific products/services. In this way, each process is ultimately linked to customer value, either directly (key process) or by serving the other processes. Thus, key processes represent a specific company's way of satisfying customer needs, while support processes represent more standard functionality, usually associated with a particular technology. The process of designing the system of processes is then mainly focused on establishing a *balance between the necessary dynamics of key processes on the one hand and the necessary stability of the system ensured by its maximally standard support processes on the other*.

Orientation on processes is necessary for keeping an active control over the business case in the current turbulent world. Active control means not only controlling the process but also instant improving the process based on the new technology possibilities. It requires two essential attributes of the business system: *resilience* on one hand and *stability* on the other hand.

Resilient business system in this context is such system, which can immediately react to any relevant change. There are two basic kinds of needed change: *change of client's preferences* and *new technology possibilities*. Ability to immediately accommodate the process to the specific client's needs requires the complete control over the key process on the level of client, which is not possible in the functional organization where the key processes are unconditionally determined by the organizational structure. To make the business simpler and more effective, thanks to the new technology, the organization has to perceive its business as a system of mutually interconnected processes, which determine all other organizational features including the system of competences and responsibilities.

Stable business system is a system as much as possible resistant to unnecessary changes. Building such a system thus requires at first a clear understanding of the essence of possible changes in order to be able to decide about their objective necessity. To do so, one must primarily respect the essential principles and qualities of the objective reality as a basic source of objective and thus certainly necessary needs for changes. Informatics traditionally calls such objective reality the Real World.

While resilience of the business system requires orientation on business processes, its stability has to be based on the precise ontological (conceptual) model of the corresponding business domain.

We understand the aforementioned balance between the flexibility and stability of an organization to make the organization directly linked to technological development as a real content of the concept of *process-driven transformation*.

This chapter focuses on the question of how to implement the business system model in an organization with respect to the process-driven management principles.

It focuses on other important and interrelated aspects of implementing the idea of process-driven organization in real life: the *process-driven information system*, the process of *building the process-driven organization*, and the *organizational maturity*.

5.2 Process-Driven Information System

The essential difference between key and support processes discussed above must also be supported by the information system. Differences between key and support types of the process, summarized above, actually outline the necessary classification of types of components of the information system in the process-driven organization.

On the one hand, the information system must support *all standard services represented by support processes*. These services should be standardized as much as possible to achieve the best cost-benefit ratio and to keep the information system as flexible as possible to the natural changes resulting from the development of technology. Standardization is also necessary to take advantage of possible collaboration, whether in the form of physical outsourcing or Web services or other forms of technological collaboration. From an information systems point of view, the needs of support processes should be covered by the standard functional components represented by, for example, Enterprise Resource Planning (ERP) systems. When properly designed, support processes should be considered as services rather than processes, as their internal process structures are not important for the enterprise but rather for the suppliers (or software developers).

On the other hand, the information system must also support the key processes, whose essential characteristics are contrary to the characteristics of the support processes. *Key processes* cannot be supported by standard functionality; their actual process (algorithmic) content *must be fully in the hands of the workflow manager*, and their definition must be fully in the hands of the process owner. Information system must work with key processes in a completely different way than with support processes.

Figure 5.1 shows the necessary structure of the information system of the process-driven organization. Stable parts of the information system represent relatively stable aspects of the business: the database and standard essential functions. The software component providing the necessary dynamics, the so-called workflow management system, is based on the definitions of business processes and works with the information about the current state of running processes. This allows it to combine the standard essential functions, working with the standard data structures dynamically according to the current needs of (key) processes. The basic *separation of relatively stable components of the information system from the "behavior"*

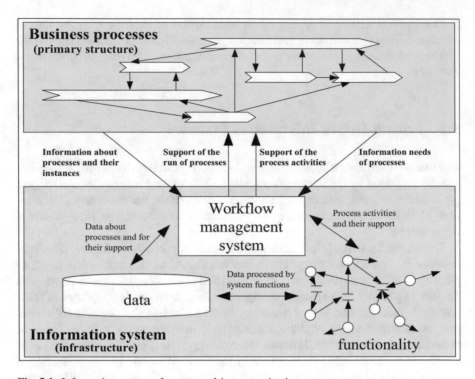

Fig. 5.1 Information system of a process-driven organization

of the information system driven by business processes *allows to create a fully dynamic information system while keeping the maximum advantage of standard ERP systems.*

For example, the key process Client Management from the process map example in Fig. 5.2 is served by two support processes Service Providing and Complaint Management, all of which belong to the key business domain Clients Care. Service Providing ensures the standard way of providing any service to the customer, while Complaint Management represents the standard way of handling complaints. Obviously, both support processes do not require any special interest in their process structure; they can be considered as standard services. The diagram also shows other related business areas: Service Management, Marketing, and Accounting. Due to their standard nature, all of these business areas (i.e., subsystems of processes) can also be considered as services without the need to care about their internal process structures. The key process ensures the provision of various relevant services to the customer throughout the customer's life cycle, including support for the "development of the customer's needs." Unlike all other support processes and domains, the key process must be subject to continuous evolution based on the experience of its instances and constant monitoring of new technological possibilities. Key processes represent the organization's flexibility. They form the field for creativity of people in direct connection with the information system.

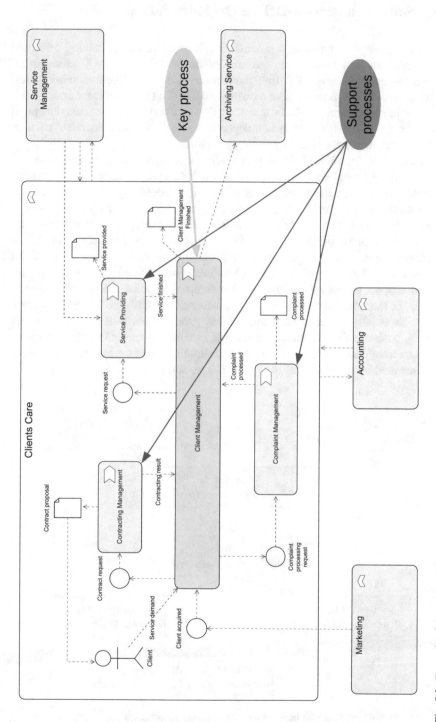

Fig. 5.2 Example of the process map

5.3   Building a Process-Driven Organization

The key challenge in building a process-driven organization is making informed decisions about how to structure business processes. This involves achieving an optimal balance: effectively fulfilling the *primary function* while maintaining simplicity, given current *technological capabilities*. The first task is a clear understanding of the intrinsic nature of the business, expressed through a system of conceptual business processes. This system is independent of real-world constraints such as technological, organizational, or regulatory factors.

Figure 5.3 outlines the MMABP process for building a process-driven organization. The *first two steps* focus on the initial analysis of the organization's process essence: identifying natural sequences of activities necessary to achieve defined business goals and analyzing the primary function to identify key processes—those that directly contribute to the primary function. In the *third step*, key processes are analyzed to eliminate supporting activities. This clarifies the process content of the business system, with key processes emphasizing the management of activities directed toward business goals, while the removed support activities represent specialized support processes designed for the internal logic of the required support services. In the first three steps, not only processes are analyzed but also business objects. Especially in the identification of key processes as well as in the process thinning, business objects play a crucial role in terms of the MMABP idea of the mutual interconnectedness of these two basic dimensions of the business system, as also illustrated by the examples in Chaps. 2, 3, 4, and 6.

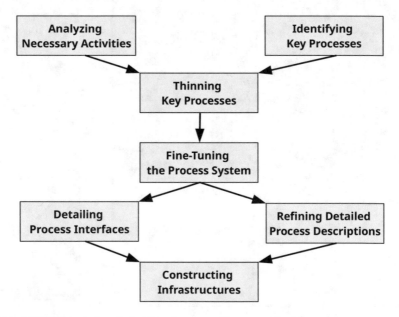

Fig. 5.3 MMABP procedure for building a process-driven organization

The *next four steps* involve implementing the process system within the organizational and technical context. Steps 5 and 7 play a key role in this process. In the *fifth step*, the interfaces between processes are detailed through Service Level Agreements (SLAs), which in the *seventh step* serve as the basis for building organizational and technical infrastructures. This comprehensive approach ensures systematic and effective transition to a process-driven organization. Further explanations of step contents follow.

Step 1: Analyzing Necessary Activities In this initial phase, basic sequences of activities are identified, focusing on the natural sequence found in workflows, legal procedures, and similar contexts. These sequences form the basis for the process system structure. The outputs include a list of potential processes/activities and their successions, along with the first version of process flow models, that outline the basic process logic.

Step 2: Identifying Key Processes The goal of this step is to uncover key processes, each of which represents the path to a specific product or service. The structure of the key processes is derived from the life cycle of the key product, emphasizing the external value to the customer. The deliverables of this step include a list of key processes and their relationships, basic attributes of key processes, and the first version of key process flow models.

Step 3: Thinning Key Processes Key processes, which initially include supporting activities, are thinned out to remove these supporting chains. Supporting activities are outsourced to stand-alone processes, resulting in a focus on the essential actions within key processes. Results include an updated version of the key process flow models and the discovery of supporting processes. The *Normalization of processes* described in Sect. 2.3.4 is the key technique to use in this step.

Step 4: Fine-Tuning the Process System After thinning out the key processes, detailed refinement and completion of the global process model take place. The structure evolves based on newly discovered supporting processes and simplified key process structures. The output is a completed Global Process Model and a detailed specification of the interfaces between the processes.

Step 5: Detailing Process Interfaces Detailed elaboration of interfaces, especially between key and supporting processes, is achieved through Service Level Agreements (SLAs). These agreements provide a universal perspective on collaboration interfaces, aligned with financial evaluations and quality metrics.

Step 6: Refining Detailed Process Descriptions Along with Step 5, key processes are revised, including events, reactions, and synchronization with the global model. Models are enriched with actors, inputs, and outputs, resulting in updated descriptions and process flows.

Step 7: Constructing Infrastructures The final step is to develop interfaces for organizational activities. The key task of this step is to analyze the requirements for both organizational and technical infrastructures based on the identified necessary interfaces between processes described as services by SLAs. Outputs include detailed specifications of products/services, cost evaluation systems, performance metrics, outsourcing decision support, information requirements, and other managerial aspects that contribute to the overall functionality of the organization. Casual detailed models of supporting processes are also developed in this step.

In the following section, we pay special attention to the service in terms of SLA, the key concept for the construction of all infrastructures.

5.3.1 Concept of Services

The conceptual model shown in Fig. 5.4 delineates a portion of the service universe within the business process domain. It is important to distinguish between the *Business Process Definition* and the *Business Process Instance*. The latter represents a specific business process running at a specific time with specific actors, inputs, outputs, and so on. Business processes can collaborate with each other, and this collaboration is represented in the model using the *Process Interface* class, which represents the association between two processes where one has the role of *Supplier* (producer of the service) and the other has the role of *Customer* (consumer of the service). In specific process interactions, the process interface acts as a contract template.

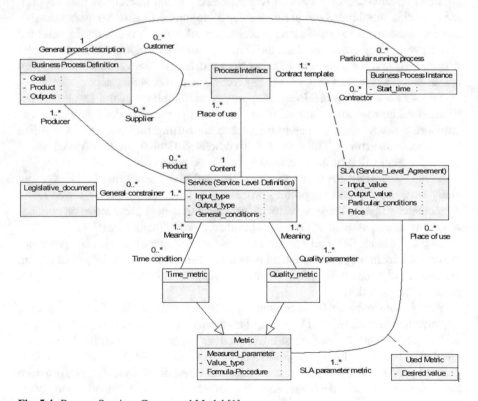

Fig. 5.4 Process Services Conceptual Model [1]

In essence, the *Business Process* can be a *Producer* of one or more *Services* (as seen in the direct association between the classes *Business Process Definition* and *Service*).

There must be an integrity constraint in the model that expresses that there should be a direct association between the *Business Process Definition* and the *Service* taking place within the *Process Interface* where that business process acts as a *Supplier*. In simpler terms, each business process must be the producer of all services it provides in different contracts.

The *Services* themselves may be subject to multiple *Legislative documents*; they must be associated with at least one *Quality metric* and may be associated with one or more *Time metrics*. This means that there must always be a measurable notion of the quality of the service, and some services must also be time limited. Each service metric is characterized by the *Measured parameter*, its value type, and the method of collection, whether it is a formula or a procedure.

Every Service Level Agreement (SLA) should include a product description (service characteristics, meaning, value, sense), basic product parameters in measurable units, product quality metrics (how to measure quality as a general product attribute), and the product "price," which reflects the necessary cost of the supporting process or offered service.

The Service Level Agreement concretizes the general attributes of the *Service* with particular attributes in the SLA. General *Input* is represented in the SLA by input data, *Output* by Output data, and *General conditions* of the service with *Particular conditions* in the contract. The SLA also includes the desired values of the service metrics and an additional attribute—the price of the service, which is determined during the negotiation as it depends on various situational factors, generally referred to as the *Market*.

This way of describing the interface between two processes is essentially a real business agreement between these processes. It erases the line between "internal" and real outsourcing, in line with the concept illustrated in Step 3 of the Procedure for the design of the business process system. This mindset prepares the ground for potential outsourcing of all support processes, where appropriate.

The distinction between key and support processes is fundamental to the application of specialization in the process-driven organization. First, it separates the management of key processes from support activities, allowing specialization of key processes in the management of the key processes (primary value chains according to Porter [2]). Second, it frees support activities from responsibility for the context of their use, allowing focus on the internal logic of support service delivery and maximum standardization of support activities/processes/services. This specialization does not compromise the integrity of key processes, a critical issue in traditional hierarchical organizations.

5.4   Organizational Maturity and Maturity Models

Process-driven transformation [3] is a complex, multi-dimensional, and uncertain endeavor. Managing this transformation requires careful attention to the impact of change across all relevant dimensions. In the field of process-driven management, this challenge gave rise to the concept of the organizational maturity model, which facilitates the management of transformation based on knowledge of the relevant aspects and consequences at a given level of organizational maturity.

The first maturity model for process-driven transformation by R. Nolan [4] led to the development of several contemporary models. M. Hammer's [5] model, known for its harmonization of process and organizational maturity, stands out as the most comprehensive. This model forms the basis of a methodology for organizational development through technology progress management [6], which, when applied, significantly helps mitigate the associated risks.

Several authors have extensively reviewed maturity models and compared individual criteria. Notable models such as Goncalves', Lockamy and McCormack's, and Hertz's maturity models compared by Palmberg in [7] focus on process definition, performance measurement and evaluation, process improvement, organizational structure, two-way communication, and information security. Many of these models are inspired by the Capability Maturity Model (CMM, CMMI [8]).

Fischer's model, which integrates dimensions such as strategy, control, processes, people, and information technology, is often cited [9]. It delineates levels of process management in each dimension, defining the company's level of process management ranging from limited expansion to integration at the tactical management level and forming part of an intelligent hierarchical network.

Závadská in [9] critically reviews a number of maturity assessment models in her article and lists models identified in management practice, including Hammer's Process and Enterprise Maturity Model (PEMM), 8 Omega by the Business Process Transformation Group, CAM-I PBM Assessment by the International Consortium for Management, BPM Maturity Framework by Gartner Company, Rosemann and Bruin's maturity model, and others.

Among these, *Michael Hammer's maturity model PEMM* is often cited and considered easy to apply. It is known for delivering immediate results in improving process-based management systems and business processes.

In his article [5], Hammer emphasizes the need for organizations to mature their business processes to ensure that they can deliver higher performance over time. He identifies two types of characteristics for development: *Process Enablers* (characteristics of individual processes) and *Enterprise Capabilities* (characteristics of the entire organization).

Process Enablers include:

- Design (comprehensiveness of process specification)
- Performers (skills and knowledge of process executors)
- Owner (responsibility of senior executive for the process)
- Infrastructure (support of the process by information and management systems)

- Metrics (measures used to track process performance)

Enterprise Capabilities include:

- Leadership (support from senior executives for process creation)
- Culture (values of customer focus, teamwork, personal accountability, and a willingness to change)
- Expertise (methodology for process redesign and skills for using it)
- Governance (mechanisms for managing complex projects and change initiatives)

Hammer's system assesses organizational maturity by considering the characteristics of process enablers and enterprise capabilities. The overall quality of an organization is viewed as a complex characteristic in which both process enablers and enterprise capabilities express necessary conditions for quality. Therefore, process maturity should be aligned with enterprise capabilities and vice versa for meaningful organizational development.[1]

Hammer outlined four levels representing the maturity of an organization and its processes, each characterized as shown in Fig. 5.5:

1. *Traditional Management* At this level, the organization recognizes the concept of processes, but the understanding and acceptance of the term "process" remain unclear and not universally embraced.

   Symptoms of this state are:
   - Constructed processes cover only fragments of the complete business case.
   - Emphasis is on partial/local improvement and personal contributions within the line organization.
   - Infrastructure remains fragmented based on the line organization structure.
   - Metrics and their usability are limited because of this organizational fragmentation.

2. *Activities as Parts of Processes* This level introduces a process-oriented view of the organization's activities, where each specific activity is viewed as part of a larger process that indicates its contextual value. At *this stage*, the processes become the central criterion, value, and common denominator for all definitions, descriptions, behaviors, approaches, attitudes, infrastructures, and metrics.

---

[1] It does not make sense for the organization to feel the high level of maturity of its processes without considering the appropriate level of its capabilities. For example, it is quite common for a company to consider its process system as perfect but at the same time keep all processes subordinate to its traditional hierarchical organization. This fact is more a proof of a fatal misunderstanding of the basic principles of process-based management than a serious message about the company's maturity.

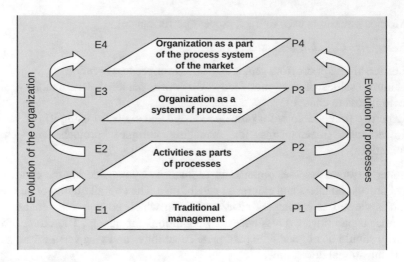

Fig. 5.5 Model of maturity of organization and its processes according to M. Hammer

3. *Organization as a System of Processes* At this stage, each process is fundamentally viewed as a component of the organization's process system. The organization becomes the primary criterion, value, and common denominator for all definitions, descriptions, behaviors, approaches, attitudes, infrastructures, and metrics.

   Symptoms of this state are:
   • All goals and meanings of activities are related to the organization.
   • Individual processes are viewed in a broader, shared context.

4. *Organization as a Part of the Process System of the Market* At the highest level, processes are viewed not only in the context of the organization but also in terms of their target significance for customers. Decisions extend beyond the boundaries of the organization to customers and collaborators, aligning the structure of processes with the overall context of customer needs.

   Symptoms of this state are:
   • Actor's behavior, approaches, and attitudes are aligned with values provided outside the organization.
   • Infrastructures are organized according to professional and technological standards to be compatible with customer and collaborator infrastructures.
   • Metrics are designed and continuously linked to the strategy.

This maturity model represents a progression from a basic recognition of processes to an advanced stage where the organization is closely linked to the market context and customer-centric values.

The maturity of the organization is a key factor that needs to be taken into account in the process of putting the idea of a process-driven organization into practice. Without respecting the maturity level of the organization, the transformation project is destined to fail. Hammer's "process audit" presented in [5] provides both the global understanding of the key success factors of such a project and their interrelationships, as well as the practical details that need to be analyzed and covered by the relevant actions in the respective milestones of the organization's maturity development process. Based on Hammer's maturity model PEMM [5], the method for developing a process-organized organization has also been developed and published as a CEABPM (Central-European Association for Business Process Management) standard [6].

5.5   Further Readings

A key resource for exploring business process and workflow management is van der Aalst and van Hee's *Workflow Management: Models, Methods and Systems* [10]. The concept of maturity models originated with Nolan's "Managing the Computer Resource: A Stage Hypothesis" [4]. Hammer's seminal work on the Process and Enterprise Maturity Model (PEMM) is detailed in the article "The Process Audit" [5], and the paper entitled "Role of the Concept of Service in Business Process Management" [1] introduces the use of the service concept as a foundation for building a process-driven organization.

5.6   Summary

This chapter provides a comprehensive view of implementing a process-driven organization, from information systems to organizational maturity, emphasizing the need for balance, flexibility, and systematic approaches.

The introductory section underscores the need for a *balance between dynamic key processes and stable support processes*, essential for organizational resilience and stability. *Resilience* requires control over key processes to adapt swiftly to client preferences and technological changes, framing the organization as a system of interconnected processes. *Stability* relies on a precise ontological model of the business domain. The section focuses on implementing a business system model based on process-driven principles, addressing various facets such as process-driven information systems, organizational construction processes, and organizational maturity, culminating in a holistic understanding that the delicate equilibrium between flexibility and stability is the essence of process-driven transformation, aligning organizations with technological advancements while maintaining stability through meticulous modeling and maturity considerations.

Section 5.2, Process-Driven Information System, delves into the critical role of information systems in implementing key and support processes within a process-driven organization. It highlights the dichotomy between these two types of processes, asserting that while support processes can be treated as standardized services, key processes require a different approach. Key processes, essential for organizational flexibility, cannot rely on standard functionality; instead, their algorithmic content must be under the control of the workflow manager and process owner. In the information system of a process-driven organization, stable components such as the database and essential standard functions coexist with the "workflow management system" that operates based on real-time information about running processes. This structural separation allows for a *fully dynamic information system* while retaining the advantages of standard ERP systems. In such a system, key processes serve as the backbone of organizational flexibility and are the main subject of continuous development and technological adaptation.

In Section 5.3, Building a Process-Driven Organization, we describe the challenges and steps involved in building a process-driven organization, focusing on the *MMABP process* shown in Fig. 5.3. It emphasizes the importance of balancing effectiveness and simplicity when structuring business processes, starting with a conceptual understanding of the nature of the business. The steps include analyzing and identifying key processes, thinning out supporting activities, refining the process system, *detailing interfaces through service level agreements (SLAs)*, and building infrastructures. In particular, the text emphasizes the concept of services, detailing a conceptual model (Fig. 5.4) that distinguishes between a business process definition and a business process instance. The Service Level Agreement is seen as a true business agreement that erases the boundary between internal and outsourced processes. The final distinction between key and support processes allows for specialization, separating the management of key processes from support activities, leading to a process-driven organization with specialized management and maximum standardization without compromising the integrity of key processes.

Section 5.4, Organizational Maturity and Maturity Models, explores the intricacies of process-driven transformation and emphasizes the importance of managing this complex endeavor through an organizational maturity model. It traces the evolution of maturity models, focusing on *M. Hammer's PEMM model*, and outlines the characteristics of process enablers and enterprise capabilities that are critical to assessing organizational maturity. Hammer's four-level maturity model (traditional management, activities as parts of processes, organization as a system of processes, organization as part of the market process system) is detailed, with symptoms defining each level. The highest level envisions processes that are aligned with customer needs, reflecting a customer-centric approach. The text emphasizes the critical role of organizational maturity in the success of a transformation project and introduces Hammer's "Process Audit" as a tool for understanding key success factors and their interrelationships. It also mentions the development of a methodology, CEABPM, as a standard for building a process-organized organization based on Hammer's PEMM model.

References

1. Řepa, V.: Role of the Concept of Service in Business Process Management Information Systems Development, pp. 623–634. New York, Springer, LNCS (2011)
2. Porter, M.E.: Competitive Advantage: Creating and Sustaining Superior Performance, 1st edn. Free Press, New York (1998)
3. Hammer, M., Champy, J.: Re-engineering the Corporation: A Manifesto for Business Revolution. Harper Business, New York (1993)
4. Nolan, R.L.: Managing the computer resource: a stage hypothesis. Commun ACM. **16**, 399–405 (1973)
5. Hammer, M.: The process audit. Harv Bus Rev. **85**(4), 111–123 (2007)
6. Řepa, V., Satanová, A., Lis, M., Kořenková, V.: Organizational development through process-based management: a case study. Int J Qual Res. **10**(4), 685–706 (2016) ISSN 1800-6450
7. Palmberg, K.: Experiences of implementing process management: a multiple-case study. Bus Process Manag J. **16**(1), 93–113 (2010)
8. Chrissis, M.B., Konrad, M., Shrum, S.: CMMI for Development: Guidelines for Process Integration and Product Improvement; [CMMI-DEV, Version 1.3]. Addison-Wesley, Upper Saddle River, NJ (2011)
9. Závadská, Z.: Audit of the process-based management system. Výkonnosť podniku. **3**(1), 6–15 (2013)
10. van der Aalst, W., van Hee, K.M., van der Aalst, W.: Workflow Management: Models, Methods and Systems. MIT Press, Cambridge, MA (2004)

Chapter 6
MMABP Use Case

Abstract The chapter unfolds the practical application of the Methodology for Modeling and Analyzing Business Processes (MMABP) through a real-world example focused on transportation services within an enterprise. Beginning with an overview of the transportation domain and the global process map, subsequent sections meticulously demonstrate the MMABP methodology through model of concepts, process maps, and process flow models. The model of concepts illustrates object relationships, classifications, and cardinalities in the business domain, with a deep dive into the Transportation Batch life cycle model. Process flow models at the conceptual level, presented in BPMN notation, provide detailed insights into the main processes and culminate with an introduction to support processes, highlighting their symbolic internal structures and their adaptability to different implementations. The last part navigates the transition from the conceptual to the technological level using the CAMUNDA workflow management system, which acts as both a process engine and a prototyping platform. The discussion hints at upcoming topics on language extension for execution, providing insight into transformed models and their seamless integration into a comprehensive system. To encourage hands-on experience, the inclusion of source code invites readers to run prototypes, fostering a practical understanding of the intricacies and potentials of process-driven organization.

In this chapter, we present the use of MMABP models in the practical example with respect to its *minimal architecture* principle. For simplification, we do not present the functional analysis for a relevant information system (i.e., Data Flow Diagram) and focus only on a conceptual specification of the business system covered by model of concepts, process map, object life cycle models, and process flow models. We only shortly discuss the main information system functions following from detailed business process models.

To be particular as much as possible, we nevertheless transform the conceptual process flow models to their implementation form in the selected workflow engine environment CAMUNDA. This allows to provide the reader with the source code of

© The Author(s), under exclusive license to Springer Nature
Switzerland AG 2024
V. Řepa, O. Svatoš, *Fundamentals of Business Architecture Modeling*, The
Enterprise Engineering Series, https://doi.org/10.1007/978-3-031-59035-1_6

process models that can be run in the CAMUNDA environment. Such an experience is very important to understand the real-time aspects of business processes, namely, their natural parallelism. Regarding the temporal nature of business processes, their *real-time aspects must necessarily be a subject of interest even in the analysis stage.*

We also do not illustrate the MMABP procedure as a way to make crucial initial decisions about key and support processes and their contents. We kindly ask the reader to take the presented models as a result of precisely made process and object analyses in terms of the MMABP procedure, with use of the techniques presented in relevant chapters of this book.

All the omitted aspects, such as information system functional analysis, process analysis including the Process Normalization Technique, business system ontology analysis, and others, are special subjects of interest in particular chapters of this book.

6.1   Description of the Business Field

As an illustration of a real system consisting of mutually cooperating business processes, we present a functional fragment focused on transportation within an enterprise. Figure 6.1 provides a high-level overview of the domain ontology in the form of a model of concepts. A transportation request can be made for either delivering an Order to the company's customer or transporting Material from the supplier to the company. Multiple transportation requests are grouped into a Transportation batch. Each Transportation batch should be transported by a single Vehicle, and this relationship is labeled as Transport, with possible outcomes of Successful, Failed, or Delayed.

Figure 6.2, the process map, displays the relevant processes within this functional domain and their interdependences. The Key process in the transportation functional area is *Transportation Request Management*. It serves as a liaison to other functional areas of the enterprise, such as *Order Management* from the

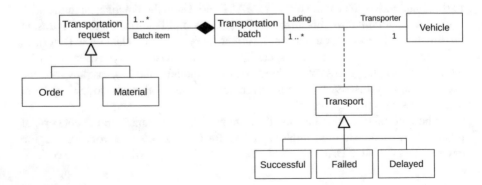

Fig. 6.1   Fragment of the Transportation model of concepts

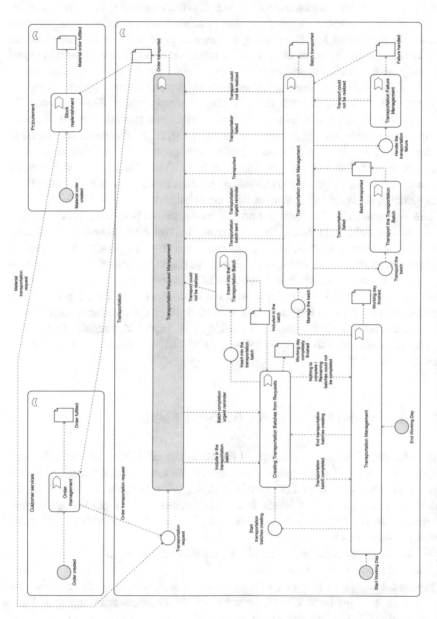

Fig. 6.2 Process map of the functional area Transportation (TOGAF Event Diagram)

Customer Services area and *Stock Replenishment* from the *Procurement* area. The *Order Management process* requires transporting the final product of a customer's order to the enterprise's customer, while the *Stock Replenishment* process focuses on transporting ordered stock from the supplier to the enterprise. The transportation processes' task is to optimize transportation by assembling optimized transportation batches from requests for transporting orders and materials. Optimization means maximizing the workload of the particular transport and optimizing (minimizing) the transportation path simultaneously.

The *Transportation Request Management* process receives transportation requests and coordinates with the *Creating Transportation Batches from the Requests* process to include them in the appropriate transportation batch. It monitors the entire transportation process for each request, from inclusion in the batch to sending it after batch completion, and tracks its progress until it reaches its destination, accounting for various possible scenarios. The *Creating Transportation Batches from Requests* process continuously assembles transportation batches from transportation requests and optimizes their composition.

The *Transportation Management* process is the main operational process in the transportation field, responsible for organizing the entire working day. It initiates the work in the transportation functional area by triggering the *Creating Transportation Batches from Requests* process at the beginning of the day and concludes at the end of the day. It manages the individual-created batches by sending them for transport using the *Transport the Transportation Batch* service and addresses any unforeseen transportation failures through the *Transportation Failure Management* service. Throughout the working day, it provides regular updates on the transport outcomes to the corresponding Key process, *Transportation Request Management*.

6.2   Conceptual Model of the Business Field

In this section, we show the conceptual model of the given business field. For this example, we model just the relevant part of the business field, determined by the business processes in the process map in Fig. 6.2. Moreover, we focus only on the part determined by the processes from the functional area of *Transportation*. Therefore, we omit the objects from related functional areas such as *Customer Order*, *Supplier*, *Stock*, *Store*, etc.

We mean by the conceptual models the traditional conceptual data model with the life cycle models of relevant objects.

Figure 6.1 shows the fragment of a high-level Transportation model of concepts. This model specifies basic objects (entities) of the business field and their basic modal relationships. Cardinalities of associations between objects are related to their general meaning determined by the business field. For instance, the existence of the *Transportation batch* makes sense only in terms of its role in *Lading*, meaning if it is to be transported. Therefore, the cardinality of its association with Vehicle

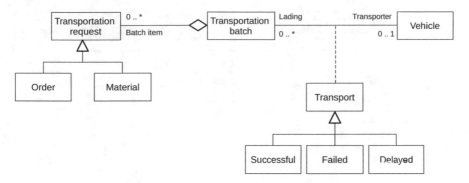

Fig. 6.3 More general version of the Transportation model of concepts

in the role of *Transporter* is 1 (precisely one mandatory *Vehicle* related to each *Transportation batch*). Once we regard possible business actions and events, we have to admit also the *Transportation batch* unrelated to any *Vehicle*. For instance, ordering the vehicle before the transportation batch is completed is unnecessary. Similarly, we should admit the possible existence of the batch without any *Transportation request* as a *Batch item* when the batch is created but not yet filled. And finally, a *Vehicle* can be a subject of other business actions besides its role as a *Transporter* so that we should regard it as a standalone object not necessarily related to the *Transportation batch*.

Figure 6.3 shows a more general version of the model, modified concerning the above-discussed business facts. One can see there changed cardinalities to express also possible empty transportation batch, the batch not related to any vehicle, and the vehicle not ordered for any transportation batch. Also, the aggregation relationship between the *Transportation batch* and the *Transportation request* was changed from a "strong" aggregation (alias composition) to a regular ("weak") aggregation since the *Transportation batch* can exist independently of any request, which follows from the cardinality 0 of the request in the *Batch item* role.

Application of the business actions view naturally leads to the distinction of the particular sub-types of the Transportation batch that represent its temporally distinct states. Such a distinction can explain the meaning of different cardinalities of relationships to other objects, namely, their optionality (i.e., possible zero cardinality). Figure 6.4 shows the class model enriched by this classification. *Empty* transportation batch is the state of the batch in which there is no transportation request. In all other states, there must be some related request. The state *Being transported* similarly represents existing related *Vehicle,* while in all other states, this relationship is irrelevant. Since such a generalization structure represents so-called dynamic generalization [1], the sub-types are labeled with ≪*phase*≫ and ≪*end*≫ stereotypes.[1]

Dynamic generalization means the sub-types should not be regarded as different stand-alone objects but just as life phases of a single object, whose identity they

---

[1] For a more detailed explanation of the stereotypes used, see the introductory part of Chap. 3.

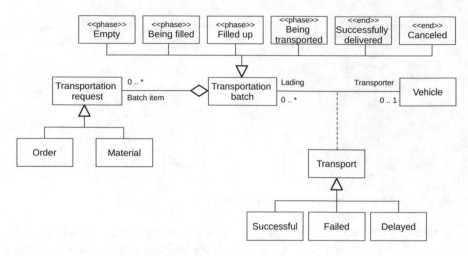

Fig. 6.4 Sub-types of the class Transportation batch

share (see Sect. 3.1). Thinking about the life phases necessarily leads to thinking about their temporal dependencies, about the life cycle of the given object. Figure 6.5 shows the life cycle model of objects of the class *Transportation batch*.

The object life cycle model defines the part of the Real-World causality determined by the business system and related to the object's life. It shows the possible ordering of the life phases of the object under various circumstances. Every possible transition between states is described by a pair of values: reason/action. The reason is usually a business event or a conditioned business event. The action represents the relationship to the business processes, an action that belongs to the particular business process or more processes as process task, a part of the task, or a set of process tasks.[2]

In this example, the life cycle model shows that only in the phase *Empty* the batch can be canceled without the need to compensate the consequences. Cancellation of the batch in both remaining relevant phases (*Filled up* and *Being transported*) necessarily requires some compensation because there are some consequences coming from the revocation or fail of the transport since the transport has been already ordered. The model also shows that once the transport starts, the batch cannot be changed anymore, only successfully delivered or canceled. There are also some transitions that do not represent the change of life phase even so they exist and represent some change: adding and removing the requests from the batch in the phase *Being filled*, handling the transport fail or delay[3] in the phase *Being transported*.

---

[2] Specifying the business action as an attribute of the transition between life phases always means the relation to some business process, which makes the life cycle model dependent on the business process. Therefore, MMABP does not regard the action as a required part of the transition specification. If we need to specify the life cycle independently of any business process, we can specify just an event part (reason) in every transition.

[3] If the transport fails or is delayed, an attempt is made to handle the failure/delay, resulting in either a successful transport or a canceled transport.

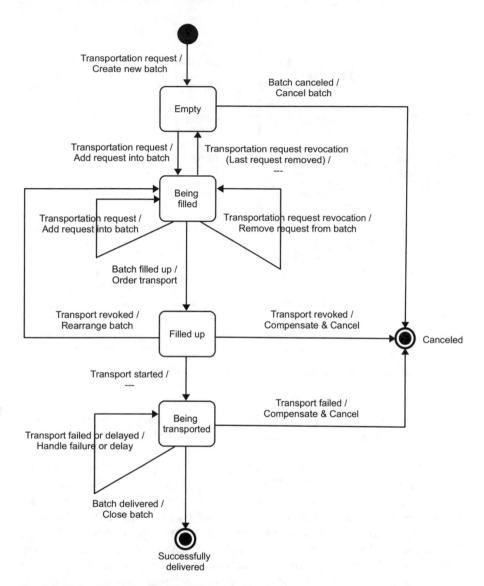

Fig. 6.5 Object life cycle of the class Transportation batch

Figure 6.6 shows a more specific version of the Transportation model of concepts that fully reflects the *Transportation batch* life cycle. The life cycle shows that the aggregation relationship between the *Transportation batch* and *Transportation request* is irrelevant in the *Empty* phase. Therefore, we introduced an additional phase *Nonempty*, which covers all three later phases. Excluding the *Empty* phase, we can regard the relationship with *Transportation requests* as a

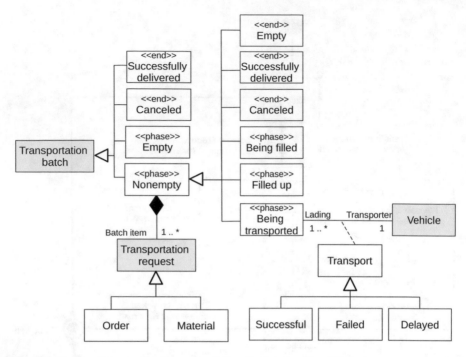

Fig. 6.6 Transportation model of concepts fully reflecting the object life cycle

strong aggregation—a composition. Similarly, the relationship with the *Vehicle* is relevant only in the *Being transported* phase. Moreover, it is mandatory in this phase.

To be systematic, we should reflect a two-layer specialization of the *Transportation batch* even in the life cycle model. Figure 6.7 shows how the new inter-type *Nonempty* manifests in the life cycle model. The life cycle of the *Transportation batch* is simplified to just a two-state model, and the *Nonempty* phase is specified with a stand-alone model. In this example, such a modification is unnecessary since it does not bring new information. Nevertheless, working with two models represents a new perspective that can bring some inspiration for the further analysis and development of the models in future stages of the project.[4]

In general, the life cycle model makes the conceptual model more precise by more detailed targeting of relationships. It allows to specify mandatory associations to just some phases instead of the former optional general association to the object as a whole. Moreover, the life cycle model contains additional information about relevant transitions and reasons for them, which is impossible in the class model.

---

[4] In terms of the MMABP multi-viewpoint principle

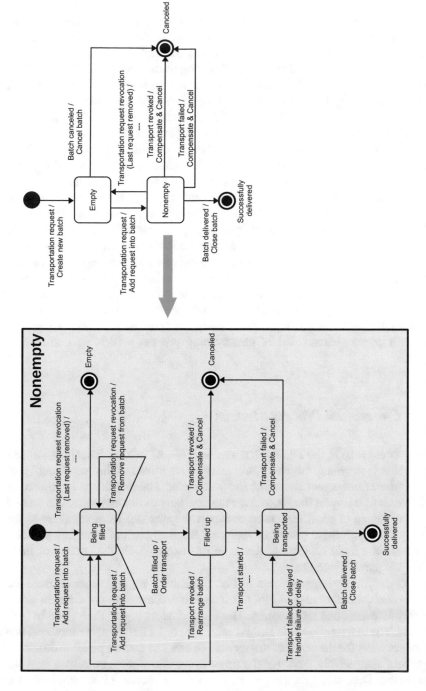

Fig. 6.7 The layered object life cycle model of the class Transportation batch

6.3   Business Field Conceptual-Level Process Flow Models

In this subchapter, we show the detailed models of basic business processes in the business domain. The process models are written in BPMN notation, which is reduced in the sense of the MMABP "minimality principle."

Process models on the conceptual level belong to the "conceptual" layer of the "Three Architectures" (see the principle of the Three Architectures in the Sect. 1.3), which means that they aim to focus only on the real content of processes and abstract all their non-conceptual features. In particular, these process models define the activities that represent the necessary actions to be performed to achieve the process goal, but do not address how these activities are performed. In the conceptual-level model, we assume that the process activities have access to the information they need and do not worry about how to store and retrieve the data to implement this access. We also assume that the events are recognized in the processes without defining how to implement a recognition of them such as messages or triggers.

The abstraction of non-conceptual features of processes also leads to the need to reduce the BPMN language, as it contains many such features. The necessary reduction of BPMN for its use as a language for conceptual-level process modeling can be found in Sect. 2.3 In Sect. 6.4.1, we describe a necessary extension of the reduced language for transforming conceptual-level process flow models into executable (i.e., technology-level) form. Finally, Sect. 6.4.3 describes how to deal with the natural parallelism of business processes using the "process inversion" technique, which is a very important part of transforming process models into an executable form.

6.3.1   Conceptual Process Models

As the process map in the Fig. 6.2 shows, the business field of transportation services, which is the main subject of this example, is linked to the "customer" processes *Order Management* and *Stock Replenishment*. The first one is the source of requirements to transport the goods from the company to its customers. The second one is the source of requirements to transport the material from suppliers to the company. Although these processes represent the end users of transport services, they are not the main subject of interest in this example. So the content of these processes is purely symbolic.

The *Order Management* process in Fig. 6.8 is only slightly different from the *Stock Replenishment* process in Fig. 6.9. The two processes do not differ in structure, only in events and task content. The basic process logic is the same in both processes. The first reaction to the initial event is to order the transport service. Then the process waits for the result of the service. In order to avoid a possible deadlock, the process alternatively waits for the timer event that signals no response in the given period. Depending on the occurred event, the process either continues the

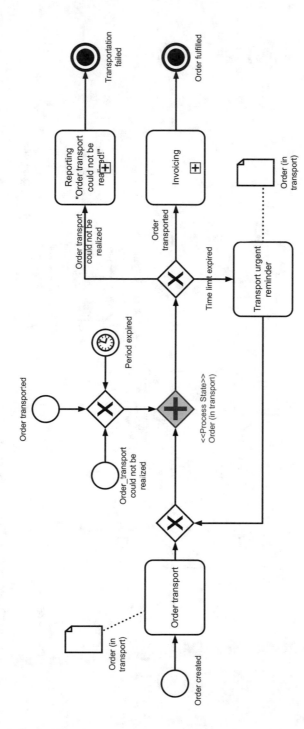

Fig. 6.8 Order Management conceptual-level process model

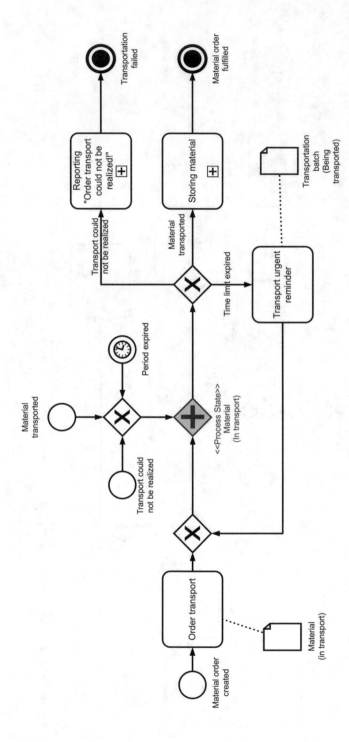

Fig. 6.9 Stock Replenishment conceptual-level process model

regular action (*Invoicing* in the case of the customer order or *Storing material* in the case of the material delivery) or reports the unsuccessful transport attempt or creates the urgent reminder.

The *Order Management* and *Stock Replenishment* processes represent the interests of the *Customer Services* and *Procurement* business functions in the field of transportation. Their task is to control the delivery time of the ordered service through urgent reminders and to react appropriately to the result of the service.

The key process of the *Transportation* business function is the *Transportation Request Management* process. As a key process, it is representative of the main service of this business function, which is to ensure the ordered transport with respect to the particular parameters of the order (such as the delivery time), including the solution of all possible problems.

Transportation Request Management process (see Fig. 6.10) is started with either order transportation or material transportation request. The process reacts to the starting event with the request for inclusion of the request to the transportation batch, which is a service or the supporting process *Creating Transportation Batches from Requests* (see Fig. 6.12). As the model in Fig. 6.10 shows in the process state *Transportation request processed*, there are four possible results of this service: either the request was successfully included in the transport batch or it was included as the last request in the batch and the physical transport of the batch was started or the transport could not be realized or nothing happened in the given time period. If the request was only included in the batch, the process remembers it and returns to the same process state. If the batch was sent, the process moves to the following state *Transportation batch on the way*. If the transport of the batch could not be realized, the process reports the cancellation of the request to the customer process and ends. If nothing happens in the given time period, the process sends the urgent reminder and returns to the same process state. There are two types of reminder. If nothing has happened to the request before the reminder, the process reminds the request to be included in the batch. If the request has already been included in the batch, the process reminds to complete the batch and start the physical transport.

In the following state *Transportation batch on the way*, which the process will only reach if the batch has been sent, the process expects four possible events: either the transport has been successfully completed, it has failed, the transport could not be realized, or nothing has happened in the given time period. If the transport was successful, the process reports this to the client process and exits. If the transport failed, the process just returns to the same state and waits for the solution, while the event *Transport could not be realized* means necessary cancellation of the request. If nothing happens in the given time, the process sends the urgent reminder and returns to the same process state.

The instance of the key process *Transportation Request Management* is related to the particular transportation request. Its role is to take care of the processing of the request and to monitor the specified deadlines.

The main operational process of the *Transportation* business function is the *Transportation Management* process (see Fig. 6.11). It is not the key process because it is not directly driven by customer requirements, so it is formally a

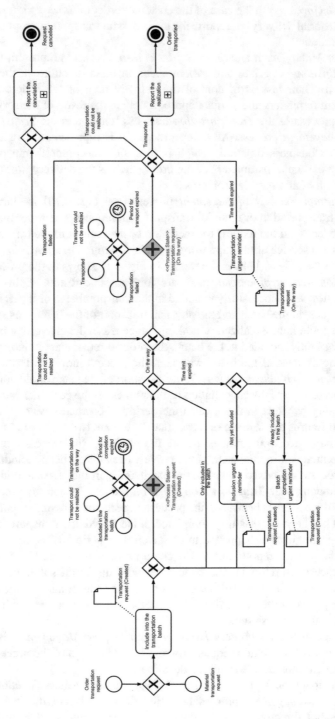

Fig. 6.10 Transportation Request Management conceptual-level process model

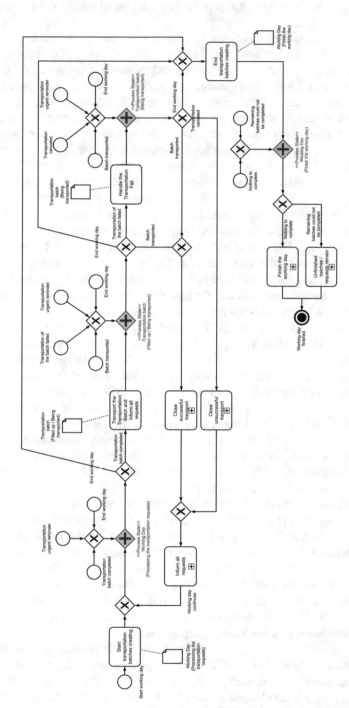

Fig. 6.11 Transportation Management conceptual-level process model—first version

support process. Nevertheless, this process plays a critical role in the operation of this business function.

The instance of the *Transportation Management* process is related to the working day. It is responsible for handling all transportation requests during the working day. The process starts with the working day, and its first task is starting the support process *Creating Transportation Batches from Requests* (see Fig. 6.12), which is its main supporting process. As can be seen in the process map in Fig. 6.2, the process *Creating Transportation Batches from Requests* captures the requests for inclusion in the transportation batch from the *Transportation Request Management* processes and includes these requests in the transportation batches according to their parameters (such as destination, direction, time limit, etc.) with the constant effort to optimize the operation. Once the transportation batch is ready to be sent, the process reports this fact to the *Transportation Management* process (via the event *Transportation batch completed*), which takes care of the batch and manages its transport and related issues (such as finishing the transport, possible transport failures, reminders, etc.). Each issue with the batch is reported by the T*ransportation Management* process to the corresponding *Transportation Request Management* processes whose requests are included in the given batch (see the *Inform all requests* task). After handling the given batch, the process returns back to the state *Creating the transportation batch* and waits for another batch.

At the end of the working day, the Transportation Management process initiates the service by the Creating Transportation Batches from Requests process "End transportation batches creating." The Creating Transportation Batches from Requests process then forces the completion and shipment of the remaining yet unsent batches. The process also sets a specific deadline for the completion of unfinished shipments. If a batch is not delivered within this period, it is marked as unfinished. Therefore, the process Creating Transportation Batches from Requests in this phase also monitors the possible expiration of the set completion period (see the process state Completing remaining batches). The final result of the service reported back to the Transportation Management process is then either Nothing to complete or Remaining batches could not be completed.

The action *Insert into the Transportation Batch* in the *Creating Transportation Batches from Requests* is performed as a service of the support process *Insert into the Transportation Batch* (see Fig. 6.13). The reason for this lies in the ontological distinction between the creation of batches, which is primarily related to the concept of batch, and the insertion of the request into the batch, which is related to the concept of transportation request. The importance of the ontological distinctions of the main subjects of interest of the processes for the organization of the processes in the process system is also briefly discussed as a multidimensional problem in Sect. 6.4.

The process *Insert into the Transportation Batch* is a simple process that, from an MMABP perspective, is a single process step. This process represents very important "internal intelligence" of the process system, an ability to optimize the transportation batches from multiple perspectives. Nevertheless, no matter how sophisticated it is, it is an elementary step from the process-oriented point of view as it does not require any collaboration with other processes.

Further analysis of the content of the *Transportation Management* process from an ontological point of view (represented by the conceptual model) revealed the

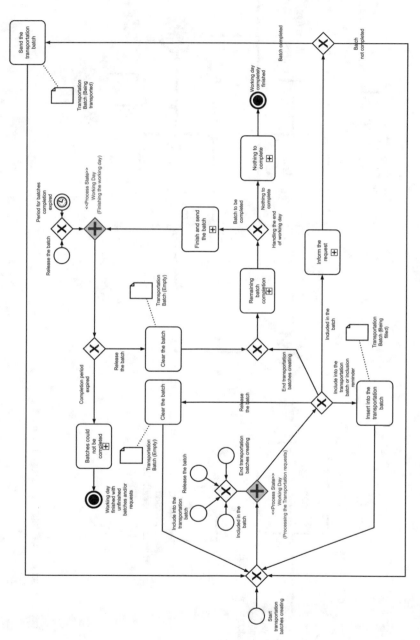

Fig. 6.12 Creating Transportation Batches from Requests conceptual-level process model

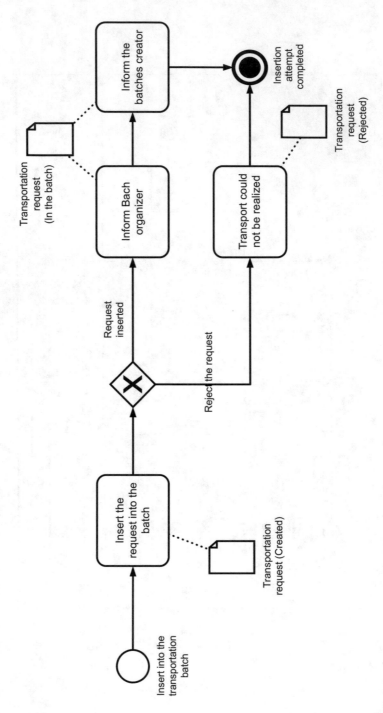

Fig. 6.13 Support process Insert into the Transportation Batch

need to remove from the process also those activities related to the *Transportation Batch* concept, since this concept is also many-to-one related to the *Working Day* concept, to which this process instance is primarily related. As a result, the new support process, *Transportation Batch Management*, has been created, and the original content of the *Transportation Management* process has been simplified (see Figs. 6.14 and 6.15).

The new *Transportation Batch Management* support process in Fig. 6.14 is started by the *Manage the batch* event. It supports the *Transportation Management* process by providing services for sending the batch monitoring the transport and handling the possible failure of the batch. The instance of this process is related to the *Transportation Batch* concept so that in this way, several transportation batches may be handled at the same time.

The instance of the new version of the Transportation Management process in Fig. 6.15 is related to the *Working Day* concept. This process now only starts the working day and then handles the completed transportation batches using the services of the *Transportation Batch Management* support process until the end of the working day. At the end of the working day, the process handles this event as in the previous version.

In MMABP, we call the process of designing the processes according to the ontological substance of the object they manipulate the "Process Normalization Technique." Therefore, we call this version of the process "normalized." See Sect. 2.3.4 for details of the technique.

The process map in Fig. 6.2 shows that the *Transportation Management* process also uses the services of the support processes *Transport the Transportation Batch* and *Transportation Failure Management*. The use of these services corresponds to the *Transportation Management* process states *Transportation batch on the way* and *Transportation Failure Management*.

The internal structure of both these support processes is just symbolic as can be seen in Fig. 6.16. They differ just in the contents of the process steps. The process *Transport the Transportation Batch* represents all possible kinds of the transport. The process *Transportation Failure Management* represents all possible kinds of handling the transportation failure. They also differ in the possible end results; while the first process may result in a successful of failed transport, the second one, representing the second attempt to transport the batch, may result in either a successful transport or its ultimate cancellation.

Both processes can be implemented in various ways according to the technological nature of the transport, transporter, supplier, etc., which is precisely why they are considered typical support processes, covering a number of variants and associated different implementations.[5]

---

[5] For example, some instances of the *Transport the Transportation Batch* process may be performed by company's own vehicles, and other instances may be performed as a sub-delivery by a shipping company. Choosing the right mode of transport can be one of the criteria for optimizing the performance of the transportation business function and, consequently, may be different for different transportation batches at the same time. Nevertheless, the logic of the process remains in all cases the same. Similarly, there are various possible ways, in which the second process may handle the transportation failure depending on the given specifics.

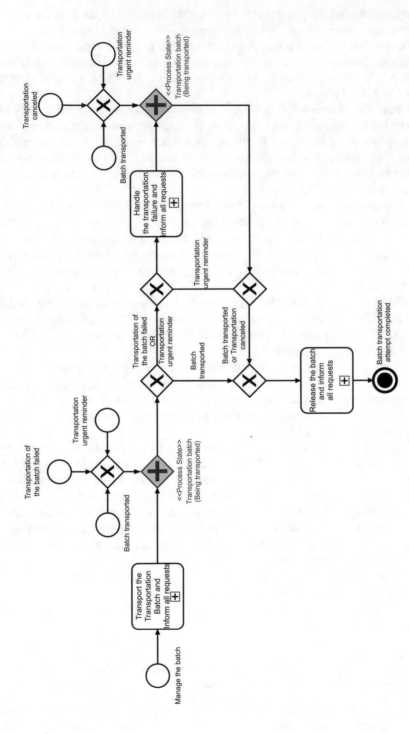

Fig. 6.14 Transportation Batch Management conceptual-level process model

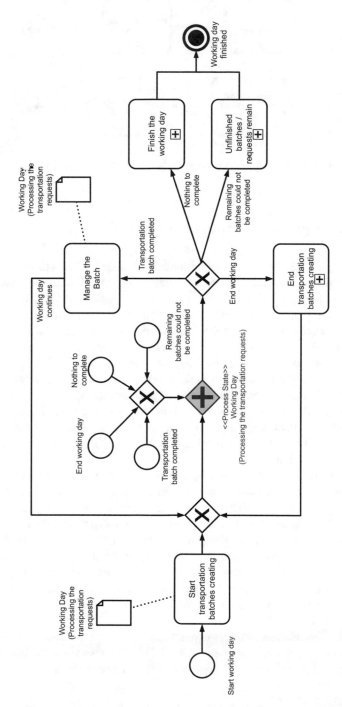

Fig. 6.15 Transportation Management normalized conceptual-level process model

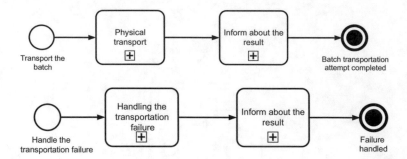

Fig. 6.16 Processes Transport the Transportation Batch and Transportation Failure Management—conceptual version

6.4   Technology-Level Process Flow Models

In this subchapter, we show the detailed models of basic business processes in the business domain transformed from the conceptual level to the technology level. The aim of the transformation is to take into account the specifics of the given technology (in this case, a particular workflow management system) while preserving the content of the processes defined at the conceptual level of the process flow models.

In this example, we use the CAMUNDA workflow management system. CAMUNDA is an open-source application, based on the JAVA environment, which fully respects the required openness in different meanings. It is open both technically (open source application) and in terms of standardization, both in terms of the environment (JAVA and related common standards) and the modeling language it supports (BPMN). This openness perfectly supports the necessary flexibility of the systems based on this platform, which is essential for the process-oriented management of the organization.

CAMUNDA is primarily the process engine (i.e., workflow engine as a crucial part of the process-driven information system of an organization). Its very useful and important feature is the ability to work as a platform for prototyping the processes on the level of their models. The ability to prototype the model contents of the model is very important especially in the case of business processes designed according to the principles of process-driven organization. As also shown in the MMABP principles, the process-orientation leads to the division of logical processes according to their ontological substance,[6] which causes the need to handle the natural parallelism of processes that follows from this ontology. This problem is a main topic of Sect. 6.4.3.

In the following chapter, we first explain how to extend the modeling language to be able to execute the processes in CAMUNDA. Then we show the transformed models and explain how they work together as an integral system.

---

[6] Better speaking: to the ontological substance of the crucial subjects of interest of the processes

This book includes the source code for the processes in this example. We strongly recommend the reader to run the prototype of this example in CAMUNDA process environment, as it will help understand the essential features and problems related to building the system of process-driven organization.

6.4.1   Transforming Conceptual-Level Process Flow Models to an Executable Form

To make the example easily comprehensible, we must first explain how to utilize the specific process implementation environment to adhere to the principles of the MMABP methodology. MMABP employs the BPMN language as a de facto standard for process modeling. However, since BPMN does not completely align with all MMABP principles, we utilize a minimal version of BPMN, containing only essential elements and augmented with the process state implementation, which is absent in BPMN.

In this example, we present the workflow engine CAMUNDA as our preferred process implementation environment. CAMUNDA strictly adheres to BPMN v2.0 and does not allow the use of constructs not present in the standard. Additionally, it mandates the use of standard-defined constructs even when they may not be the most suitable. To accommodate our requirements, we have to extend our minimal version of BPMN to facilitate process implementation in the CAMUNDA engine.

Figure 6.17 displays the basic BPMN v2.0 activity types that we must utilize. For process communication, we need to create events that trigger the necessary reactions of other processes. CAMUNDA realizes this as a "call activity" indicated by an envelope icon. By such activity, CAMUNDA enables us to call its "object correlation" function, facilitating the creation of events. To distinguish between activities performed by human actors (Interactive application task) and those executed automatically by the system (Automated application task), we utilize specific types of task. The "automated task," also known as a "script task," allows us to invoke a script, while the "interactive task" allows using an inbuilt interactive forms generator provided by CAMUNDA.

Figure 6.18 shows how we implement the process state in CAMUNDA. The process state serves as a point of communication between the process and its environment, whether it is another process or an actor. Technically, it represents the time the process waits for one of the possible events to occur. In MMABP, we model the process state as synchronization of the process flow with the awaited event using the

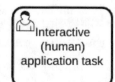
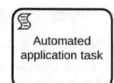

Fig. 6.17 Accommodation of MMABP to the CAMUNDA BPMN v 2.0

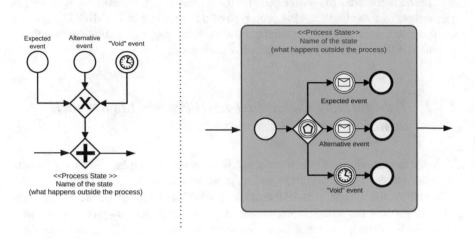

Fig. 6.18 Accommodation of MMABP to the CAMUNDA BPMN v 2.0—Process State

BPMN "parallel gateway" in the synchronization mode, which means more input flows per single output flow (see the left side of Fig. 6.18). The process is synchronized with one of the possible awaited events. Therefore, all possible events are connected by the XOR gateway.

Since BPMN does not explicitly recognize the concept of a process state, we utilize the BPMN element called the "Event-based gateway" (see the right side of Fig. 6.18). This is the only element of BPMN v 2.0 that allows the internal process flow to be properly linked to events, which represent the actions of collaborating processes. To avoid any potential confusion, we model the process state as a stand-alone expanded sub-process comprising only the gateway and the expected events. The process state retains its original name and is marked the stereotype ≪*Process State*≫.

According to MMABP, the decision about the next process step must be made immediately after the process state. This is implemented in Camunda BPMN 2.0 by using the common variable (*CurrentEvent* in this example), which contains the name of the last occurred event. Each event in the process model contains the setting of this variable to the name of the event as an output parameter.

For an explanation of the purpose, the ontological meaning of the process state, and how to use it, refer to Sect. 2.3.2., "Modeling Business Processes."

Other Arrangements Necessary to Make the Models Executable

Making the models executable requires some other arrangements and additions.

- The need for information sharing in the process requires the *use of variables*. Variables are needed to:

- Transfer the *information about the occurred event in the process state* to an immediately following decision about the next process step.
- Transfer the *information between different process steps and activities*. Even the fact that we have to distinguish different types of activities—calling, interactive, and automated—requires to transfer the information between them. For example, information about the decision made in the interactive task, which causes the event to another process, must be transferred to the following calling task since an interactive task cannot perform a calling action. Similarly, we need to transfer the information from an automated to calling task.
- Transfer the *information needed for the decision*. Any process decision is made based on the value (values) of some variable (variables). The variables are set either by the activities of the process or by other processes and shared with them as "global" variables.

• Implementation of process actions *requires programming,* which means the use of some programming language. For instance, CAMUNDA can interpret the code in more Java-based programming languages, namely, JavaScript and Groovy since it is written in Java. There are various specific Java object libraries in CAMUNDA that can be used for realizing many process-related operations. From the MMABP principle of minimal architecture, the following types of operations can be regarded as generally necessary:

- Contacting other processes in the process system (creating events).
- *Collaborating with other applications and systems* (calling external applications as sub-routines and calling CAMUNDA processes from external applications), typically *user interface* applications, *ERP system interface* applications, and *database interface* applications. Particularly, CAMUNDA uses the standard Java Database Connectivity (*JDBC*) to allow processes to work with relational databases, standard application interfaces *REST API and Java API* for integration of the process system with external systems, and specialized *External Task Client* for asynchronous execution of external tasks.

• *The need for information sharing among different processes requires* the *use of global data stores*. The most general and natural way of implementation of the global data store is to use the database. CAMUNDA supports this way by the standard database interface Java Database Connectivity (JDBC) and related functions, which can be used in special tasks like script task to manipulate data in the database. The use of the database adds complexity to the models and requires additional technical effort that is not relevant for simple prototyping. Unfortunately, CAMUNDA does not support global sharing of variables between processes, which would solve the need for global data storage. The only way to transfer data between independent processes is to use a so-called correlate function, which represents the event in the process system. Since events should represent the real events in the real world, such a use of events to simulate global access to information cannot be regarded as methodologically correct. In our example, we simulate the missing database by a special "technical" process, the Batch Organizer, which provides other processes in the system with the simplified database-like services to the minimal extent that satisfies the information needs of the processes in the system.

6.4.2 Technology-Level Models

As can be seen in Figs. 6.19, 6.20, 6.21, 6.22, 6.23, 6.24, and 6.25, implementation of processes requires the use of special types of BPMN tasks and events:

- All starting events are implemented as so-called Start message events, and all events in process states are implemented as so-called Intermediate message events or Intermediate timer events.
- Tasks that represent a human-related action (either the input of some information or the process message targeted to the human user) are implemented as so-called User task, which represents the user form requiring the response from the user.
- Tasks that represent an automated action performed by the machine, not requiring any human activity, are implemented as so-called Script task containing the JavaScript code that manipulates data in the variables.
- Tasks that represent the process output for another process, which actually means creation of the event for the target process, are implemented as so-called Message task containing the expression with the Camunda function *correlate()*.

Figure 6.19 shows the technology-level model of the key process of the *Transportation* business function, *Transportation Request Management*. The process is initiated by one of the events from either the *Order Management* or *Stock Replenishment* process. The very first action of the process is a call for the service *Include into the transportation batch*.

Through this call, the process creates the event *INCLUDE INTO THE TRANSPORTATION BATCH*, which is targeted to the support process *Creating Transportation Batches from Requests* using the Camunda function *correlate()*:

```
#{execution.getProcessEngineServices().getRuntimeService()
.createMessageCorrelation('INCLUDE_INTO_THE_TRANSPORTATION_BATCH')
.setVariable("Request_ID",Request_ID).correlate()}
```

By the function *setVariable()*, the calling process relies the called process the *Request_ID* variable with the identifier of the request (number of the customer or material order). The identifier of this so-called message correlation is the name of the event.

Other two "message tasks" are at the ends of the process. By these tasks, the process creates the events for its "customer" process to inform it about the result of the service. Expression in the *Report the realization* task:

```
#{execution.getProcessEngineServices().getRuntimeService()
.createMessageCorrelation('ORDER_TRANSPORTED')
.processInstanceBusinessKey(Request_ID).correlate()}
```

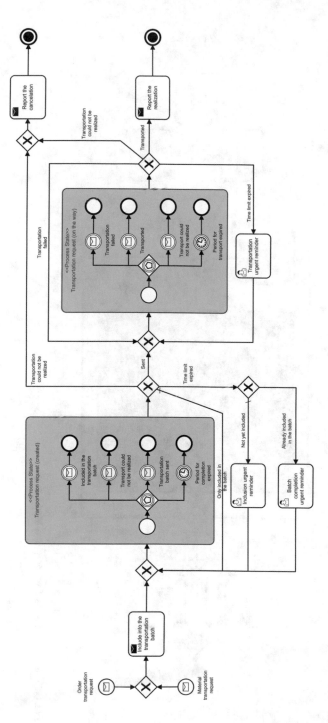

Fig. 6.19 Key process Transportation Request Management

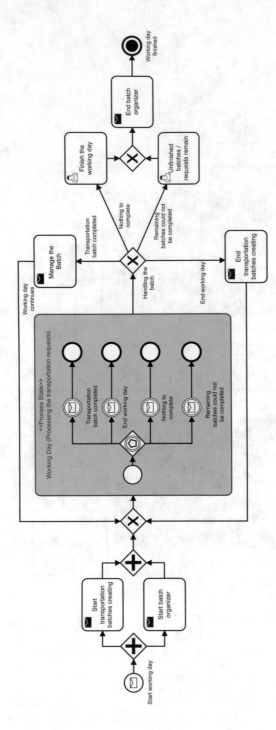

Fig. 6.20 Support process Transportation Management

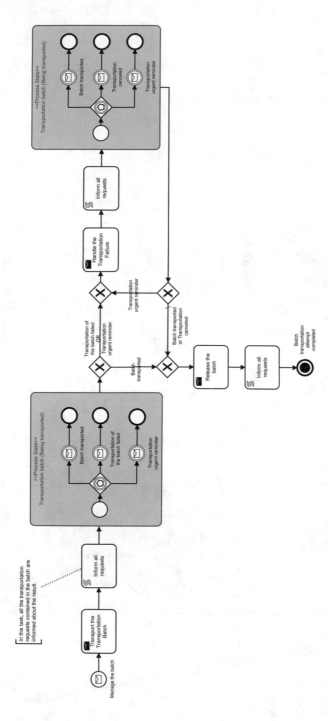

Fig. 6.21 Support process Transportation Batch Management

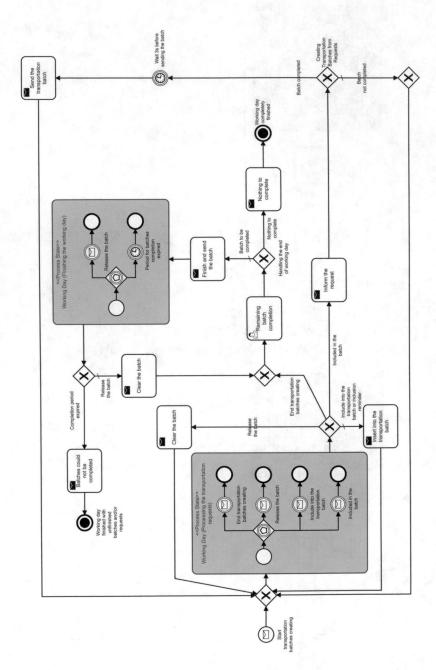

Fig. 6.22 Support process Creating Transportation Batches from Requests

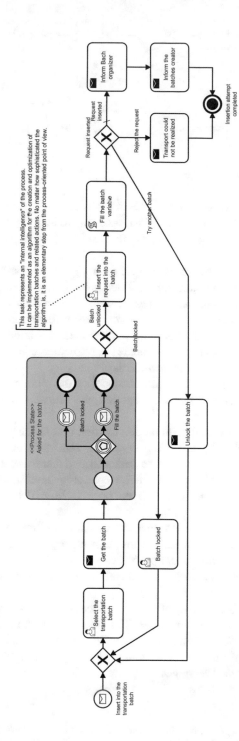

Fig. 6.23 Support process Insert into the Transportation Batch

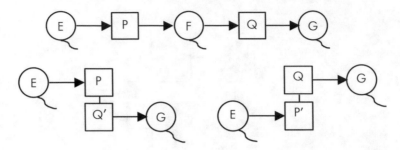

Fig. 6.24 Program inversion technique

In this expression, the process uses the identifier of the request in the Request_ID variable in the function *processInstanceBusinessKey()* to identify the target instance of the "customer" process since each active request has its own instance of the calling process.[7]

The remaining tasks in the process are the reminders, which are activated by the "timer" event when the time limit expires. Each process state contains a timer. The timer in the *Transportation request processed* state represents two possible reminders, the *inclusion* reminder and the *batch completion* reminder. This is possible because the difference in what should be reminded is contextual, so it is always clear what should be reminded. All reminders are implemented as "human tasks" to remind the human actors of the unwanted delay.

Figure 6.20 shows the technology-level model of the main operational support process of the *Transportation* business function, the *Transportation Management* process.

In contrast to the conceptual-level model, the first task in the process is complemented by the parallel task *Start batch organizer. Batch organizer* is a technical process that compensates for the lack of a database, and therefore, it has no meaning as a real business process. It exists only on the technology level and has to be started together with the *Transportation Management* process. More details about this technical process can be found in Sect. 6.4.4.

The process state in this process does not contain the timer event because the time limits are monitored individually from the perspective of each request by the *Transportation Request Management* processes.

Figure 6.21 shows the technology-level model of the support process *Transportation Batch Management.*

Each process step before and after both process states is implemented as a sequence of "message" and "script" tasks. The "message" task invokes the relevant service (*Transport the Transportation Batch, Handle the Transportation Failure*), and the "script" task informs all requests in the batch (i.e., all relevant instances of the *Transportation Request Management* process) of the invoked service. The main fragment of the script in this task:

---

[7] The same Request_ID also identifies the instance of the *Transportation Request Management* process. There must also be a special instance of this process for each request, as it serves that particular request.

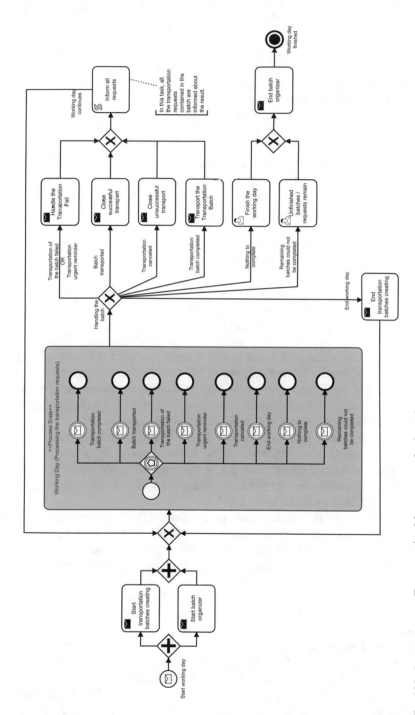

Fig. 6.25 Support process Transportation Management after inversion

```
// Informing all real requests from the variable Batch_content

if (Batch_content["Req1"] != "empty")
{CurrentRequest = Batch_content["Req1"];
execution.getProcessEngineServices().getRuntimeService()
.createMessageCorrelation(CurrentResult)
.setVariable("Batch_ID",Batch_ID)
.setVariable("Batch_content",Batch_content)
.processInstanceBusinessKey(CurrentRequest)
.correlate()};
if (Batch_content["Req2"] != "empty")
{CurrentRequest = Batch_content["Req2"];
execution.getProcessEngineServices().getRuntimeService()
.createMessageCorrelation(CurrentResult)
.setVariable("Batch_ID",Batch_ID)
.setVariable("Batch_content",Batch_content)
.processInstanceBusinessKey(CurrentRequest)
.correlate()};
if (Batch_content["Req3"] != "empty")
{CurrentRequest = Batch_content["Req3"];
.....
```

The algorithm iterates through the cells of the *Batch_content* field and copies each non-empty value into the *CurrentRequest* variable, using this value as the identifier of the instance of the *Transportation Request Management* process that it needs to inform. The name of the event created is taken from the *CurrentResult* variable, making the algorithm universally applicable for different events.

The instance of this process is related to the respective transportation batch, which allows several transportation batches to be operated simultaneously. The need for this parallelism comes from the ontological difference between the concepts *Transportation* Batch and *Working Day* (see the model of concepts in Fig. 6.6) and is discussed in more detail in Sect. 6.4.3.

Like the *Transportation Management* process, also this process does not monitor the deadlines for requests as these are monitored individually from the perspective of each request by the *Transportation Request Management* processes.

Figure 6.22 shows the technology-level model of the support process *Creating Transportation Batches from Requests*.

The process steps are mainly implemented as the "message" tasks that create the events—requirements to other processes—to insure the creation of batches, force the transport of completed tasks, and inform other processes.

The forced completion of the remaining tasks at the end of the working day is implemented as a "human" form task. Like the *Transportation Management* process, also this process does not monitor the deadlines for requests as these are monitored individually from the perspective of each request by the *Transportation Request Management* processes. However, it does monitor the possible expiry of the deadline for completion the remaining batches at the end of working day in the process state *Completing remaining batches.*

As in the technical process *Batch organizer* (see Sect. 6.4.4), also in the process *Creating Transportation Batches from Requests*, we have to delay the process flow between the tasks *Inform the request* and *Send the transportation batch* using the purposeless timer before creating the event *SEND THE BATCH.* It is because CAMUNDA suspects that the process *Transportation management* is not ready to accept the event[8] and rejects this action. It is important to keep in mind that this necessary delay is only a technical issue that has nothing to do with the logic of the real business processes and that the timer used for the implementation of the delay has nothing to do with the real business event.

Figure 6.23 shows the technology-level model of the support process *Insert into the Transportation Batch.*

The need for realizing the insertion of the request into the transportation batch as an extra support process lies in the ontology distinction of the objects (concepts) *Transportation Batch* and *Transportation Request* (see the model of concepts in Fig. 6.6) combined with the fact that the process *Creating Transportation Batches from Requests* handles both objects. As Fig. 6.23 shows, the insertion can take a while due to the human tasks and especially due to the fact that the batch may be temporarily locked, which does not allow the insertion to be completed. Support process *Creating Transportation Batches from Requests* handles all existing insertion requests together with all existing transportation batches at the same time. Certain requests are related to particular batches and not to other batches, so the insertion of some requests is synchronized with the creation of some batches and asynchronous with the others, which in real time can cause the conflicts and, ultimately, in some unfortunate combinations, lead to a deadlock.[9] The sure way to solve this problem is to free the insertion of requests into batches from the manipulation of batches. Particular insertions are handled independently of batch manipulation and potential conflicts of parallel requests to modify the same batch can be handled by locking the batches for the currently active request. Once the request is inserted (or rejected), the batch is passed to the *Creating Transportation Batches from Requests* process for further manipulation.

Support process Insert into the Transportation Batch contains also the process state due to the needed cooperation with the technical process Batch organizer,

---

[8] Which is physically possible in view of the fact that the instance of the *Transportation Management* process can be related to several instances of the *Creating Transportation Batches from Requests* process at the same time, as follows from the ontology of the field. This can lead, in special situations, to the inability of the receiving process to accept the event at the moment when it is serving the same event from another instance. In the real-world implementation of the process system, such an error should be detected by the user interface application, which then applies the necessary delay. In the prototype implementation, we need to use the delay directly in the model.

[9] In this case, the possible deadlock manifests itself as an error since CAMUNDA uses to reject the requested correlations, which could result in the situation that the target process instance is not ready to accept the correlation request.

which is responsible for keeping data consistent by locking the batches for the currently active requests.

The parallelism of different instances of processes discussed in the previous paragraphs is a natural property of the process system that follows from the ontological substance of the business system in which the processes operate. This leads to the necessary further distinction between the conceptual and the technological model of the process, which is discussed in the following chapter.

6.4.3   Dealing with the Natural Parallelism of Business Processes

As discussed in the previous chapter, the business processes in the process system are naturally parallel, as this follows from their ontological substance, which is determined by the ontology of the Real World. The basic methodological way of dealing with the natural parallelism of business processes in MMABP is the Process Normalization Technique mentioned above. However, not all aspects of parallelism are usually uncovered at the conceptual level of analysis. Some of these may manifest themselves at the technology level as a malfunction of the process system. In such a case, the needed corrections are usually made directly in the technology-level models of processes without the proper care of the conceptual meaning of the changes. Through such changes, the original conceptual logic of the process can be hard-coded into the work with variables, making it explicitly invisible. This can ultimately jeopardize the fundamental value of process-driven management, by preventing some future changes directly in the process definitions, without the need to re-code the process implementation. The best example of this hard-coding of process logic is what we call the "process inversion." The process inversion is a way of implementing multiple logical, interacting processes in a single routine. This technique is analogous to the "program inversion technique" described by Michael Jackson in his seminal work Principles of Program Design [2].

In Jackson Structured Programming [2], the author introduces his approach to the program development based on working with data structures and a special technique for solving the of so-called structure clash problem: program inversion.

> The JSP technique for dealing with a structure clash is to decompose the original program into two or more programs communicating by intermediate data structures. A boundary clash, for example, requires a decomposition into two programs communicating by an intermediate sequential stream. [2]
> The underlying idea of program inversion is that reading and writing sequential files on tape is only a specialized version of a more general form of communication. In the general form, programs communicate by producing and consuming sequential streams of records, each stream being either unbuffered or buffered according to any of several possible regimes. The choice of the buffering regime is, to a large extent, independent of the design of the communicating programs. But it is not independent of their scheduling. [3]

Later, in Jackson System Development JSD [3], the author generalizes the inversion technique as the main principle for developing the system of concurrent programs.

Figure 6.24 shows how the inversion technique works. The problem of the boundary clash between the structures of streams E and G can always be solved by dividing the processing to two programs P and Q (see the upper part of Fig. 6.24). P creates an intermediate stream F consisting of such parts of stream E that are compatible with the structure of the stream G. Q can then simply process the stream F and produce the stream G. The lower part of Fig. 6.24 shows two basic possibilities of inversion. The scheme on the left side shows the inversion of Q with respect to the stream F. The scheme on the left side shows the inversion of P with respect to the stream F. The former routine Q exists there as a subroutine Q', which is called repeatedly in the process of processing the stream E. The former routine Q is interrupted by the processing of E. The repeated interruption requires the storage of the information about the state of an interrupted process in the data structure called "state vector," which contains the identification of the state and other important data (attributes) related to the process state. The scheme on the left side shows the inversion of P with respect to the stream F. The former routine P exists there as a subroutine P', which is called repeatedly in the process of processing the stream G. From an operational point of view, both options are equivalent; we can prefer the one which is better from another point of view, for example, from the point of view of algorithmic logic.

Sequential streaming is a natural feature of business processes. It is a consequence of the flow of time as a natural dimension of the Real World. The definition of the process determines the behavior of its actors valid for all possible instances of the process. In the reality, the process exists only in the form of instances, each of which is anchored in a particular time slot. All instances are thus ordered in a sequential stream and the operation of the process over multiple instances is actually the processing of the sequential stream of starting events. Since the execution of the process instance takes some time, the parallel existence of multiple instances is natural. Thus, the typical situation in the real-world business processes corresponds exactly to Jackson's problem of structure clash, and the use of the program inversion is fully relevant there. (For a more detailed reflection of Jackson's program inversion technique in the field of business processes, see [4].)

Jackson's Program Inversion Technique shows an essential difference between the algorithmic logic and the implementation form of the computer program. We see this as an important contribution to the general "principle of three architectures," which expresses the need to distinguish between the pure logic and the possible ways of its implementation in the computer system. However, in the context of the process-driven management, the inversion of processes is highly undesirable since it directly contradicts its principles.

Process-driven management is based on the idea that the development of the algorithmic essence of the system is done through models, which are as close as possible to the natural shape of the business processes. The necessary re-coding of these algorithmic models into machine-understandable form is done by direct interpretation rather than by human re-coding, which would create a barrier of understanding between coders and business people. The part of the information system that directly interprets the process models, the "workflow management system," is therefore the crucial part of the system. Such a system also requires the process models in the form to be as close as possible to the real business processes. Any "optimization" of the process algorithmic structure obscures the essence of the business and is a certain opportunity for misunderstanding. Moreover, in the context of the natural parallelism of business processes, such a transformation can also lead to incorrect functionality as a result of future process changes, as illustrated in the following example and the notes on its application in Sect. 6.4.4.

Figure 6.25 shows the process *Transportation Management* after we have inverted the process *Transportation Batch Management* with respect to the event flow *Manage the Batch*, and before it, we have internally inverted the process *Transportation Batch Management* with respect to the event flow in the state *Handling the Transportation Failure* so that we have integrated both internal states into a single one. In this way, we eliminated the need for the *Transportation Batch Management* process.

After this change, the process system works in exactly the same way as before. The only difference is that the logic of the managing transportation batches is not explicitly visible in this process. It is hidden in the data stored in internal variables that allow distinguishing between particular logic steps of the management of the batch and respecting this invisible logic.

This example illustrates one of the most important features of the process-driven management, as opposed to the traditional management supported by the monolithic IT applications such as traditional ERP systems. Process-driven management allows to actively involve the managers to the process of development and evolution of the IT support (information system). The process models explicitly show the original logic of the business processes in a way that is understandable to business people, rather than hard-wiring it into the IT application. This allows the business people to actively collaborate on the evolution of the system by directly proposing the changes of the process models, which eliminates the traditional need for detailed understanding of the business by IT people and/or detailed understanding of IT by business people.[10] The active collaboration of IT and business people in the development[11] of the organization's information system hand in hand with the development of the business itself is the essence of so-called digital transformation.

6.4.4   Technical Notes to the Execution of the Prototype

This book contains as a supplement the complete source codes of the processes in this example, allowing the reader to run and control the prototype, which effectively helps understand the complexity of the creating the process system design. The

---

[10] Which is typically rather a misunderstanding, an essence of a typical gap between business and IT
[11] In this context, rather a genuine "evolution"

prototype can be run in the CAMUNDA process engine environment version 7.x (all sub-versions) [5].

The complete set of source codes consists of:

- Basic business processes in the system
  - Order Management process
  - Stock Replenishment process
  - Transportation Request Management process
  - Transportation Management process
  - Transportation Batch Management process
  - Creating Transportation Batches from Requests process
  - Insert into the Transportation Batch process
  - Transport the Transportation Batch process
  - Transportation Failure Management process
- Complementary inverted version of the *Transportation Management* process
- Auxiliary technical processes
  - Event generator process
  - Batch Organizer process

Basic business processes are described and explained in the previous chapters.

Auxiliary technical processes are not business processes. They simply support the process system by providing additional functions that enable and/or facilitate the operation and control of the system. In this example, the *Batch Organizer* process (see Fig. 6.26) compensates for the lack of a database, the implementation of which would unnecessarily increase the complexity of the example. The *Event generator* process (see Fig. 6.28) creates the events for operating the system. This allows the example to be used in a natural, business-oriented rather than technical way.

The batch organizer process (see Fig. 6.26) takes care of the common data about batches that are shared among different processes and process instances in order to keep them consistent. It actually represents a missing database. The process holds the common data of the process system in its local variables and supports the other processes by providing services for their use. It also locks and unlocks the variables to prevent possible data mismatching caused by multiple parallel accesses.

There is the only instance of this process in the system initiated by the *Transportation Management* process at the beginning of the working day. At the beginning, the process initiates its variables by filling them with "empty" values. Then the process continuously captures the data manipulation requests and reacts to them as described in Table 6.1:

As shown in the model in Fig. 6.26, this process is "fully automated." It does not contain any human activity. In the very first task, all local process variables are initiated as "output parameters" of the task (see Fig. 6.27).

There are five structured variables (arrays of the CAMUNDA type "Map") *Batch1* to *5* for storing the contents of the batches and one array *CurrentBatch* for handing off the contents of the required batch to the requesting process. Similarly, there are five single logic variables *Batch1Locked* to *Batch5Locked* for the

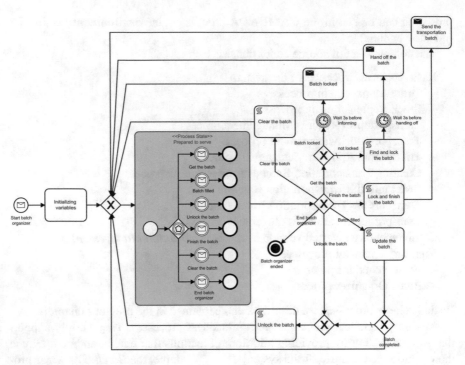

Fig. 6.26 Auxiliary technical process Batch organizer

Table 6.1 Events and how they are handled by the Batch Organizer process

Event (data manipulation request)	Reaction (Batch organizer service)
Get the batch (the process requires the access to the batch)	Reports if the batch is locked; otherwise hands off the batch contents to the requiring process (by creating the event *Fill the batch*) and locks it to prevent changing it by other processes
Batch filled (the process requires to change the batch data)	Updates the batch by new values from requiring process and unlocks it
Unlock the batch	Only unlocks the required batch
Finish the batch (action at the end of working day)	Locks the batch to prevent changing it by other processes and creates the event *Send the transportation batch* to report that the batch can be transported
Clear the batch (the variable of the already sent batch should be released for other requests)	Re-initiates the batch by filling it with "empty" values.
End Batch organizer	Ends its own run

information about whether the given batch is locked and the variable *Locked* for handing off this information to the requesting process. Finally, there are five string variables *Batch1LockedBY* to *Batch5LockedBy* for the information about which request locked the batch and the string variable *BatchLockedBy* for handing off this

Fig. 6.27 Initializing the
local variables as "Output
parameters" in the task
Initializing variables

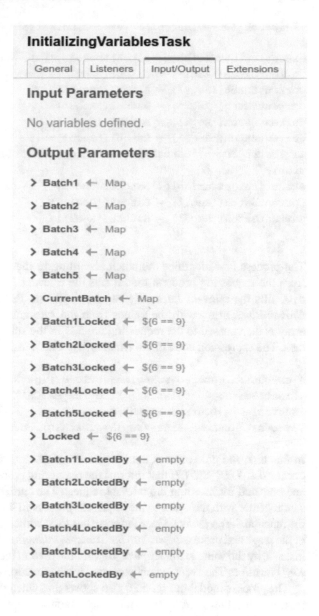

information to the requesting process. All variables are filled with the initial value
empty and *false*. The remaining tasks are either of the "script" or "send" type. All
"script" tasks in the process contain the JavaScript code that ensures the relevant
data manipulation. The fragment of the code in the *Find and Lock the Batch* task
follows:

```
if (Batch_ID == 'Batch1') {execution.setVariable('Batch1Locked',
true);
execution.setVariable('Batch1LockedBy', Request_ID);
CurrentBatch['Req1'] = Batch1['Req1'];
CurrentBatch['Req2'] = Batch1['Req2'];
CurrentBatch['Req3'] = Batch1['Req3'];
CurrentBatch['Req4'] = Batch1['Req4'];
CurrentBatch['Req5'] = Batch1['Req5']; };
if (Batch_ID == 'Batch2') {execution.setVariable('Batch2Locked',
true);
execution.setVariable('Batch2LockedBy', Request_ID);
CurrentBatch['Req1'] = Batch2['Req1'];
CurrentBatch['Req2'] = Batch2['Req2'];
...
```

The process first identifies the batch according to the *Batch_ID* variable received from the requesting process; then it sets the relevant *Locked* variable to the value *true*, fills the relevant *LockedBy* variable with the *Batch_ID* value, and fills the *CurrentBatch* array with the values from the relevant *Batch* array. *CurrentBatch* array is then passed to the requesting process in the subsequent *Hand off the batch* task. The expression code in the *Hand off the Batch* task:

```
#{execution.getProcessEngineServices().getRuntimeService()
.createMessageCorrelation('FILL_THE_BATCH')
.setVariable("CurrentBatch",CurrentBatch)
.processInstanceBusinessKey(Request_ID).correlate()}
```

In this task, the process uses the function *createMessageCorrelation()* to create the event *FILL_THE_BATCH* that informs the requesting process that the batch is locked and prepared for inserting the relevant request. The current contents of the batch are sent together with the event to the requested process in the variable *CurrentBatch* by the function *SetVariable()*. Since the event has to be addressed to the particular instance of the requested process *Insert into the Transportation Batch*, the process identifies the instance by the value in the *Request_ID* variable used in the *processInstanceBusiness-Key()* function. The event is finally created by the function *correlate()*.

The process model in Fig. 6.26 also shows that when the process responds to the request *Get the batch* from the data manipulating process *Insert into the Transportation Batch*, the response must be delayed for several seconds. Even if the logic of the processes does not allow it, CAMUNDA suspects that the requesting process is not ready to accept the response and rejects this action. This pseudo-problem is completely solved with a simple purposeless delay. This complication is related to the fact that the process is only a technical and fully automated routine. The necessary delay is only a technical issue that has nothing to do with the logic of the real business processes. Similarly, the BPMN "intermediate timer event" used for the implementation of the delay has nothing to do with the real business events.

The *Event generator* auxiliary process (see Fig. 6.28) offers creation of the relevant events in the given situation. The Process map in Fig. 6.2 shows that there are

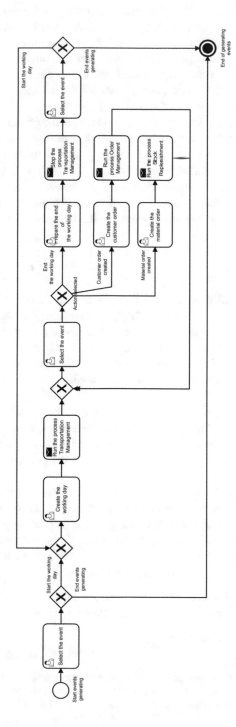

Fig. 6.28 Auxiliary technical process Event generator

only four objective (external) events, i.e., events incoming to the process system from the external world: *Start working day*, *Customer order created*, *Material order created*, and *End working day*. The first and the last one are captured by the *Transportation Management* process. The remaining two events represent the actions of the customers.[12] The *Customer order created* event starts the *Order Management* process, and the *Material order created* event starts the *Stock Replenishment* process. The *Event generator* process offers in the first task only the *Start working day* event or ending the generating of events. Once the working day is started, the process offers the events *Customer order created*, *Material order created*, or *End working day*. After ending the working day, the process offers only starting the new working day or ending the generating of events. As well as creating the events, this process ensures that the correct attributes are created, such as time limits and request identifiers.

With the help of this auxiliary process, the process system prototype can be operated in a way that is close to the real behavior in the business system.

Running the Prototype

To run the prototype, all process models must first be deployed to the running CAMUNDA Process Engine using the "deploy" option in the Camunda Modeler. The only process that needs to be run manually is the *Event generator*. All other process instances will be started by the events created by this process. The very first event created must be the *Start working day* event. After that, the *Order created* and *Material order* created events can be created repeatedly until the event *End working day* event is created.

As the prototype runs, the processes periodically pause in process states and "interactive human tasks" (forms) waiting for the user's response. That is an opportunity to observe the process models, their running instances, and the contents of their variables, which helps understand all aspects of the process system operation in depth.

For a deeper understanding of the problem of parallel instances and the consequent need to distribute the work among support processes according to their ontological differences, as well as the need to preserve the original logic of processes up to their implementation in order to achieve the value of the process-driven management, we strongly recommend experimenting with the complementary inverted version of the *Transportation Management* process model:

- Remove the original *Transportation Management* and *Transportation Batch Management* processes from Camunda Process Engine by deleting their deployments.

---

[12] These are the customers of the *Transportation* business function. While the *Customer order created* event represents the action of the company's customer, the *Material order created* event represents the action of the *Procurement* business function, i.e., an "internal" customer, part of the same company.

- Deploy the inverted version of *Transportation Management* process and run the system by creating the event *Start working day*. See how the system works the same way as with the original versions of processes.
- In the process states, observe the internal variables of the *Transportation Management* process, and see how the logic of handling the transportation batches, previously explicitly visible in the *Transportation Batch Management* process, is now transformed to the working with values in variables.
- Try to implement the change of the logic of handling the transportation batches in the inverted version of the *Transportation Management* process.
  - If the failed transport batch fails a second time, insert the human decision whether to reject the batch or make an additional attempt to transport the batch (instead of the automatic rejection in the original version).
- Replace the deployment of the *Transportation Management* process with the improved one. Run the system and test how it now works.
  - Create several parallel batches to see if the process system can handle them. Test the situation when the decision on a second time failed transportation batch is postponed and the system turns its attention to other batches.
- Face the problem of handling parallel process instances in relation to the single process instance.
- Try to implement the change of the logic of handling the transportation batches in the original (not inverted) version of processes. See how the required change can be implemented easily and safely in this version of the processes.
- Remove the inverted *Transportation Management* process deployment and deploy the new version of *Transportation Management* and *Transportation Batch Management* processes. Run the system and see how it handles multiple batches in parallel.

The experiment described above shows the importance of preserving the original logic of processes until they are implemented. This makes it possible to make changes to processes in a natural, simple, and secure way that is easily understood by business people. Moreover, the changes of processes in the multi-instance environment, covering the one-to-many relationships of process instances, require the perfect understanding of their business meaning, without which it is almost impossible to implement them. The experiment also shows that the implementation of process changes in the process-driven information system only minimally affects the process definitions. If the design of the process system and the distribution of work among the supporting processes is well done, the required change usually affects only one process definition without affecting the others. This significantly increases the safety of the changes in terms of the traditional "principle of minimal coupling" from computer system design theory.

6.5 Summary

This chapter demonstrates the application of the Methodology for Modeling and Analysis of Business Processes (MMABP) through a practical example focused on transportation services within an enterprise.

Section 6.1, Description of the Business Field, illustrates the transportation domain within an enterprise and provides a high-level overview of the domain ontology, including the global process map.

Sections 6.2 and 6.3 provide a comprehensive demonstration of the MMABP methodology in the context of transportation services within an enterprise. The MMABP models, including the model of concepts, process map, object life cycle models, and process flow models, are used to illustrate the conceptual specification of the business system.

The model of concepts specifies the basic objects and their relationships in the business domain, including their basic classification and the cardinalities of their associations. A detailed examination of the object life cycle model of the Transportation Batch is presented, outlining its basic states and transitions between them. We then delve into conceptual-level process flow models, represented in BPMN notation. The main processes, such as Order Management, Stock Replenishment, Transportation Request Management, and Transportation Management, are described in detail. The conceptual process models focus on the actual content of the processes, abstracting non-conceptual features and assuming access to necessary information. This part concludes with an introduction to support processes such as Creating Transportation Batches from Requests, Transportation Batch Management, Transporting the Transportation Batch, and Transportation Failure Management, emphasizing their symbolic internal structures and flexibility for different implementations.

Section 6.4, Technology-Level Process Flow Models, then deals with the transition of detailed business process models from a conceptual to a technological level, using the CAMUNDA workflow management system. CAMUNDA, an open-source JAVA-based application, is introduced as a versatile tool that complies with technical and standardization openness. Notably, it serves as both a process engine and a platform for prototyping process models, a crucial aspect in the context of process-driven organizations. The chapter previews upcoming discussions on extending the modeling language for CAMUNDA execution and provides insight into the transformed models and their integration within a comprehensive system. The availability of the source code encourages the reader to run prototypes in CAMUNDA, thus fostering a practical understanding of the features and challenges of process-driven organization.

6.6   Further Reading

A very important factor of business process analysis and design is proper respect of the difference between process specification (model) and process instance. This factor creates the need for the prototype as a regular part of the analysis process. This is because in processes, we must constantly deal with the natural parallelism of instances, combined with the need to manage the required parallelism that comes from the content of the business system. This combination leads to a number of possible situations that are difficult to handle during conceptual analysis without prototyping the operation of the process system. This problem is addressed and discussed in more detail in the paper [4].

Another specific process design factor related to parallelism and an essential distinction between the conceptual model and its implementation is the problem of "process inversion." For a deeper understanding of this important distinction, we recommend M.A. Jackson's "program inversion technique," described in [2] and generalized for the process system in [3].

Not only the implementation but also the process prototyping requires the transformation of the conceptual model into the technological form, which is always related to the particular operating environment. A comprehensive documentation of the CAMUNDA platform used in this example can be found at [5].

References

1. Guizzardi, G.: Ontological Foundations for Structural Conceptual Models. Telematics Instituut/ University of Twente. Centre for Telematics and Information Technology, Enschede (2005)
2. Jackson, M.A.: Principles of Program Design. Academic Press, London (1975)
3. Jackson, M.A.: System Development. Prentice/Hall, Englewood Cliffs, NJ (1983)
4. Řepa, V.: Coping with natural parallelism in business process models. In: Joint Proceedings of the BIR 2022 Workshops and Doctoral Consortium co-located with 21st International Conference on Perspectives in Business Informatics Research (BIR 2022), pp. 24–34. CEUR-WS, Aachen (2022)
5. CAMUNDA Platform: https://camunda.com/

Appendix: Solutions to Exercises

A.1   Solutions for Chap. 1

There were no exercises/solutions in this chapter.

A.2   Solutions for Chap. 2

A.2.1 Process Map

1. a), d)
2. c)
3. b)
4. d)
5. b)

6.
7. a),b),c),d)
8. a),b)
9. a)
10. g),k)

A.2.2 Process Flow Model

 1. b)
 2. a)
 3. c)
 4. c)
 5. b)
 6. a),b),c)
 7. c)
 8. a),b)
 9. a)
10. a)
11. a),d)
12. a)

A.3   Solutions for Chap. 3

A.3.1 Model of Concepts

1. a), b), d)
2. a), c), e)
3. a), b)
4. b), d), e)
5. d)
6. a), b)
7. b)
8. d)
9. b)

A.3.2 Object Life Cycle Model

1. a), b)
2. a), d)
3. b), d)
4. a), b), c), d)
5. a)
6. b)
7. a), b)

A.4   Solutions for Chap. 4

1. a), c)
2. b)
3. b)
4. a)
5. b)
6. a), c)
7. c)
8. a)
9. b)
10. a), b), c), d), e)

A.5   Solutions for Chap. 5

There were no exercises/solutions in this chapter.

A.6   Solutions for Chap. 6

There were no exercises/solutions in this chapter.

Printed in the United States
by Baker & Taylor Publisher Services